Study and Revise
GCSE Key Stage 4
Physics

Jim Breithaupt

KEY TO SYMBOLS

As you read through this book you will notice the following symbols. They will help you find your way around the book more quickly.

 shows a handy hint to help you remember something

 shows you some key facts

 means remember!!!

 gives worked examples to help you with calculations and equations

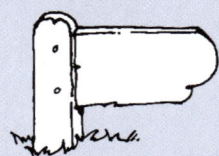 points you to other parts of the book where related topics are explained

Copyright © Jim Breithaupt 1997, 2004

First published in this edition 2004
exclusively for WHSmith by
Hodder & Stoughton Educational
338 Euston Road
London NW1 3BH

All rights reserved. Apart from any use permitted under UK copyright law, no part of this publication may be reproduced or transmitted in any form or by any means, electronic or mechanical, including photocopying, recording or any information storage and retrieval system, without permission in writing from the Publisher.

Impression number   10 9 8 7 6 5 4 3 2 1
Year   2010 2009 2008 2007 2006 2005 2004

Illustrations: Peter Bull, Simon Cooke, Chris Etheridge, Ian Law, Joe Little, Andrea Norton, Mike Parsons, John Plumb, Dave Poole, Chris Rothero, Anthony Warne

Prepared by Starfish, London

Printed and bound in the UK by Scotprint

A CIP record for this book is available from the British Library

ISBN 0 340 85864 8

Contents

GCSE Physics and this Study and Revise book — 1

1 Beyond the Earth — 2
  1.1 Gravity — 3
  1.2 The Solar System — 4
  1.3 Life as a star — 6
  1.4 The expansion of the Universe — 8

2 Energy resources and energy transfer — 11
  2.1 Work and energy — 12
  2.2 More about kinetic and potential energy — 13
  2.3 Power and efficiency — 14
  2.4 Heat transfer — 15
  2.5 Controlling heat transfer — 16
  2.6 Energy resources — 17

3 More about materials — 20
  3.1 Density — 20
  3.2 Specific heat capacity and specific latent heat — 22
  3.3 The gas laws — 25

4 Waves — 29
  4.1 What is a wave? — 29
  4.2 Transverse and longitudinal waves — 30
  4.3 Measuring waves — 31
  4.4 Wave properties — 32

5 Sound waves and seismic waves — 34
  5.1 Properties of sound — 34
  5.2 Ultrasound — 36
  5.3 Seismic waves — 37
  5.4 Resonance — 38

6 Light — 42
  6.1 Reflection — 43
  6.2 Refraction — 44
  6.3 Fibre optics — 45
  6.4 Light and colour — 46

7 Optics — 50
  7.1 Waves and rays — 50
  7.2 The eye — 53
  7.3 Optical instruments — 55

8 Electromagnetic spectrum — 57
  8.1 Using electromagnetic waves — 57
  8.2 Electromagnetic waves in medicine — 59
  8.3 Communications — 60

9 Force and motion — 63
  9.1 Speed and distance — 64
  9.2 Acceleration — 65
  9.3 On the road — 66
  9.4 Force and acceleration — 67
  9.5 Work and energy — 68

10 Forces in balance — 71
  10.1 Equilibrium — 72
  10.2 Strength of solids — 74
  10.3 Pressure and its measurement — 75
  10.4 Hydraulics — 76

11 Additional mechanics — 78
  11.1 Dynamics equations and graphs — 78
  11.2 Force and momentum — 80
  11.3 More about forces — 83

12 Electric charge — 86
  12.1 Electrostatics — 87
  12.2 Electrostatics at work — 89
  12.3 Current and charge — 90
  12.4 Electrolysis — 91

13 Electric circuits — 93
  13.1 Current and potential difference — 94
  13.2 Resistance — 95
  13.3 Components — 96
  13.4 Mains electricity — 97
  13.5 Electrical safety — 98

Contents

14 Electromagnetism — 101
- 14.1 Magnetism — 102
- 14.2 The electric motor — 103
- 14.3 Electromagnetic induction — 104
- 14.4 Transformers — 106

15 Electronics and communications — 109
- 15.1 More about components and electric circuits — 109
- 15.2 Electronic control — 114
- 15.3 Communication systems — 117

16 Radioactivity — 121
- 16.1 Inside the atom — 121
- 16.2 Radioactive isotopes — 123
- 16.3 Radioactive emissions — 124
- 16.4 Half-life — 125
- 16.5 Using radioactivity — 126
- 16.6 Nuclear reactors — 127

17 More about the atom — 130
- 17.1 Electrons — 130
- 17.2 More about the nucleus — 132

Answers — 137

Equations and symbols you should know — 155

Index — 156

GCSE Physics and this Study and Revise book

This *Study and Revise GCSE Physics* book is not intended to replace your school textbooks. As tests and examinations approach, however, many students feel the need to revise from something a good deal shorter than their usual textbook. This book is intended to fill that need. It covers all the GCSE Physics syllabuses for the different Examining Groups.

Make a timetable for revision, using the contents list to ensure you cover all the topics on your syllabus. Planned use of time and concentrated study will give you time for other activities and interests as well as work.

Each chapter begins with a set of Test yourself questions to give you an idea of how well you have already grasped the topic. In addition, each topic (or related topics) includes a concept map that shows how the main ideas in the topic link together. There is a set of Round up questions at the end of each chapter. Work out your improvement index from your score on the Round up questions compared with your score on the Test yourself questions.

When the exam arrives, you should have confidence if you have revised thoroughly. In the examination room, attempt all the questions you are supposed to answer and make sure you turn over every page. Many marks have been lost in exams as a result of turning over two pages at once. If you suffer a panic attack, breathe deeply and slowly to get lots of oxygen into your system and clear your thoughts. Above all, keep your examination in perspective – it is important but not a matter of life or death!

I wish you success.

Jim Breithaupt

Chapter 1 — Beyond the Earth

PREVIEW

At the end of this topic you will be able to:

- recall the main features of the planets
- interpret data about the planets
- use the theory of gravity to explain the motion of the planets, the Moon, satellites and comets
- describe the life cycle of a star
- describe evidence for the expansion of the Universe
- describe how the future of the Universe depends on the amount of mass present.

Test yourself

1. List the planets Mars (M), Jupiter (J), Neptune (N), Uranus (U) and Venus (V) in order of *increasing* distance from the Sun. [5]

2. State two factors that determine the force of gravity due to the Sun on a planet. [2]

3. Why does the brightness of a planet vary? [2]

4. Why can you see different constellations in the night sky during the year? [2]

5. a) Of the planets Mercury, Venus, Mars and Jupiter, which one is rocky and further from the Sun than Earth is? [1]

   b) Which of the above four planets does not have a solid surface? [1]

6. A comet X orbits the Sun once every 76 years. It was last seen from Earth in 1985 when it was visible for about a year. By the year 2050, is it likely to be

   a) slowing down or speeding up? [1]

   b) moving towards or away from the Sun? [1]

7. What is the name of the process that releases energy in the core of a star? [1]

8. What is a supernova? [2]

9. What is meant by 'red shift'? [2]

10. What did the astronomer Edwin Hubble discover? [2]

CONCEPT MAP Page 10.

How much do you already know? Work out your score on page 137.

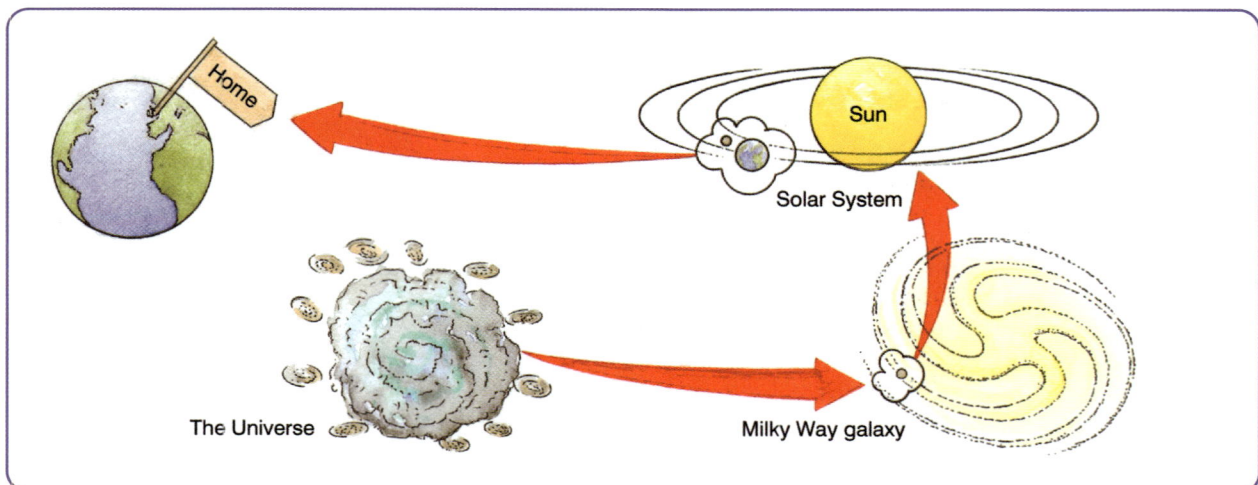

Where do you fit in?

Beyond the Earth

1.1 Gravity

A mysterious force

Any two objects attract each other. This force of attraction is called **gravity**. The greater the masses of the two objects or the closer they are, the stronger the force of gravity between them. The planets, the Moon, satellites and comets all stay in their orbits because of the force of gravity. You stay on the Earth because of the force of gravity between you and the Earth.

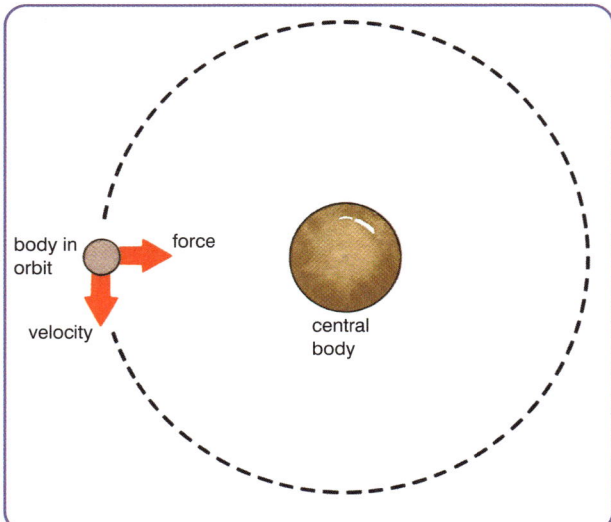

In orbit

Comets

★ Comets move round the Sun in elliptical orbits, usually in a different plane from the Earth's orbit.

★ As a comet approaches the Sun, it moves faster because the Sun's gravity is stronger closer in.

★ It also becomes visible near the Sun because solar heating raises the comet's temperature until it glows.

★ A comet usually develops a tail when it is near the Sun, as particles streaming from the Sun 'blow' glowing matter away from the comet.

★ Comets disappear into darkness as they move away from the Sun, but the Sun's gravity pulls them back towards the Sun again.

Scaling down

If the Sun was represented by a football, the Earth would be a pea 50 metres away from it. Pluto would be a small seed over 2 km away, still held in the Solar System by the force of gravity between it and the Sun.

Satellites

★ **Artificial satellites** are kept in their orbits because of the Earth's gravity. The greater the radius of orbit, the longer its **time period** (the time it takes to go round Earth once).

★ **Communication satellites** orbit the Earth at a certain height above the equator, with a time period of 24 hours. This means that they are always in the same place as seen from the Earth.

★ **Polar satellites** are in low orbits which take them over both poles once every few hours. They have a wide range of uses, including weather forecasting, surveying and spying.

★ **The Moon** is a natural satellite of the Earth. Its radius of orbit is so great that it takes over 27 days to orbit the Earth once.

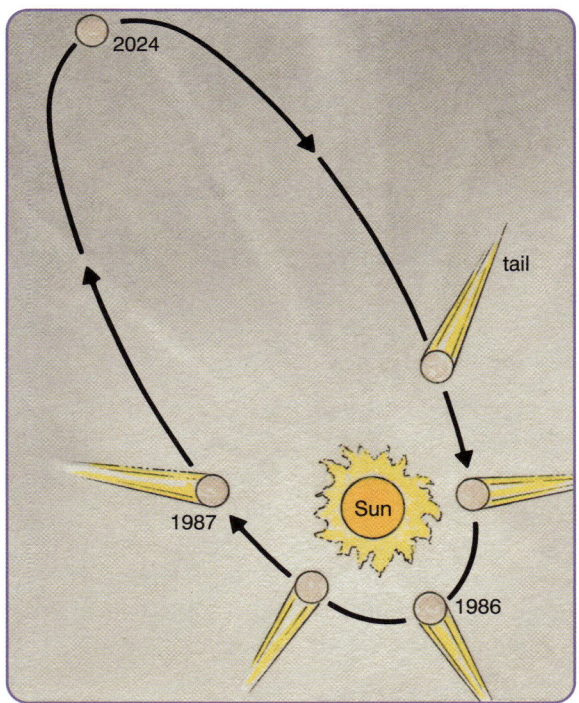

A comet orbit

Beyond the Earth

1.2 The Solar System

Planets in perspective

★ The planets all move round the Sun in the same direction.

★ Their orbits are almost circular, except for Pluto, and in the same plane as the Earth's orbit.

★ The planets reflect sunlight, which is why we can see them.

★ The further a planet is from the Sun, the longer it takes to go round its orbit.

★ When we observe the planets from Earth, they appear to move through the constellations as they go round the Sun.

★ The brightness of a planet varies as its distance from Earth changes and the amount of its sunlit surface we can see changes.

On another planet

Mercury and **Venus** are called the 'inner planets' because they are closer to the Sun than Earth is. They are rocky, without moons. **Mars** is a rocky planet like the Earth and the inner planets. **Jupiter**, **Saturn**, **Uranus** and **Neptune** are giant spinning balls of fluid. **Pluto** is a small rocky planet.

Handy hint

To remember the order of the planets from the Sun, use the mnemonic '**M**ake **V**ery **E**asy **M**ash, **J**ust **S**tart **U**sing **N**ew **P**otatoes'!

Wandering stars

Ancient astronomers called the planets 'wandering stars' because they move through the constellations gradually. This is because the time each planet takes to move round its orbit is different for each planet. Seen from the Earth, the position of a planet against the constellations therefore changes because it moves round its orbit at a different speed from the speed of the Earth.

Questions

1. Use the chart of the planets opposite to answer each of the following questions:
   a) Which planets do not have any moons?
   b) Which planets have just one moon each?
   c) Which planet has a ring system that can be seen from Earth?

2. Use the table of data opposite to answer each of the following questions:
   a) What is the closest distance, in astronomical units, that the Earth and Venus come to each other?
   b) How much bigger in diameter is the Sun than Jupiter?
   c) How much greater in mass is the Sun than Jupiter?

3. Use the information in the chart to explain why Saturn's rings can be seen from Earth whereas Jupiter's rings cannot.

Welcome to Sedna!

Astronomers in 2004 claim to have discovered a tenth planet which has been called 'Sedna' after the Inuit goddess of the oceans. Sedna is thought to be about the same size as Pluto but three times further from the Sun than Pluto.

Answers

1 a) Mercury and Venus b) Earth and Pluto c) Saturn
2 a) 0.3 AU b) 10 times c) 1040 times
3 Saturn's rings reflect sunlight much better than Jupiter's ring system.

Beyond the Earth

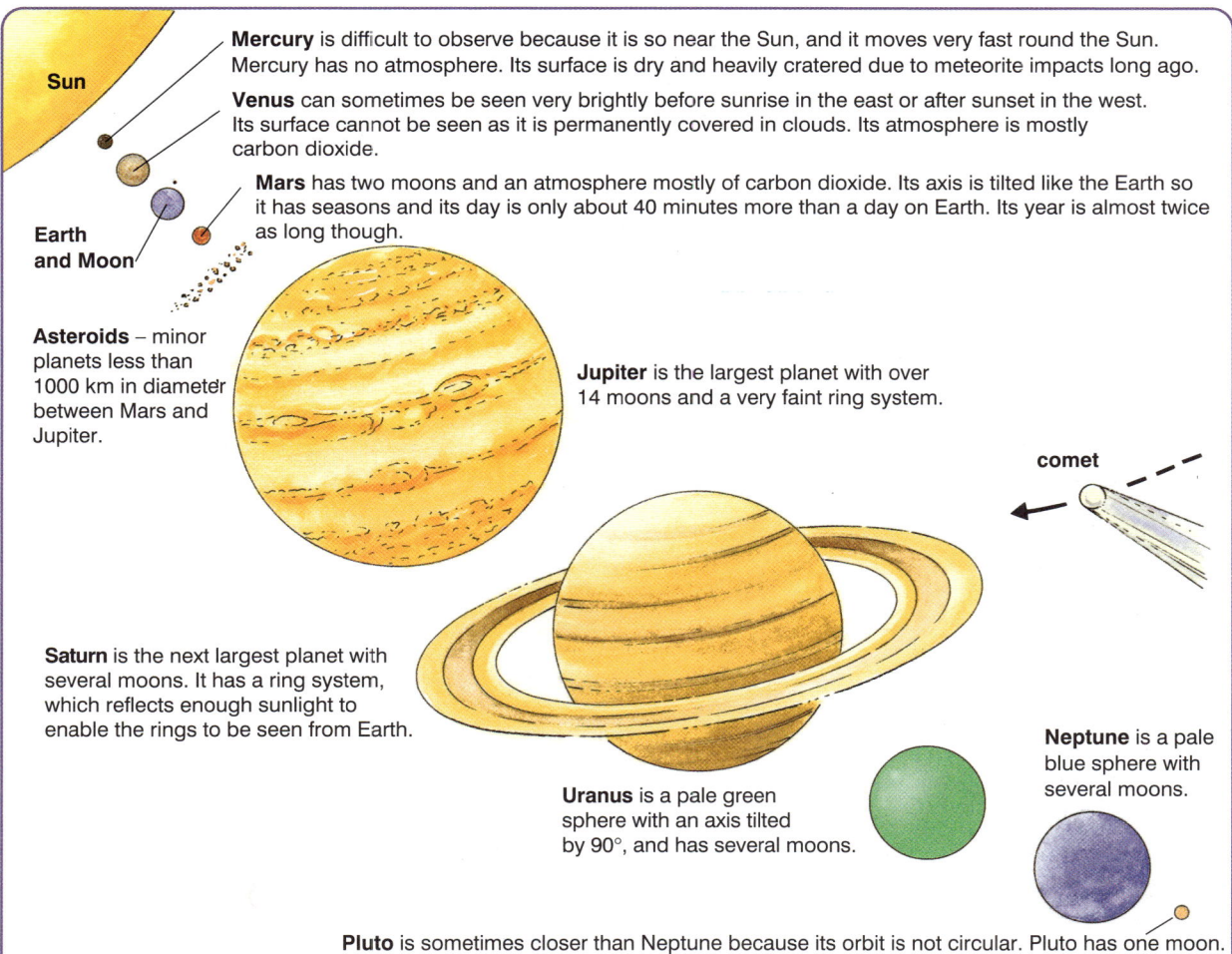

Mercury is difficult to observe because it is so near the Sun, and it moves very fast round the Sun. Mercury has no atmosphere. Its surface is dry and heavily cratered due to meteorite impacts long ago.

Venus can sometimes be seen very brightly before sunrise in the east or after sunset in the west. Its surface cannot be seen as it is permanently covered in clouds. Its atmosphere is mostly carbon dioxide.

Mars has two moons and an atmosphere mostly of carbon dioxide. Its axis is tilted like the Earth so it has seasons and its day is only about 40 minutes more than a day on Earth. Its year is almost twice as long though.

Asteroids – minor planets less than 1000 km in diameter between Mars and Jupiter.

Jupiter is the largest planet with over 14 moons and a very faint ring system.

Saturn is the next largest planet with several moons. It has a ring system, which reflects enough sunlight to enable the rings to be seen from Earth.

Uranus is a pale green sphere with an axis tilted by 90°, and has several moons.

Neptune is a pale blue sphere with several moons.

Pluto is sometimes closer than Neptune because its orbit is not circular. Pluto has one moon.

The planets

Planet	Distance from the Sun in AU	Time to orbit the Sun in years	Mass of planet / Mass of Earth	Diameter of planet / Diameter of Earth
Mercury	0.4	0.24	0.06	0.4
Venus	0.7	0.61	0.8	1.0
Earth	1	1	1	1
Mars	1.5	1.9	0.11	0.5
Jupiter	5.2	11.9	318	11.2
Saturn	9.5	29.5	95	9.5
Uranus	19.2	84	15	3.7
Neptune	30	165	17	3.5
Pluto	39	250	0.002	0.4

1 astronomical unit (AU) = 150 million km
mass of Sun = 330,000 × mass of Earth
diameter of Sun = 110 × diameter of Earth

Beyond the Earth

1.3 Life as a star

★ The stars we see are at different stages of evolution and they vary in size, brightness and lifetime.

★ Massive bright stars last no more than a few million years.

★ Small dim stars shine for thousands of millions of years.

★ The Sun is thought to be a typical middle-aged star about halfway through its life cycle of about 10 000 million years.

Formation
- A star forms from dust and gas in space pulled in by its own gravity.
- As its density rises, it becomes hotter and hotter due to the release of gravitational energy.
- The planets are thought to have formed from the dust clouds left over at this stage.

Birth
- At a temperature of about 10 million degrees, the nuclei of hydrogen atoms fuse together, releasing nuclear energy.
- This energy keeps the star temperature high enough for nuclear fusion to continue. A star is born!

Equilibrium
- For most of its life, the star gradually fuses the hydrogen nuclei in its core into heavier nuclei such as helium.
- The nuclear reactions in the core release vast amounts of electromagnetic and particle radiation.
- The inward gravitational attraction on the core is balanced by outward pressure due to this radiation.

Expansion
- Eventually, the hydrogen in the core is used up and the star expands to become a **red giant**.
- This is thought to occur because the helium nuclei and other light nuclei formed from the hydrogen nuclei fuse to form heavier nuclei, releasing more radiation, which forces the star to swell out.

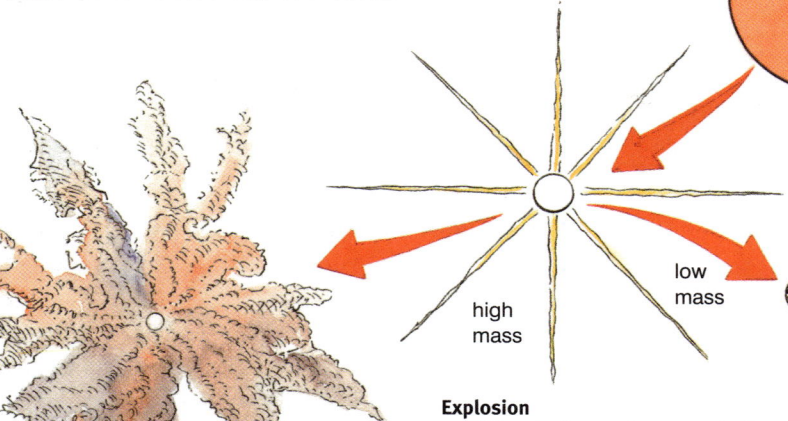

Collapse
- Once there are no more light nuclei to fuse together, the star collapses due to its own gravity.
- It becomes very hot, very dense and very small. It is now referred to as a **white dwarf**.

Explosion
- If the star is massive enough, its collapse is followed by a massive explosion in which huge amounts of matter and radiation are released in a very short time. This event is known as a supernova because the star suddenly outshines entire galaxies.
- Heavy atoms (e.g. lead, uranium) are formed in the explosion as light atoms are fused into heavier atoms by the force of the explosion.
- The supernova event is thought to leave behind an extremely dense object known as a **neutron star**, which is composed only of neutrons.
- If the star was very massive, a **black hole** is left behind. Nothing can escape from a black hole, not even light, because its gravity is so strong.

The life cycle of a star

Sandaluk II

Supernovae are rare events. The Crab Nebula in the constellation Taurus is thought to be the remnants of an eleventh century supernova. In 1987, a supernova was observed in the Andromeda galaxy. It was thought to be the death throes of a star called Sandaluk II.

In a supernova explosion, large heavy nuclei are formed from the fusion of lighter nuclei. Dense elements like uranium found in the Earth mean that the Earth and the Sun probably formed from the debris of a supernova explosion.

SETI, the search for extra-terrestrial intelligence

★ Astronomers now know that planets orbit other stars. Large telescopes enable astronomers to see planets in orbit round nearby stars. Some stars 'wobble' because of the gravitational pull of a planet too small to see.

★ Other solar systems exist, probably containing small planets like Earth. They are too far away for space travel.

★ Radio telescopes are being used to find out if intelligent life exists beyond Earth, capable of transmitting radio signals. This search for extra-terrestrial intelligence (SETI) has not discovered any such signals yet.

★ Life in the form of microbes might exist or have existed on the other planets of our own solar system. Evidence of microbes has been found in a meteorite discovered in Antarctica, and thought to be from Mars. Space probes sent to one or two areas of Mars have not yet found evidence of life.

Are we alone?

About one in ten stars might have planets. About one in ten planets could be Earth-like. Intelligent life perhaps exists on a planet for about ten thousand years, a period of time less than a millionth of its existence. Even though our galaxy contains about a billion stars, intelligent life may not exist elsewhere in our galaxy at the present time.

Questions

1. When a star forms from dust clouds, it becomes so hot that its nuclei fuse together and release more energy. Why does it become hot when it forms from dust?
2. List the main stages in the life cycle of a massive star.
3. What evidence is there that the Sun and its solar system formed from the remnants of a supernova?
4. List the main points in support of the view that
   a) life probably exists elsewhere in our galaxy,
   b) life in our galaxy beyond Earth, if it exists at all, may not be intelligent.

Answers

1. The dust clouds attract each other due to their own gravity and become more and more dense. Gravitational potential energy is converted into kinetic energy of the dust particles, which become very hot when they collide with each other.
2. Formation from dust and cloud; heating up until fusion starts; steady emission of light as a star; sudden expansion as a red giant; collapse to a white dwarf; sudden explosion as a supernova.
3. Atoms heavier than iron atoms are present in our solar system. These atoms can only be formed in a supernova explosion. Therefore, our solar system must have formed from the remnants of a supernova explosion.
4. (a) Evidence of microbes in a meteorite thought to have come from Mars; about 1 in 100 stars probably have Earth-like planets, (b) SETI radio telescopes have not detected any extra-terrestrial radio signals yet.

Beyond the Earth

1.4 The expansion of the Universe

Galaxies

★ The Sun is just one of billions of stars in the Milky Way galaxy.

★ There are many other galaxies.

★ The nearest galaxy is about 10 million light years away.

★ The furthest is about 12 000 million light years away.

The red shift

The spectrum of light from a star is crossed by dark vertical lines. These are caused by substances in the star's outer layers absorbing light of certain wavelengths. **Edwin Hubble** discovered that the absorption lines due to the same substances in the light spectra of distant galaxies are red-shifted towards longer wavelengths in the spectrum. This is because these galaxies are moving away from us very quickly so their light waves are lengthened.

Hubble made precise measurements and discovered that the speed of a galaxy is greater the more distant the galaxy is. This important discovery is known as **Hubble's law**.

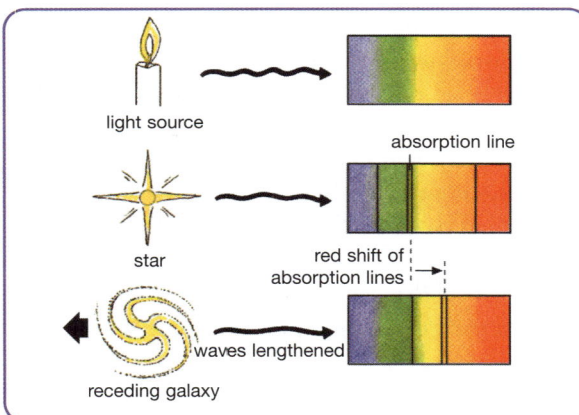

Starlight spectra

Question

If the age of the Universe at 15 000 million years was scaled down to start 24 hours ago, when would life on Earth (one million years ago) have started?

The Big Bang

In the beginning

All the distant galaxies are rushing away from us. Scientists think the Universe is expanding. This would explain why distant galaxies are moving away faster and faster the further they are from us. The expansion started about 15 billion years ago in a huge explosion called the **Big Bang**. At present, it is not known whether the expansion will continue indefinitely or reverse – ending perhaps in the Big Crunch!

The Big Bang theory was only accepted after astronomers detected background microwave radiation from **all** directions in space. Before this discovery, many scientists doubted the Big Bang theory and they favoured the **Steady State** theory. This theory is based on the idea that the Universe has always existed and is the same now as it always was. Matter was thought to be entering the Universe at so-called 'white holes' in space, pushing the galaxies away from each other. The Steady State theory could not explain the presence of background microwave radiation whereas the Big Bang theory predicts its presence as radiation released in the Big Bang.

The future of the Universe

★ No object can travel faster than light. Light from the Big Bang defines the edge of the Universe, which is expanding at present. Hubble estimated that the edge of the Universe is about 12 000 million light years away!

★ The expansion of the Universe could continue forever or slow down and reverse, depending on the total mass of the Universe, which is not known at present. If the mass of the Universe is sufficiently large, the expansion will slow down and reverse leading to the Big Crunch! If it is too small, the expansion will continue forever at a decreasing rate of expansion.

Recent measurements suggest an increasing rate of expansion, indicating the existence of a cosmic repulsion force.

Answer

7 seconds ago.

Beyond the Earth

ROUND UP

How much have you improved? Work out your improvement index on page 137.

1 a) Explain why the planets of the Solar System do not leave the Solar System. [2]

  b) Why does the Earth orbit the Sun whereas the Moon orbits the Earth? [1]

2 During the night, the constellations move across the sky. Explain why this happens. [2]

3 a) Stars produce their own light but planets do not. Explain why we can see the planets. [1]

  b) The diagram shows the planet Venus in two different positions on its orbit relative to the Earth. A sketch was made of Venus in each of these positions, viewed through a large telescope. Decide which sketch is for which position, and explain your reasons. [2]

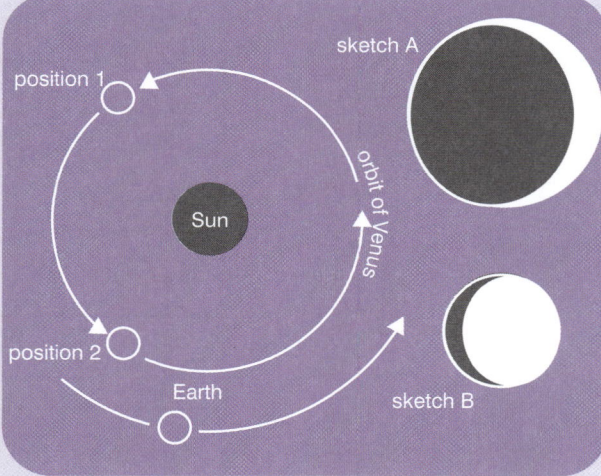

4 List the following astronomical objects in order of increasing distance from Earth:

Andromeda galaxy, Moon, Pole star, Sun [4]

5 a) Draw a sketch to show the relative positions of the Sun, the Earth and Jupiter when Jupiter is easily visible in the night sky. [1]

  b) State four differences between the Earth and **(i)** Mars **(ii)** Jupiter **(iii)** Saturn. [12]

6 a) Mercury is very difficult to observe. Why? [3]

  b) Pluto is the most distant planet, yet it can be closer than Neptune to the Sun. Why? [2]

  c) Uranus is closer to the Sun than Neptune is. Which takes longer to go round the Sun? [1]

  d) Why do comets disappear and then return? [3]

7 a) Betelgeuse is a red giant star. Why is it described as a red giant? [2]

  b) Describe what will happen to the Sun when it uses up all the hydrogen nuclei in its core. [4]

  c) What is a supernova? [2]

8 a) Why is it difficult to launch satellites into orbit? [3]

  b) The Earth's surface gravity is 10 N/kg. The Moon's surface gravity is 1.6 N/kg. Why is the Moon's gravity smaller? [2]

9 The Universe is thought to be expanding. Describe the evidence for this. [4]

10 a) What is the Big Bang theory and how does it explain the expansion of the Universe? [2]

  b) If the total mass of the Universe is less than a certain amount, what will be the future of the Universe? [2]

  c) Write a short account of the possibilities of life in the Universe beyond Earth. [5]

Well done if you've improved. Don't worry if you haven't. Take a break and try again.

Beyond the Earth

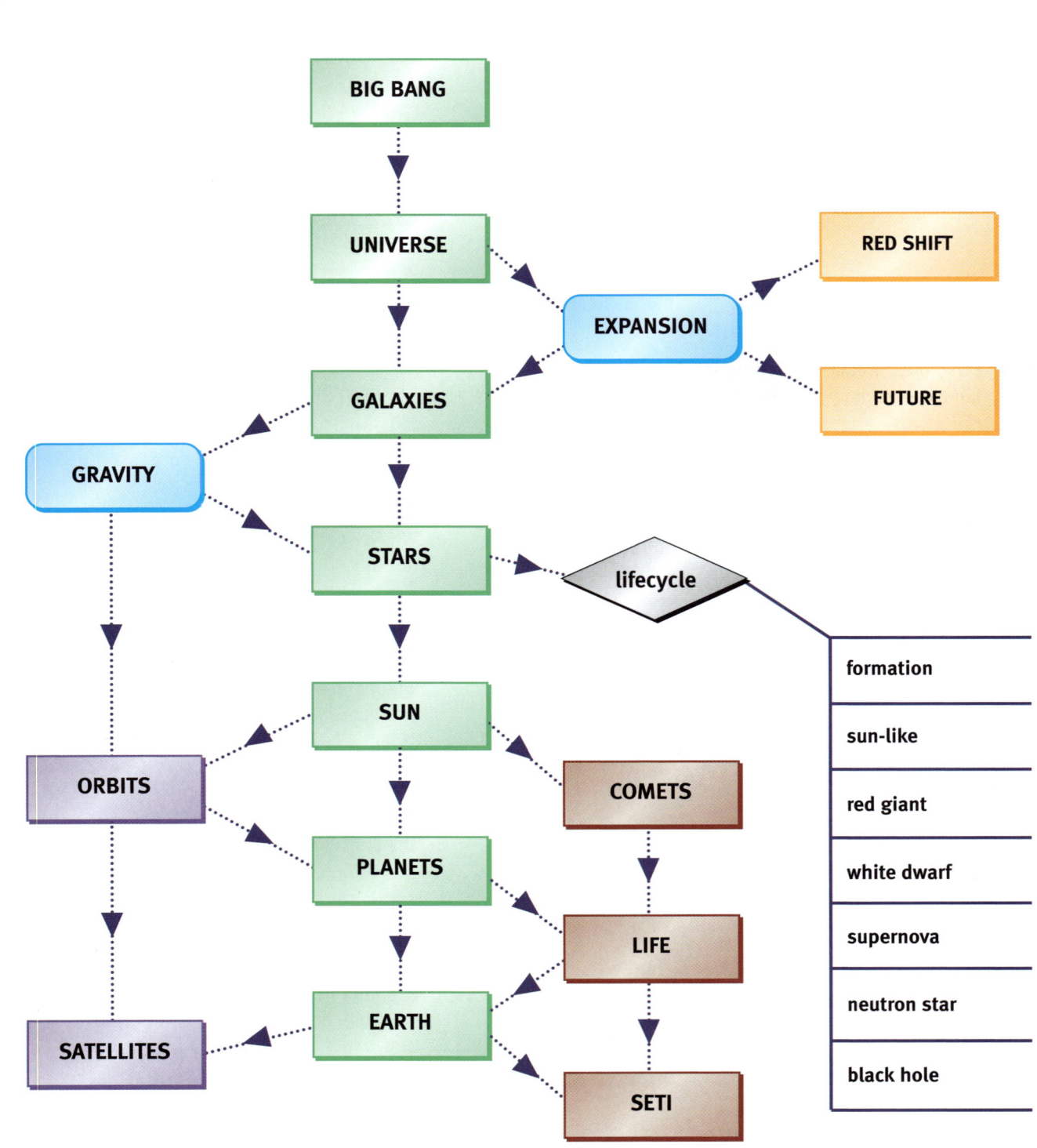

Concept map: the Earth in space

Energy resources and energy transfer — Chapter 2

PREVIEW

At the end of this topic you will be able to:

- describe different forms of energy
- explain what is meant by work, energy and power
- describe the energy changes when work is done or when heat transfer takes place
- explain what is meant by conservation of energy, efficiency and energy waste
- carry out calculations using the formulae for kinetic energy, potential energy, power and efficiency.

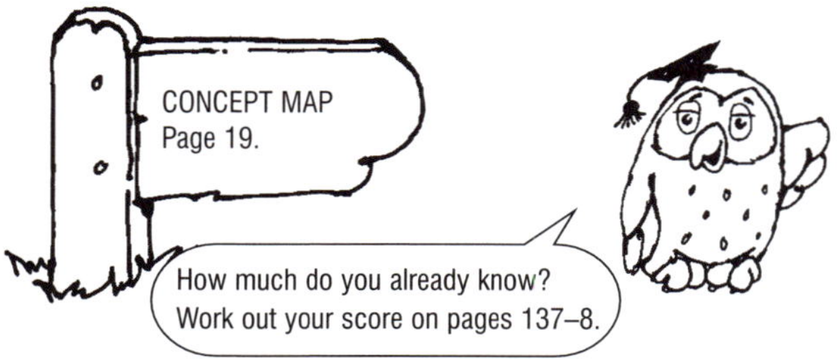

CONCEPT MAP Page 19.

How much do you already know? Work out your score on pages 137–8.

Test yourself

Assume $g = 10$ N/kg where necessary.

1. A cyclist freewheels down a road and eventually comes to rest. Which one of the following sequences **A** to **D** best describes the energy changes in this process?

   A chemical ⟶ potential ⟶ kinetic
   B potential ⟶ kinetic ⟶ thermal
   C potential ⟶ chemical ⟶ kinetic
   D chemical ⟶ kinetic ⟶ thermal   [1]

2. State the correct units for weight and power, respectively.   [2]

3. A weightlifter raises an object of mass 60 kg from the floor to a height of 2.0 m. Calculate the gain of potential energy of the object.   [1]

4. An object of weight 2.0 N is held 4.0 m above a floor and then released. Calculate its kinetic energy and its potential energy in joules
   a) when it is 1.0 m above the floor   [2]
   b) just before it hits the floor.   [2]

5. A person uses a 1.0 kW electric heater for 4 hours and a 3.0 kW electric oven for 2 hours. Calculate the total number of kilowatt hours used.   [2]

6. A trolley of mass 20 kg is released at the top of a slope of height 10 m and allowed to run down the slope. Its speed at the bottom of the slope is 5.0 m/s. Calculate the ratio of the trolley's loss of potential energy to its gain of kinetic energy.   [3]

7. Why are metals good conductors of heat?   [3]

8. Home heating bills may be reduced by installing
   a) double glazed windows instead of ordinary windows
   b) felt insulation in the loft
   c) draught excluders round the door frames.

   Which of the above measures reduces heat loss due to thermal conduction or thermal radiation?   [2]

9. Which of the above measures reduces heat loss due to thermal convection?   [1]

10. A falling weight is used to turn an electricity generator which is used to light a bulb, as shown in the diagram. Complete the energy flow diagram below.   [5]

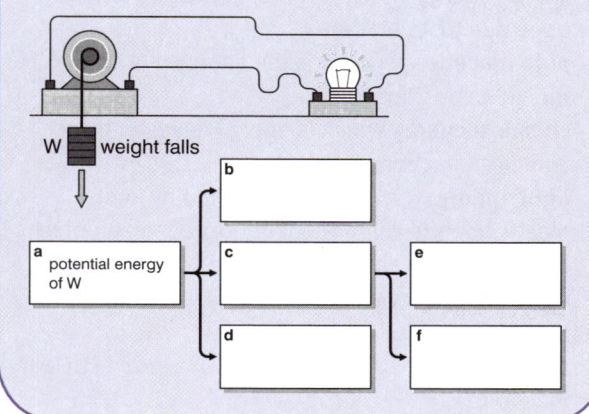

11

Energy resources and energy transfer

2.1 Work and energy

Time for work

Work is done when a force makes an object move. The greater the force or the further the movement, the greater the amount of work done. For example, the work done to lift a box to a height of 2 m is twice the work done to lift the same box to a height of 1 m.

Energy is the capacity to do work. A battery-operated electric motor used to raise a weight does work on the weight. The battery therefore contains energy because it has the capacity to make the motor do work.

Heat is energy transferred due to a difference of temperature. Heat and work are two methods by which energy can be transferred to or from a body. Work is energy transferred due to force and heat is energy transferred due to temperature difference. Heat as a method of transferring energy is discussed in more detail on pages 15–16.

Energy can be changed from one form into other forms.

Forms of energy

Energy exists in different forms, including:
- **kinetic energy** which is the energy of a moving body due to its motion
- **potential energy** which is the energy of a body due to its position
- **chemical energy** which is energy released by chemical reactions
- **light energy** which is energy carried by light
- **elastic energy** which is energy stored in an object by changing its shape
- **electrical energy** which is energy due to electric charge
- **nuclear energy** which is energy released in nuclear reactions
- **sound energy** which is energy carried by sound waves
- **thermal energy** which is the energy of an object due to its temperature.

Temperature is the hotness of an object and is measured in degrees Celsius (°C).

The Celsius scale of temperature is defined in terms of **ice point**, 0°C, which is the temperature of pure melting ice, and **steam point**, 100°C, which is the temperature of steam at atmospheric pressure.

Measuring energy

Work and energy are measured in joules (J), where one joule is defined as the work done when a force of one newton acts over a distance of one metre in the direction of the force.

The following equation is used to calculate the work done (or energy transferred) by a force:

work done (or energy transferred) = force × distance moved in the direction of the force

$$W = F \times s$$
(in joules) (in newtons) (in metres)

Questions

a) A student applies a force of 600 N to a wardrobe and pushes it a distance of 2.0 m across a floor. Calculate the work done by the student.

b) If the wardrobe had been emptied, it could have been pushed across the floor using a force of 200 N. How far could it have been moved for the same amount of work?

c) Describe the energy changes in the picture below.

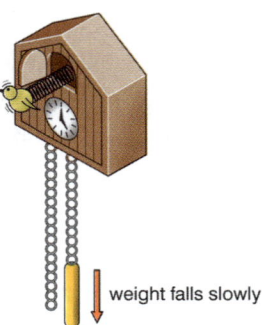

weight falls slowly

Answers

a) 1200 J b) 6.0 m
c) Potential energy of the weight ⟶ kinetic energy of the moving parts of the clock + sound

2.2 More about kinetic and potential energy

Gravitational potential energy (GPE)

For an object of mass m raised through a height h, its

gain of potential energy = mgh

where g is the gravitational field strength.

Note that for an object of mass m, its **weight** = mg because g is the force of gravity per unit mass on an object. Also, the mass must be in kilograms and the height gain in metres to give the gain of potential energy in joules. The value of g on the Earth is 10 N/kg.

Kinetic energy (KE)

For an object of mass m moving at speed v, its

kinetic energy = $\frac{1}{2}mv^2$

Proof of this formula is not required at GCSE. Note that the mass must be in kilograms and the speed in metres per second to give the kinetic energy in joules.

> **Questions**
>
> 1. How much gravitational potential energy does a 60 kg swimmer gain as a result of climbing a height of 15 m?
>
> 2. a) If the swimmer in question **1** dives from a diving board 15 m above the water, how much kinetic energy does the swimmer have just before impact?
>
>   b) Calculate the swimmer's speed just before impact.

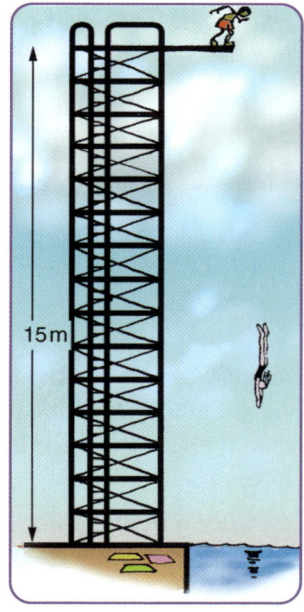

A very important principle

The principle of conservation of energy states that in any change, the total energy before the change is equal to the total energy after the change. In other words, the total amount of energy is conserved, even though it may change from its initial form into other forms as a result of the change.

Consider the energy changes if a 100 N weight is released at a height of 1.0 m above the floor.

★ Its initial potential energy (relative to the floor) is mgh = 100 N × 1.0 m = 100 J.

★ Its potential energy (relative to the floor) just before impact = 0, since its height is effectively zero just before impact.

It loses 100 J of potential energy as a result of falling to the floor. Just before impact, its kinetic energy is therefore 100 J since it had no kinetic energy at the start and all its potential energy is transformed into kinetic energy – assuming no air resistance!

But

The trouble with energy is that it tends to spread out when it changes from one form into other forms. For example, in a bicycle freewheeling down a slope, friction at the wheel bearings causes the bearings to become warm. Some of the initial potential energy is therefore converted into thermal energy. Such thermal energy is lost to the surroundings and can never be recovered and used to do work. The thermal energy is therefore wasted.

Even where energy is concentrated, such as when a car battery is charged, energy is wasted in the process. For example, the electric current passing through a car battery when it is being charged would warm the circuit wires a little.

> **Answers** 1 9000 J 2 a) 9000 J b) 17 m/s

Energy resources and energy transfer

2.3 Power and efficiency

Power is defined as the work done or energy transferred per second.

$$\text{power (in watts)} = \frac{\text{energy transferred (in joules)}}{\text{time taken (in seconds)}}$$

The unit of power is the **watt** (W), equal to one joule per second. Note that one kilowatt (kW) equals 1000 W and one megawatt (MW) equals 1 000 000 W.

Question

1. Calculate the muscle power of a student of mass 50 kg who climbs a height of 5.0 m up a rope in 10 s. (Hint: remember that weight = mass × g where g = 10 N/kg. Also, the student uses both arms to climb the rope.)

Electrical power

The electrical power supplied to an electrical appliance is the electrical energy transferred per second to the appliance. For example, a 1000 W electrical heater is supplied with 1000 J of electrical energy each second. This is changed into thermal energy by the heater.

The electrical power of an appliance depends on the current and potential difference (i.e. voltage), in accordance with this equation:

electrical power = current × potential difference
P = I × V
(in watts)   (in amperes)   (in volts)

The unit of electrical energy used to cost mains electricity is the **kilowatt hour**, sometimes written as kWh. One kilowatt hour is the electrical energy supplied to a 1000 W appliance in one hour and is equal to 3.6 million joules (1000 W × 3600 s).

The electrical energy supplied to a mains appliance in a certain number of hours is calculated by multiplying the power of the appliance in kilowatts by the number of hours. For example, the electrical energy used by
- a 3.0 kW heater in 2 hours is 6.0 kWh,
- a 100 W light bulb in 24 hours is 2.4 kWh (= 0.1 kW × 24 hours).

Electrical energy supplied in kWh
= power in kilowatts × the number of hours

Notes

1. The kilowatt hour (kWh) is the unit which is used to cost electricity.
2. The cost of the electrical energy supplied = the number of 'units' used × the cost per 'unit'.

Machines at work

A machine is a device designed to do work. Energy is supplied to a machine enabling it to do **useful work**. The useful work done by a machine is always less than the energy supplied to it because of friction between its moving parts. This causes heating and therefore wastes energy. Energy may be wasted in other ways in a machine as well as through friction.

Efficiency

The efficiency of a machine is the proportion of the energy supplied to the machine which is transferred to useful work. This may be expressed as an equation:

$$\text{efficiency} = \frac{\text{useful work done by the machine}}{\text{energy supplied to the machine}}$$

Notes

1. Efficiency is sometimes expressed as a percentage (the fraction above multiplied by 100).
2. The efficiency of any machine is always less than 100% because of friction.
3. Efficiency may be expressed in terms of power as

$$\frac{\text{output power}}{\text{input power}}$$

Questions

2. A pulley system is used to raise a crate of weight 500 N through a height of 2.4 m. To do this, the operator must pull on the rope with a force of 300 N through a distance of 4.8 m.

    a) Calculate (i) the work done by the operator (ii) the potential energy gain of the crate.

    b) Hence calculate the efficiency of the pulley system and give two reasons why it is not 100%.

Answers

1. 125 W
2. a) (i) 1440 J (ii) 1200 J b) 83% Heat and sound energy losses due to friction

Energy resources and energy transfer

2.4 Heat transfer

Heat transfer occurs by means of thermal **conduction**, **convection** and **radiation**. Cooling also takes place during **evaporation** from a hot liquid, and matter as well as heat is transferred in this process, which is not the case with conduction, convection or radiation.

Thermal conduction – five facts

1. Thermal conduction is heat transfer through a substance without the substance moving.
2. Solids, liquids and gases all conduct heat.
3. Good thermal conductors are also good electrical conductors. They contain free electrons which can transport both energy and charge through the substance.
4. Metals and alloys are the best conductors of heat.
5. Insulating materials such as wood, fibreglass and air are very poor conductors of heat. The presence of air pockets in an insulating material improves its insulating properties.

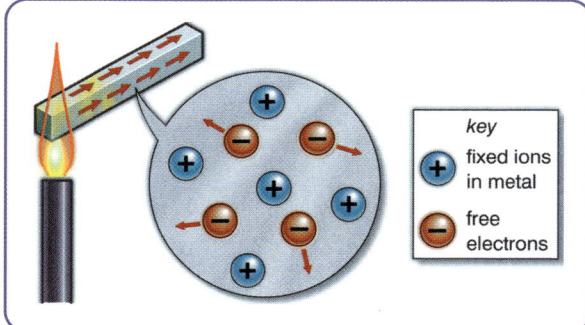
Thermal conduction in a metal

Thermal convection – five facts

1. Thermal convection is heat transfer in a liquid or a gas due to internal circulation of particles.
2. Thermal convection occurs only in fluids (liquids or gases).
3. Natural convection occurs because hot fluids, being less dense than cold fluids, rise, whereas cold fluids sink. When a fluid is heated, circulation is caused by hot fluid rising and cold fluid sinking.
4. Forced convection happens when a cold fluid is pumped over a hot surface and takes away energy from the surface.
5. Cooling fins on an engine increase the surface area of the engine and therefore enable more thermal convection to occur.

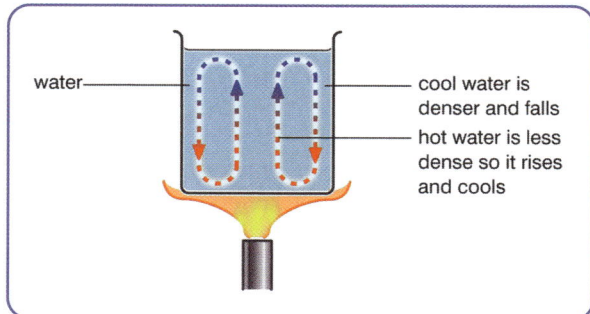
Thermal convection in water

Thermal radiation – five facts

1. Thermal radiation is electromagnetic radiation emitted by any surface at a temperature greater than absolute zero.
2. The hotter a surface is, the more thermal radiation it emits.
3. Thermal radiation can pass through a vacuum and does not need a substance to carry it.
4. A black surface is a better emitter and absorber of thermal radiation than a silvered surface.
5. A matt (rough) surface is a better emitter and absorber of thermal radiation than a shiny surface.

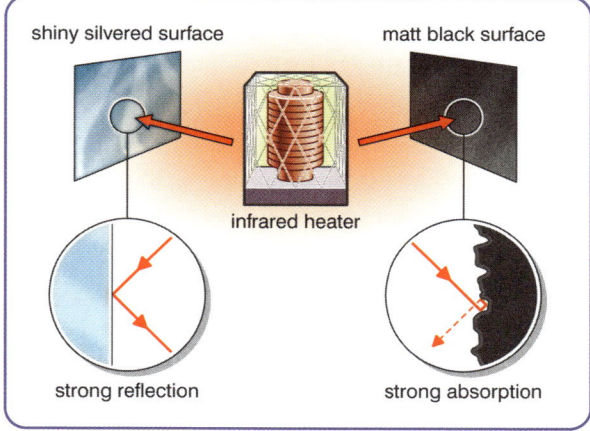
Thermal radiation

Energy resources and energy transfer

2.5 Controlling heat transfer

Designers need to take account of the thermal properties of materials when considering what materials to use in any given device or situation.

★ A car radiator transfers heat from the engine to the surroundings. Forced convection occurs as water pumped round the engine block carries away heat to the radiator. Heat is conducted through the radiator walls so the outside of the radiator becomes hot. Air circulates round the outside of the radiator, carrying away heat, and the radiator surface is blackened so it emits thermal radiation.

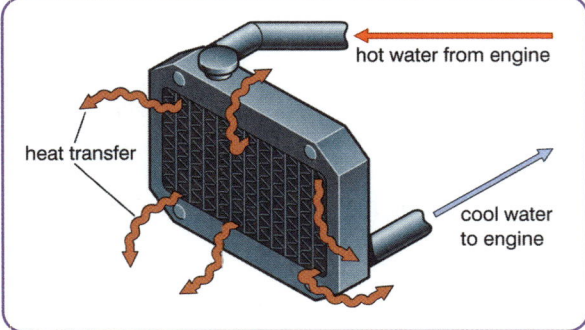

A car radiator

★ A domestic hot water tank is fitted with an insulating jacket to reduce heat losses. The outer surface of the jacket is shiny to reduce heat losses due to thermal radiation.

Keeping warm in winter

Home heating bills can be greatly reduced by fitting loft insulation and double glazing. The picture of the house shows these and other measures that can be taken to reduce fuel bills.

Question

1 Tick boxes in the table below to show which heat transfer processes have been reduced by each measure.

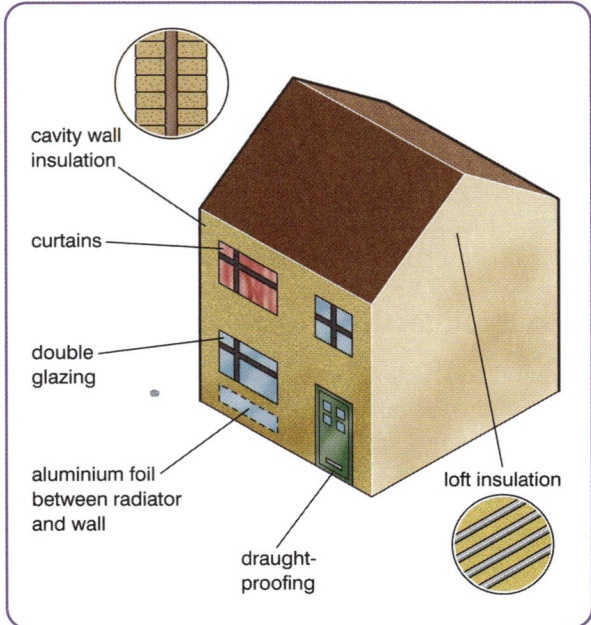

Reducing home heating bills

Maintaining body temperature

If you are outdoors in winter, you need warm dry clothing made of fibres which trap layers of air. Since air is a very poor conductor of heat, it reduces heat transfer from the body to the surroundings. A white outer surface reduces thermal radiation. A smooth shiny surface would be even better but might be expensive! In addition, the outer surface needs to be waterproof and the inner layers need to prevent water vapour caused by sweat penetrating the fibres.

Question

2 List the materials you would use to make a winter coat, giving a reason for each material chosen.

Answers

1 conduction ✓✓✓✗✗✗ radiation ✓✗✓✓✓✗ convection ✗✓✓✗✓✓
2 Wool or polyester fibres to trap layers of air; silk lining for smooth fit

	loft insulation	double glazing	cavity wall insulation	radiator foil	heavy curtains	draught excluder
conduction						
convection						
radiation						

Energy resources and energy transfer

2.6 Energy resources

Demand and supply

The total energy demand for the United Kingdom in one year is about 10 million million million joules. This works out at about 5000 joules per second for every person in the country.

Fuels are substances which release energy as a result of changing into another substance. Fuels cannot be reused.

- Fossil fuels – coal, oil, gas
- Nuclear fuels – uranium, plutonium

Renewable energy resources are sources of useful energy which do not change the substances involved, allowing them to be reused. The energy usually comes from the Sun.

★ Solar-driven resources – solar panels for water heating, solar cells.

★ Weather-driven resources (indirectly powered by the Sun's heating effect on the atmosphere) – hydroelectricity, wind turbines, wave powered generators.

★ Tidal generators (powered by the gravitational potential energy between the Earth and the Moon).

★ Geothermal power (powered by thermal energy in the Earth's interior).

Electricity supplies need to be matched to demand, which is usually lowest at night and greatest at meal times.

★ Mains electricity in Britain is mostly supplied from fossil fuel and nuclear power stations.

★ Electricity power stations need to be started and stopped quickly to match sudden changes of demand during each day.

★ The start-up time of each type of power station is, from shortest to longest:

hydroelectric   gas   oil   coal   nuclear.

Energy efficiency

Reasons why energy should not be wasted:

1. Fuel supplies are finite and cannot be renewed once used.
2. Fossil fuels release carbon dioxide gas, which is thought to be causing global warming, resulting in melting icecaps and rising sea levels. Sulphur dioxide from power stations is a cause of acid rain.
3. Nuclear fuel creates radioactive waste which must be stored safely for hundreds of years to prevent it harming us.
4. Small-scale renewable resources may damage the environment, for example turbine noise from wind turbines, and plant and animal life are affected when tidal power stations are built.
5. It costs money to make energy useful and to distribute it.

How to use energy resources more efficiently

★ Use machines and vehicles more efficiently.

★ Replace inefficient machines and vehicles with more efficient ones.

★ Improve thermal insulation in buildings.

★ Fit automatic lighting and temperature sensors to reduce unnecessary lighting and heating.

★ Supply waste heat from power stations for district heating (combined heat and power stations).

★ Use more pumped storage schemes.

★ Make energy-efficient lifestyle choices, for example teleworking, car sharing, better public transport.

A pumped storage station. Electricity is used to pump water uphill when the demand for electricity is low. Electricity is generated by allowing water to flow downhill when demand is high.

Energy resources and energy transfer

ROUND UP

How much have you improved? Work out your improvement index on page 138.

1. Describe the energy changes that take place when
   a) the alarm sounds on a battery-operated clock [1]
   b) a parachutist jumps from a plane and descends safely to the ground. [2]

2. An elevator is used in a factory to lift packages each weighing 200 N through a height of 4.0 m from the production line to a loading platform. The elevator is designed to deliver three packages per minute to the loading bay.

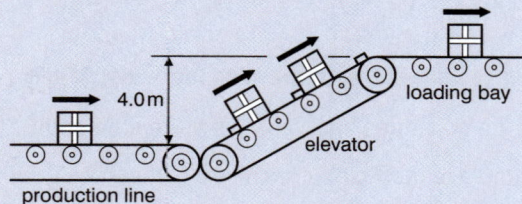

   a) Calculate
      (i) the potential energy gain of each package [1]
      (ii) the work done per second by the elevator to lift the packages. [1]
   b) A 200 W electric motor is used to drive the elevator. Calculate the efficiency of the elevator and motor system. [1]

3. a) An athlete of mass 55 kg is capable of running at a top speed of 10 m/s. Calculate the athlete's kinetic energy at this speed. [1]
   b) If the athlete could convert all the kinetic energy in a) into potential energy, how much would the athlete's centre of gravity rise? [1]

4. A passenger aeroplane of mass 25 000 kg accelerates on a level run from rest to reach its take-off speed of 80 m/s in a time of 50 s. Calculate
   a) its kinetic energy at take-off [1]
   b) the power developed by its engines to achieve this speed in 50 s. [1]

5. A student records the usage of electrical appliances in her household over a period of 24 hours.

   2.0 kW electric heater for 2.5 hours
   100 W electric light for 3 hours
   40 W electric light for 5 hours
   750 W microwave oven for 20 minutes
   3.0 kW electric kettle used 4 times for 5 minutes each time

   a) Calculate the total number of units of electricity (kWh) used by the appliances. [1]
   b) Calculate the total cost of using all these appliances if each unit of electricity costs 6.0p. [1]

6. A 12 V electric heater, rated at 25 W, is designed for use in a car and is capable of heating a flask of tea from 20°C to 50°C in 15 minutes.
   a) Calculate the energy supplied by a 25 W electric heater in 15 minutes. [1]
   b) A student decides to test the heater by filling the flask with 0.2 kg of water. She has discovered in a separate test that 4200 J of energy are needed to raise the temperature of 1.0 kg of water by 1°C. She finds that the heater takes 650 s to heat the water from 20°C to 40°C.
      (i) Calculate the energy needed to heat 0.2 kg of water from 20°C to 40°C. [1]
      (ii) Calculate the actual power of the heater. [1]

7. a) Explain whether hot tea in a china teapot would cool faster than hot tea in a shiny metal teapot. [2]
   b) Explain why hot tea cools faster in a wide-brimmed cup than in a narrow cup. [3]
   c) Explain why heat loss through a single-glazed window can be reduced by fitting double glazing. [2]
   d) (i) Condensation often forms on single-glazed classroom windows in winter. Explain how this happens. [2]
      (ii) Double glazing reduces condensation. Why? [2]

Well done if you've improved. Don't worry if you haven't. Take a break and try again.

Energy resources and energy transfer

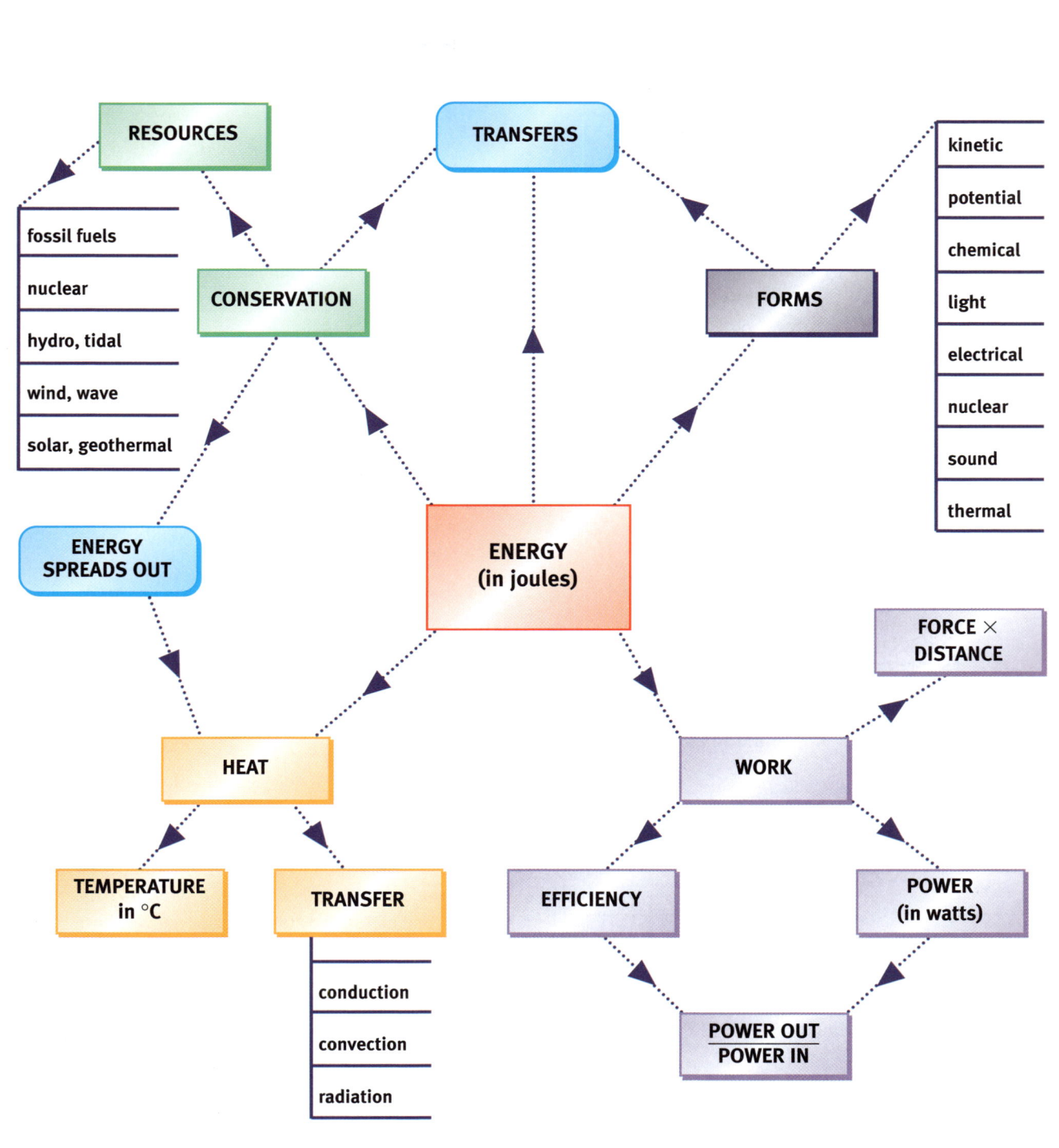

Concept map: energy

Chapter 3: More about materials

3.1 Density

PREVIEW

At the end of this topic you will:
- be able to recall that the density of a substance is defined as the mass per unit volume of the substance
- know that density is measured in kilograms per cubic metre (kg/m^3) or in grams per cubic centimetre (g/cm^3)
- be able to use the equation density = mass / volume.

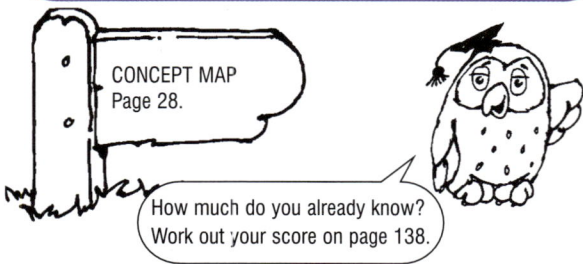

CONCEPT MAP Page 28.

How much do you already know? Work out your score on page 138.

Test yourself

1. Calculate the missing quantities in the table below. [5]

mass	1000 g		60 g	55 kg	
volume	120 cm³	25.5 m³			0.0020 m³
density		1.2 kg/m³	1.1 g/cm³	2500 kg/m³	2700 kg/m³

2. An empty plastic cup is placed on a top pan balance which then displays a reading of 75 g. The cup is removed, partly filled with water and placed on the balance again. The balance now shows a reading of 158 g.
   a) Calculate the mass of water in the cup in
      (i) grams   (ii) kilograms.
   b) The density of water is 1000 kg/m^3. Calculate the volume of water in the cup in
      (i) cubic metres (ii) cubic centimetres. [4]

3. An empty paint tin has a mass of 0.12 kg. It is filled with 1500 cm^3 of paint. The total mass of the paint and the tin is then 2.98 kg. Calculate
   a) the volume of paint in the tin, in cubic metres
   b) the mass of the paint in the tin, in kilograms
   c) the density of the paint, in kilograms per cubic metre. [3]

4. A room is 4.0 m long, 3.5 m wide and 2.5 m high.
   a) Calculate the volume of the room.
   b) The density of air in the room is 1.2 kg/m^3. Calculate the mass of air in the room. [2]

The density equation

For a mass m of volume V, its density ρ is calculated from the equation $\rho = \dfrac{m}{V}$.

1. If two of the three quantities in the density equation are known, the third quantity can be calculated. Start by writing down the known quantities and the equation.

2. Rearrange the equation to make the unknown quantity the subject.
   - To find ρ, use the equation $\rho = \dfrac{m}{V}$.
   - To find m, rearranging the equation gives $m = \rho V$.
   - To find V, rearranging the equation gives $V = \dfrac{m}{\rho}$.

3. Write the equation again with the values of the two known quantities instead of the symbols. Then use your calculator to work out the unknown third quantity.

4. Write the answer down, including its unit.

Converting units

★ **Mass:** 1 kg = 1000 g

★ **Length:** 1 km = 1000 m, 1 m = 100 cm, 1 cm = 10 mm

★ **Area:** square the conversion factor for length, for example, $1 km^2 = 10^6 m^2$, $1 m^2 = 10^4 cm^2$, $1 cm^2 = 100 mm^2$

★ **Volume:** cube the conversion factor for length, for example, $1 km^3 = 10^9 m^3$, $1 m^3 = 10^6 cm^3$, $1 cm^3 = 1000 mm^3$
   Note: *volume is sometimes expressed in litres, where 1 litre = 1000 millilitres (ml) and 1 ml = 1 cm^3.*

★ **Density:** 1000 kg/m^3 = $10^6 g / 10^6 cm^3$ = 1 g/cm^3

Calculating the volume of a regular solid

1. For a rectangular box
   volume = length × breadth × width.

2. For a uniform cylinder of radius r and length l
   volume = $\pi r^2 l$.

3. For a sphere of radius r
   volume = $\frac{4}{3}\pi r^3$.

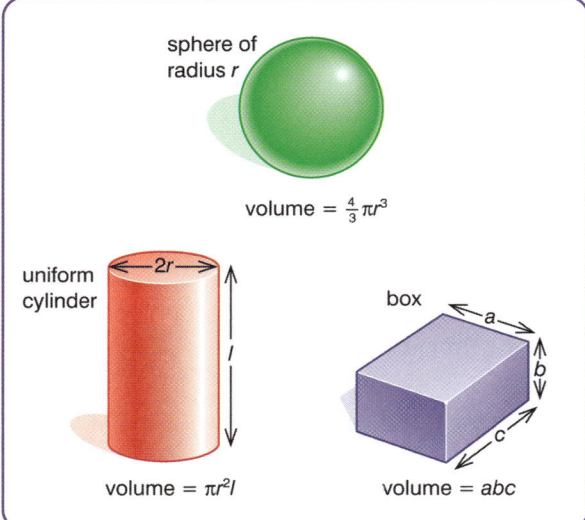

Volume formulae

Making measurements

★ **Mass:** use a top pan balance.

★ **Length** or **diameter:** use a micrometer or vernier callipers if possible.

★ **Volume** of an irregular solid: *either* immerse the object in water in a measuring cylinder and measure the change of volume of the water, *or* use a displacement can as shown in the diagram.

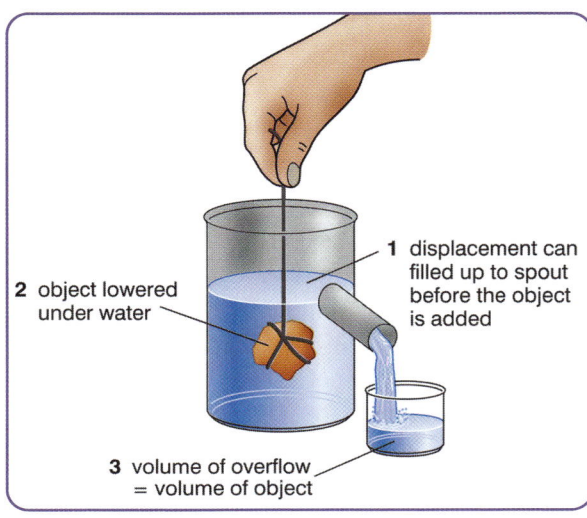

Using a displacement can

ROUND UP

How much have you improved?
Work out your improvement index on page 138.

1. A rectangular concrete paving slab of thickness 40 mm is 450 mm long and 300 mm wide.
   a) Calculate its volume in **(i)** cubic millimetres **(ii)** cubic centimetres **(iii)** cubic metres.
   b) The density of the concrete is 2500 kg/m³. Calculate the mass of the paving slab. [4]

2. A steel wire of uniform diameter 0.55 mm has a length of 1.5 m.
   a) Show that the volume of the wire is 3.6×10^{-7} m³.
   b) The density of steel is 7900 kg/m³. Calculate the mass of the wire in **(i)** kilograms **(ii)** grams.
   c) Calculate the length of wire that has a mass of 1 g. [4]

3. An oil droplet of volume 0.1 mm³ is placed on a clean water surface. It spreads out to form a circular patch of uniform thickness 350 mm in diameter. Calculate the thickness of the patch in **a)** millimetres **b)** metres. [4]

4. A scientific article in a newspaper claims that the human body is approximately 80% water.
   a) Make a sensible estimate of your own mass and volume. Assume you are a uniform cylinder to estimate your volume.
   b) The density of water is 1000 kg/m³. Use your estimate to discuss whether the newspaper claim is reasonable. [4]

Well done if you've improved. Don't worry if you haven't. Take a break and try again.

More about materials

3.2 Specific heat capacity and specific latent heat

PREVIEW

At the end of this topic you will be able to:

- describe what is meant by the specific heat capacity of a material
- relate the temperature rise of a material to its mass, its specific heat capacity and the energy supplied
- relate the temperature rise of an object containing two or more materials to the mass and the specific heat capacity of each material, and the energy supplied
- explain what is meant by latent heat
- use specific latent heat values to calculate energy transfers in a change of state
- use specific heat capacity values and specific latent heat values to calculate energy changes for materials that change state and change temperature.

How much do you already know? Work out your score on pages 138–9.

Test yourself

Where necessary, use the data from the table opposite.

1. Calculate the energy needed to raise the temperature of
   a) 5.0 kg of water from 15°C to 50°C
   b) 5.0 kg of lead from 15°C to 50°C
   c) 0.2 kg of aluminium from 10°C to 60°C
   d) 0.2 kg of oil from 10°C to 60°C. [4]

2. Explain why the temperature of the water in an outdoor swimming pool changes very little on a hot day, but the temperature of the surrounding concrete border changes more. [3]

3. a) An aluminium saucepan of mass 0.15 kg contains 1.2 kg of water at 20°C. Calculate the energy needed to heat the saucepan and the water to 100°C.
   b) A copper water tank of mass 12 kg contains 80 kg of water at 22°C. Calculate the energy needed to heat the water and the copper tank to 60°C. [6]

4. A 2.5 kW electric kettle of mass 1.6 kg is made of steel. It contains 0.8 kg of water, initially at 20°C. The specific heat capacity of steel is 470 J/kg°C. Calculate
   a) the energy needed to heat the kettle and the water to 100°C
   b) the time it takes to reach 100°C. [5]

5. Calculate the time taken to freeze 100 g of water at 0°C in a freezer which is removing energy from the water at a rate of 40 J/s. The specific latent heat of ice is 340 J/g. [2]

6. The specific latent heat of vaporisation of water is 2.3 MJ/kg. Calculate the time taken to boil away 0.5 kg of boiling water in a 3.0 kW electric kettle. [2]

How not to revise!

How to keep cool

An open-air swimming pool is a good place to be on a hot summer's day. However, standing barefoot on a paved area can be very uncomfortable if the paving material is too hot. It's much cooler in the pool! Why does the water heat up much less than the paving material does?

When a material is heated, the change of temperature depends on:
- the **mass** of the material
- the **energy** gained by the material
- the nature of the **material** itself
- the **physical state** of the material (whether it is solid, liquid or gas).

More about materials

The energy gained by the material increases the kinetic energy of its atoms. This is referred to as the **internal energy** of the material. In a solid, the atoms vibrate more as a result of gaining kinetic energy. In a liquid or a gas, the random motion of the atoms is faster as a result.

Defining specific heat capacity

The specific heat capacity of a material is the energy needed to raise the temperature of 1 kg of the material by 1 °C without a change of state of the material.

For example, the specific heat capacity of water is 4200 J/kg°C. This means that 1 kg of water must be supplied with 4200 J to raise its temperature by 1 °C. It also means that in order to cool 1 kg of water by 1 °C, 4200 J of energy must be removed from the water.

The table below gives the specific heat capacities of some common materials. Note that the specific heat capacity of water is much higher than that of the other materials in this table.

material	specific heat capacity J/kg°C
lead	130
copper	380
aluminium	900
oil	2100
water	4200

The specific heat capacities of some common substances

The following equation can be used to calculate the energy transferred to or from a material to change its temperature.

Energy transferred (in J) = mass (in kg) × specific heat capacity (in J/kg°C) × temperature change (in °C)

The equation can be written in symbols as

$$E = mc(T_2 - T_1)$$

where: E = energy transferred, m = mass of material, c = specific heat capacity of the material, T_2 = final temperature and T_1 = initial temperature.

Measuring the specific heat capacity of a metal block

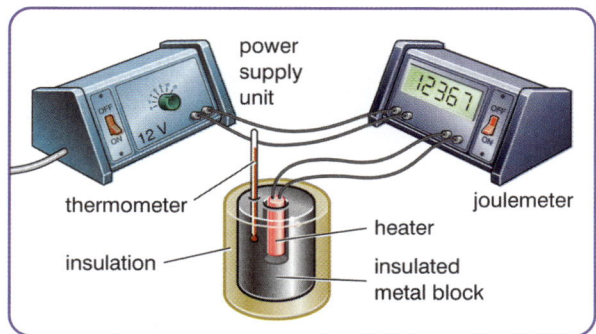

Using a joulemeter

1. The mass m of the block is measured using a top pan balance.
2. The low voltage electric heater and the thermometer are inserted in the block as shown. The block is then insulated.
3. The initial temperature T_1 of the block is measured. The joulemeter reading is recorded.
4. The heater is switched on for 5 minutes.
5. The joulemeter reading is recorded again and the highest temperature T_2 reached by the block is measured.

Sample results

Mass of block = 1.0 kg

Initial temperature = 15 °C

Initial joulemeter reading = 500 J

Final temperature = 31 °C

Final joulemeter reading = 15 200 J

Calculation

Energy E gained by the block = 15 200 − 500
= 14 700 J

Temperature rise $(T_2 - T_1)$ = 31 − 15 = 16 °C

Rearranging $E = mc(T_2 - T_1)$ gives

$$c = \frac{E}{m(T_2 - T_1)} = \frac{14\,700}{1 \times 16}$$

= **920 J/kg°C**

More about materials

Specific latent heat

Another way not to revise!

An ice lolly needs to be eaten quickly on a hot summer's day. The energy needed to melt 1 g of ice is 340 J, the same as a 100 W light bulb uses in just 3.4 seconds!

★ The **specific latent heat of fusion** of a material is the energy needed to melt 1 kg of material. For example, the specific latent heat of fusion of ice is 340 000 J/kg.

★ The **specific latent heat of vaporisation** of a material is the energy needed to vaporise 1 kg of material. For example, the specific latent heat of vaporisation of water is 2.3 MJ/kg.

★ The **energy transfer** for a change of state of a material of mass m can be found using the equation

$$\text{energy transfer} = ml$$

where l is the specific latent heat of the material for a certain change of state.

Worked example

A 2.5 kW electric kettle contains 3.0 kg of water. The specific latent heat of water is 2.3 MJ/kg. Calculate **a)** the energy needed to boil away 1.2 kg of water at 100 °C **b)** the time taken to supply the necessary energy.

Solution

a) Energy needed = ml = 1.2 × 2.3 = **2.8 MJ**

b) Power = $\dfrac{\text{energy}}{\text{time}}$ therefore

time = $\dfrac{\text{energy}}{\text{power}} = \dfrac{2.8 \text{ MJ}}{2.5 \text{ kW}} = \dfrac{2.8 \times 10^6 \text{ J}}{2500 \text{ J/s}}$ = **1120 s**

ROUND UP

How much have you improved? Work out your improvement index on page 139.

Specific heat capacity of water = 4200 J/kg °C
Specific latent heat of fusion of water (ice) = 340 000 J/kg
Specific latent heat of vaporisation of water = 2.3 MJ/kg

1. Use your knowledge about latent heat to explain each of the following observations.
   a) The chill you feel outdoors in wet weather is greater if it is windy than in still air.
   b) The skin becomes cool if it is dabbed with a small quantity of a volatile liquid such as alcohol. [5]

2. Calculate the energy needed to melt 2.5 kg of ice at 0 °C and then raise the temperature of the melted water to 20 °C. [3]

3. The heating element of a 3 kW electric kettle is just immersed when the kettle contains 0.4 kg of water. The kettle is designed to hold 1.6 kg of water when filled. Calculate
   a) the mass of water which would need to boil away after the kettle has been filled in order to expose the heating element
   b) the energy needed to boil away this mass of water
   c) the time taken by the heating element to supply this quantity of energy. [4]

4. Water flows from an electric shower at a rate of 20 g/s. The water enters the shower at 15 °C and leaves it at 45 °C. Calculate
   a) the mass of water leaving the shower in 300 s
   b) the energy needed to heat this mass of water from 15 °C to 42 °C
   c) the power of the electric heater in the shower. [4]

5. In a nuclear power station, water enters the heat exchanger at 20 °C and leaves as steam at 100 °C. Calculate
   a) the energy needed to change 1 kg of water at 20 °C to steam at 100 °C
   b) the mass of water that must enter the heat exchanger each second if heat is to be transferred at a rate of 1000 MJ/s. [5]

More about materials

3.3 The gas laws

PREVIEW

At the end of this topic you will be able to:

- explain what is meant by the absolute zero of temperature
- relate the Celsius scale of temperature to the absolute scale
- state and use the combined gas law.

How much do you already know? Work out your score on page 139.

Test yourself

1. Convert a) 100 °C to kelvins (K)
   b) 77 K to degrees Celsius (°C). [2]

2. a) State the combined gas law.
   b) A fixed mass of gas occupies a container of volume 5.0 m³ at a pressure of 120 kPa and a temperature of 300 K. The volume is reduced to 4.0 m³ and the temperature is reduced to 250 K. Calculate the pressure of this amount of gas at this new volume and temperature. [5]

3. The table below shows readings of the pressure, volume and temperature of a fixed mass of an ideal gas. Complete the table. [4]

mass/g	10	10	10	10	10
volume/m³	0.01	0.02	0.02		0.02
pressure/kPa	100		100	50	60
temperature/K	300	300		450	

4. In an electrolysis experiment, a gas was evolved at an electrode and collected. The volume of gas collected was 60 cm³ at a temperature of 17 °C and a pressure of 110 kPa.

   a) Convert 17 °C into kelvins.
   b) Calculate the volume of this amount of gas at a temperature of 0 °C and a pressure of 100 kPa. [4]

5. Use the kinetic theory to explain why the pressure of a gas in a sealed container increases when it is heated. [3]

Temperature scales

The **Celsius scale** is defined in terms of the temperature of pure melting ice (0 °C) and the temperature of steam at atmospheric pressure (100 °C).

The **absolute scale** of temperature is related to the Celsius scale by adding 273. The unit of temperature on the absolute scale is the **kelvin** (K).

temperature in kelvins = temperature in °C + 273

The lowest possible temperature is called **absolute zero**. This is −273 °C or 0 K.

Combining the gas laws

Boyle's law states that for a fixed mass of gas at constant temperature, its pressure multiplied by its volume is always the same. An ideal gas is defined as a gas that obeys Boyle's law.

Charles' law states that for a fixed mass of ideal gas at constant pressure, its volume is proportional to its absolute temperature.

The **pressure law** states that for a fixed mass of gas at constant volume, the pressure is proportional to the absolute temperature.

Below are the laws written as equations.

★ **Boyle's law:** pV =   constant
★ **Charles' law:** V/T =   constant
★ **pressure law:** p/T =   constant

The three laws can be expressed as a single equation, called the **combined gas law**. For a fixed mass of gas

$$\frac{pV}{T} = \text{constant}$$

where p = gas pressure, V = gas volume and T = absolute temperature of the gas.

More about materials

Maths workshop

Suppose a fixed mass of gas initially at pressure p_1, volume V_1 and temperature T_1 changes its pressure, volume and temperature to p_2, V_2 and T_2, respectively. Since pV/T is unchanged, then

$$\frac{p_1 V_1}{T_1} = \frac{p_2 V_2}{T_2}$$

If five of the six quantities in this equation are known, the unknown quantity can be calculated. For example, if T_2 is the unknown quantity, you can rearrange the above equation to make T_2 the subject

$$T_2 = \frac{p_2 V_2 T_1}{p_1 V_1}$$

The known values can then be substituted into the equation to find the unknown quantity.

Measurement of gas pressure

The **Bourdon gauge** measures the absolute pressure of a gas. The flexible copper tube uncoils slightly when the gas pressure is applied to it. This moves a pointer across the scale.

The **U-tube manometer** measures the excess pressure of a gas. This is its absolute pressure less atmospheric pressure. The height difference h of the two levels in the U-tube is a measure of the excess pressure. (See page 75.)

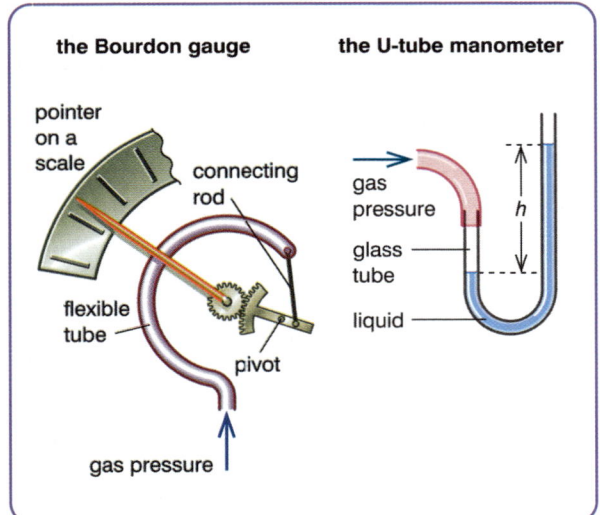

Measuring pressure

Atmospheric pressure

Some applications of atmospheric pressure are shown in the diagram. Each application works because of the force due to atmospheric pressure.

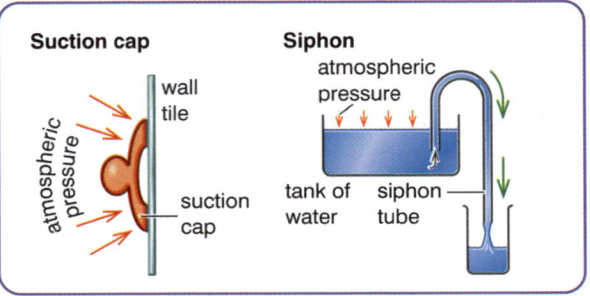

Using atmospheric pressure

Atmospheric pressure decreases with height, and changes slightly with the weather. At sea level, its mean value is 100 kPa. It can be measured using a barometer. The diagram here shows one type of barometer.

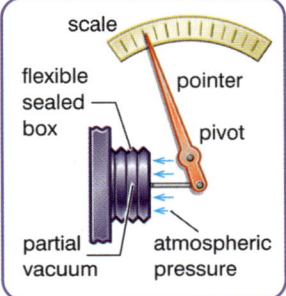

An aneroid barometer

Kinetic theory

The arrangement and movement of the particles in a solid, liquid or gas are used to explain its physical properties.

Shape and flow: the arrangement of particles in each state of matter is shown in the diagram below.

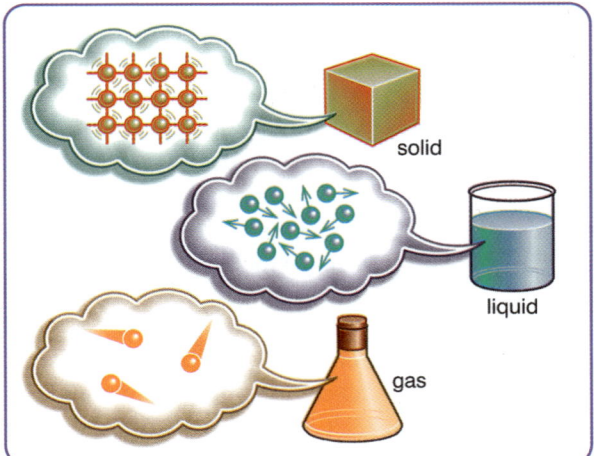

Particles in a solid, liquid and gas

More about materials

★ A solid has its own shape because its atoms are locked together by strong bonds. The atoms vibrate about fixed positions.

★ In a liquid, the atoms move about at random in contact with each other.

★ In a gas, the atoms move about at random at relatively large distances from each other.

Change of state: energy is needed to melt a solid or vaporise a liquid. This energy, called **latent heat**, is used to break bonds holding the particles together. When a vapour condenses or a liquid freezes, bonds are formed and latent heat is released.

Above a certain temperature, a gas cannot be liquefied no matter how much pressure is applied to it. This temperature is called the **critical temperature** of the gas. The term 'vapour' is used for a gas below its critical temperature.

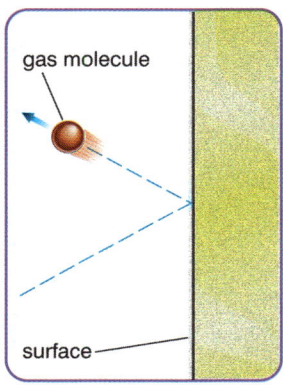

Impacts like this cause pressure

Gas pressure: the molecules in a gas move about at random very fast, colliding with and rebounding from each other and any surfaces the gas is in contact with. The pressure of a gas in a container is caused by the force of the impacts on the container surface. Raising the temperature of the gas at constant volume raises the pressure. This is because the molecules move faster when the temperature is raised, causing harder impacts at a faster rate, and hence higher pressure.

Evaporation: a liquid can evaporate below its boiling point because its molecules have a range of speeds. The faster-moving molecules are able to escape from the attraction of the other molecules. Raising the temperature increases the rate of evaporation. This is because more molecules move fast enough to escape. Evaporation only occurs at the surface of a liquid, unlike boiling which occurs throughout the liquid.

ROUND UP

How much have you improved? Work out your improvement index on page 139.

1. In a chemistry experiment, a volume of 1.20×10^{-4} cm^3 of gas is collected at a pressure of 105 kPa and a temperature of 21 °C. Calculate
   a) the volume of this gas at a pressure of 101 kPa and a temperature of 0 °C
   b) the pressure the gas would exert if its temperature was raised to 100 °C at a volume of 1.20×10^{-4} cm^3. [6]

2. A hot water tank contains 150 cm^3 (= 1.50×10^{-4} m^3) of air trapped by water at the top of the tank where the temperature is 42 °C. The pressure of this trapped air is 150 kPa.
   a) Calculate the volume of this mass of air at a temperature of 0 °C and a pressure of 100 kPa.
   b) The density of air at 0 °C and 100 kPa pressure is 1.25 kg/m^3. Calculate the mass of the trapped air. [5]

3. A sealed food can holds 10 cm^3 of air at 100 kPa pressure and a temperature of 15 °C.
   a) Calculate the pressure of this air if the temperature of the can is raised to 200 °C, assuming the volume of the air **(i)** does not change **(ii)** changes to 8 cm^3 because the food expands in the can when heated.
   b) Use the result of your calculation to explain why it is important to pierce the can before heating it. [5]

4. a) Use the kinetic theory to explain why the pressure of a gas increases when its volume is reduced at constant temperature.
   b) A cylinder of nitrogen gas contained 0.004 m^3 at a temperature of 10 °C and a pressure of 110 kPa. The cylinder was moved to a room where the temperature was 20 °C and a syringe was used to draw off 0.001 m^3 of the gas. Calculate the pressure of the gas remaining in the cylinder. [6]

Well done if you've improved. Don't worry if you haven't. Take a break and try again.

More about materials

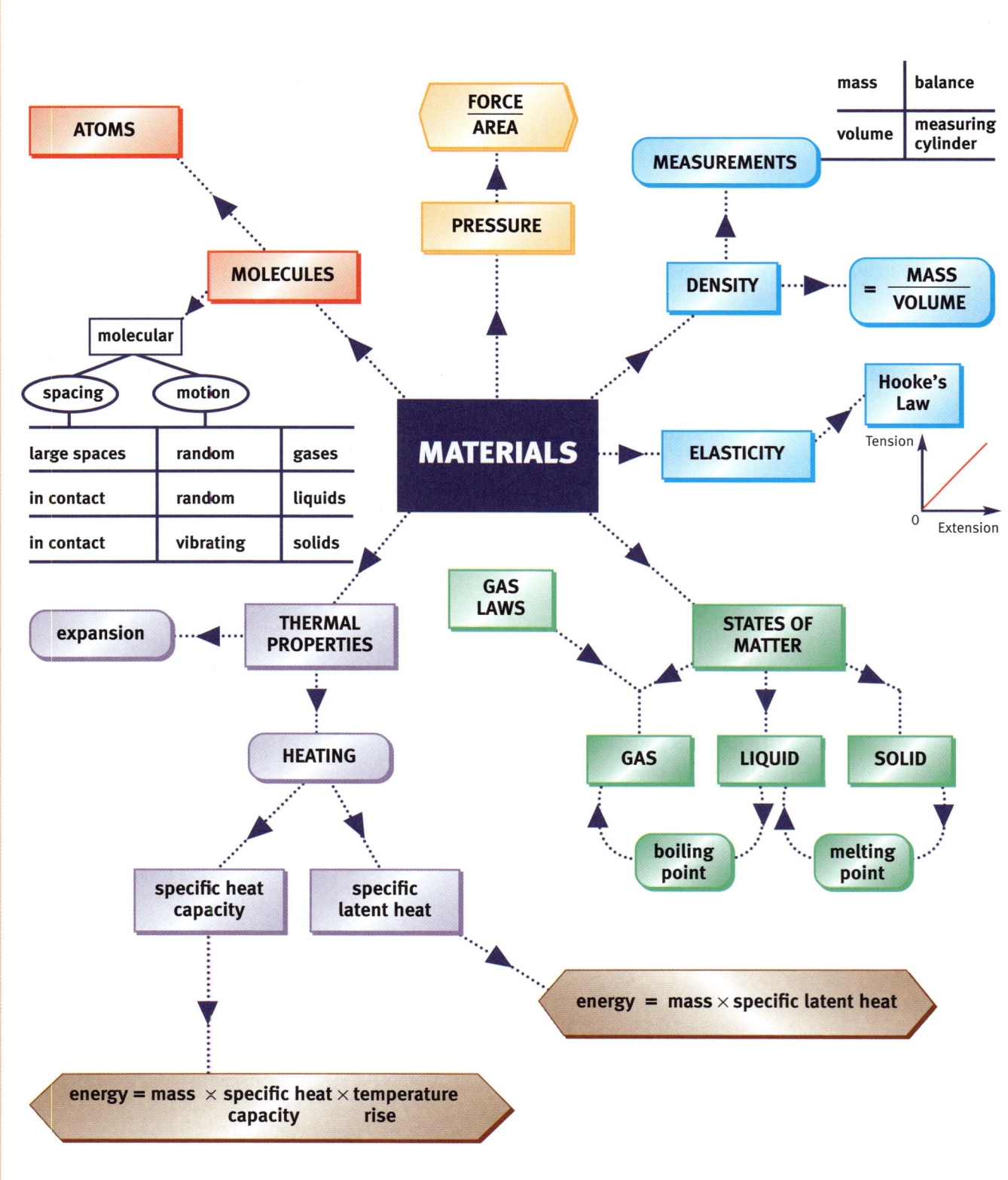

Concept map: materials

Waves — Chapter 4

PREVIEW

At the end of this topic you will be able to:
- describe different types of waves
- explain what is meant by a transverse wave and a longitudinal wave
- explain what is meant by the amplitude, wavelength and frequency of a wave
- relate the speed of a wave to its wavelength and its frequency
- describe reflection, refraction and diffraction as wave properties.

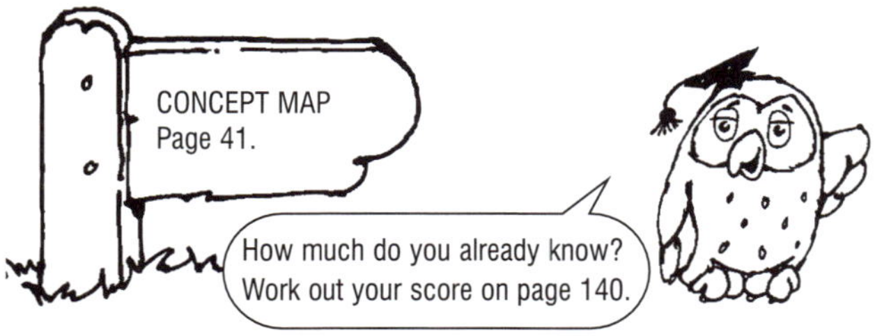

CONCEPT MAP Page 41.

How much do you already know? Work out your score on page 140.

Test yourself

1. State four different types of waves. [4]
2. a) What is the difference between a longitudinal wave and a transverse wave? [2]
   b) Is the primary component of a seismic wave longitudinal or transverse? [1]
3. State one type of wave that can travel through a vacuum, and one type that cannot. [2]
4. The diagram shows a snapshot of a wave travelling from left to right.

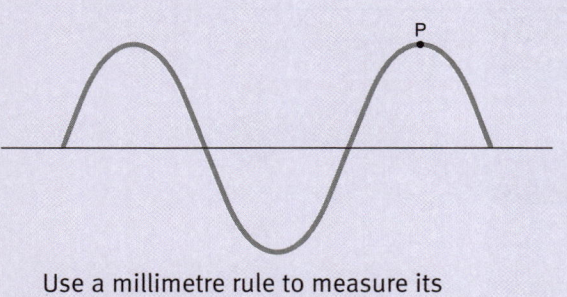

   Use a millimetre rule to measure its wavelength and its amplitude. [2]

5. If the wave in **4** is travelling at 20 mm/s, what is
   a) its frequency? [1]
   b) the number of complete cycles each point goes through in 1 minute? [1]
6. In the diagram in **4**, what is the position of point P
   a) exactly 1.0 s after the snapshot shown?
   b) exactly 4.0 s after the snapshot shown? [2]
7. Why are waves on the seashore not reflected when they run up the beach? [2]
8. What is meant by refraction of waves? [2]
9. When waves pass through a gap they spread out. Is the spreading increased or decreased when
   a) the gap is made narrower?
   b) the wavelength is decreased? [2]
10. a) Calculate the frequency of sound waves in air which have a wavelength of 0.40 m, given that the speed of sound in air is 340 m/s. [1]
    b) Calculate the wavelength of ultrasonic waves of frequency 1.5 MHz in water, given that the speed of the waves is 1500 m/s. [1]

4.1 What is a wave?

Waves can carry energy without carrying matter. Drop a stone in a pond and observe the ripples as they spread out. A small object floating on the water would bob up and down as the ripples pass it. The ripples are waves on the water surface carrying energy across the pond. A water wave is an example of a disturbance which travels through a substance. Electromagnetic waves do not need a substance to travel through; all other types of waves do.

Waves

4.2 Transverse and longitudinal waves

Different types of waves

Some types of waves are listed below. You need to know how they are produced, what they have in common and how they differ from each other. They include:
- water waves
- waves on a string or a rope
- seismic waves
- sound waves
- electromagnetic waves (radio waves, microwaves, infrared radiation, visible light, ultraviolet light, X-rays, gamma rays).

Making waves

All waves except electromagnetic waves need a substance to travel through. Waves are sent through the medium when one part of the substance is made to vibrate. For example, waves can be sent along a long stretched coil by making one end vibrate. The vibrations can be in any direction, but there are two particular ways of sending waves down the coil.

★ **Longitudinal waves** can be created by making one end vibrate to and fro along the coil. At any point, the vibrations are parallel to the direction in which the waves travel. The coil windings are squeezed and stretched as the waves pass down the coil.

★ **Transverse waves** can be created by making one end vibrate at right angles to the coil. At any point along the coil, the vibrations are at 90° to the direction in which the waves travel.

More about transverse waves

'Transverse' means 'across', so transverse waves vibrate in a direction that is across (perpendicular to) the direction in which the wave travels. Examples of transverse waves include:
- waves on a rope or a string
- electromagnetic waves
- secondary (S) seismic waves.

Transverse waves are **polarised** if their vibrations are in one plane only. However, if the plane of vibration continually changes, the waves on the rope are **unpolarised**.

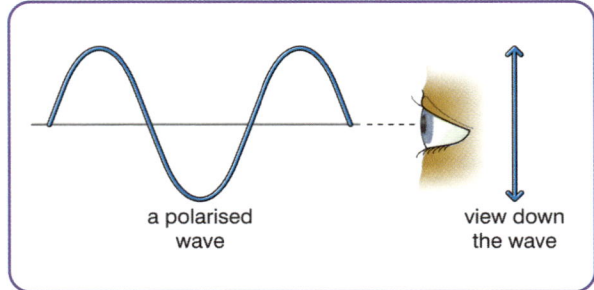

Polarisation

More about longitudinal waves

'Longitudinal' means 'along', so longitudinal waves vibrate along (parallel to) the direction in which the wave travels. They squeeze and stretch the medium. Examples of longitudinal waves include:
- sound waves
- primary (P) seismic waves.

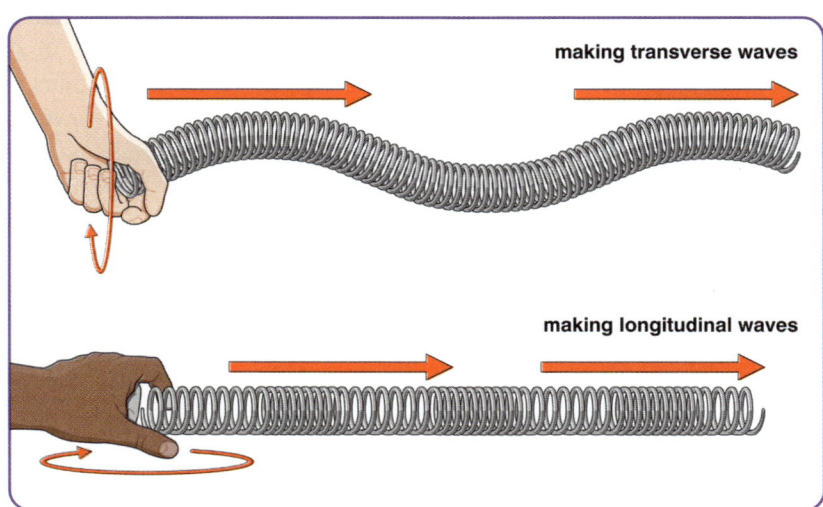

Transverse and longitudinal waves

Waves

4.3 Measuring waves

Look at the snapshot of a transverse wave in the diagram below. The wave is travelling from left to right, but you can't tell this from the snapshot. Each point on the wave vibrates at 90° to the wave direction.

★ **One complete cycle** of vibration of any point returns the point to the same position and direction it had at the start of the cycle. In this time, a wave crest at the point is replaced by the next wave crest.

★ **The amplitude of a wave** is the height of the wave crest above the centre. This is the same as the depth of a wave trough below the centre.

★ **The wavelength of a wave** (symbol λ, pronounced 'lambda') is the distance from one crest to the next crest. This is the same as the distance from a trough to the next trough.

★ **The frequency of a wave** (symbol f) is the number of crests passing a given position each second. This is the same as the number of complete cycles of vibration per second of any point. The unit of frequency is the hertz (symbol Hz), equal to 1 cycle per second.

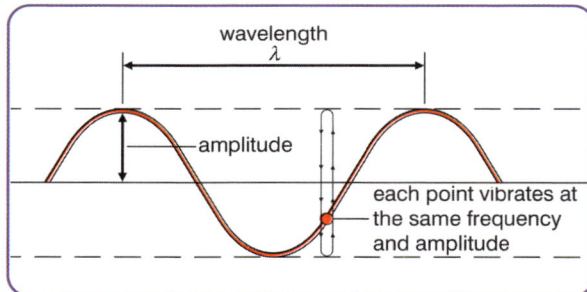

Wave measurements

Question

1. What are the wavelength and the amplitude of the wave shown above?

Speed

★ The speed v of a wave is the distance travelled by a crest in one second. The unit of speed is the metre per second (m/s).

★ The speed of a wave can be calculated from its frequency and wavelength using the following equation:

speed = frequency × wavelength
(in m/s)   (in Hz)   (in m)

Maths workshop

- The equation for speed can be written in symbols as $v = f\lambda$, where v is the speed, f is the frequency and λ is the wavelength.

- To find the frequency f from $v = f\lambda$, the equation needs to be rearranged to make f its subject.

  Start with $\quad f\lambda = v$

  then divide both sides by λ to give

  $$\frac{f\lambda}{\lambda} = \frac{v}{\lambda}$$

  then cancel λ top and bottom on the left-hand side of the equation to give

  $$f = \frac{v}{\lambda}$$

- To find the wavelength λ from $v = f\lambda$, transfer f from the top on one side to the bottom on the other side to give

  $$\lambda = \frac{v}{f}$$

Questions

2. Complete the table below by calculating the missing value of speed, frequency or wavelength.

wavelength/m	2.5	0.1			5×10^{-7}
frequency/Hz		3400	500	3750	
speed/m/s	340		80	1500	3×10^8

3. Suppose the wave in the diagram is travelling at a speed of 60 mm/s to the left. Calculate its frequency using the wavelength measurement from question **1**.

Answers

1. Amplitude = 10 mm, wavelength = 40 mm
2. 136 Hz, 340 m/s, 0.160 m, 0.40 m, 6×10^{14} Hz
3. 1.5 Hz

Waves

4.4 Wave properties

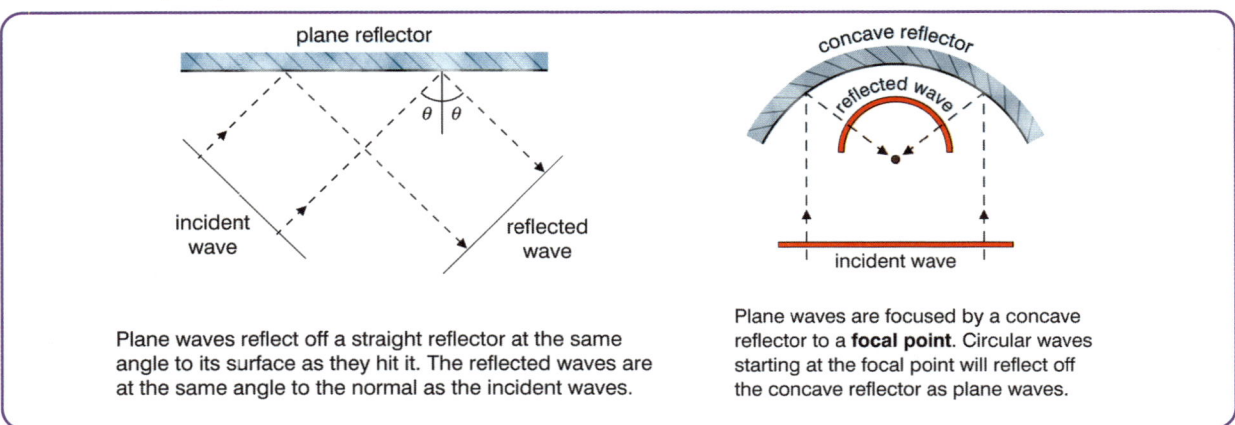

Plane waves reflect off a straight reflector at the same angle to its surface as they hit it. The reflected waves are at the same angle to the normal as the incident waves.

Plane waves are focused by a concave reflector to a **focal point**. Circular waves starting at the focal point will reflect off the concave reflector as plane waves.

Reflections on reflection

Reflection

The shape and the direction of a reflected wave depend on the shape of the incident wave and on the shape of the reflecting surface.

Note
Straight waves are sometimes called **plane waves**. A line perpendicular to a wall or boundary is called a **normal**.

Refraction

When a plane wave passes across a straight boundary:
- its wavelength changes if the wave speed changes at the boundary; the frequency does not change
- its direction of motion changes if its direction is not perpendicular to the boundary.

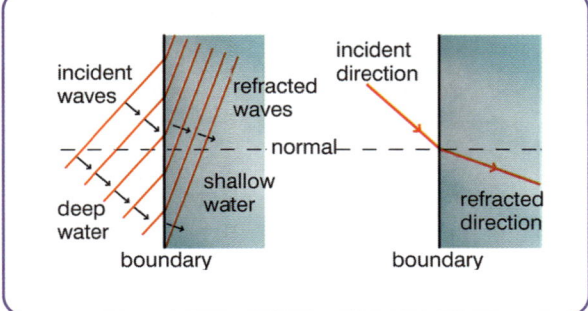

Refraction

Diffraction

★ Waves spread out when they pass through a gap or behind an obstacle. This process is called **diffraction**.

★ The spreading is greater the longer the wavelength or the narrower the gap.

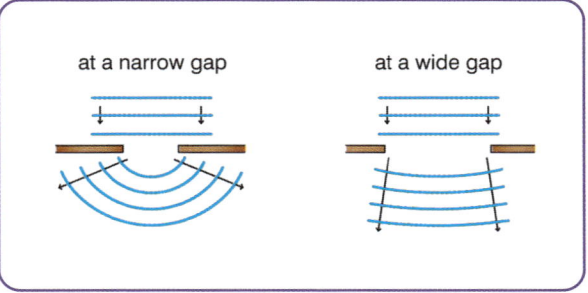

Diffraction

Questions

A satellite TV dish needs to be pointed in the correct direction to obtain a picture.

a) Using a diagram, explain how a satellite dish works.

b) Why are larger dishes needed in northern Europe than in southern Europe?

Answers

a) The dish is a concave reflector which focuses radio waves from the satellite onto an aerial at the focal point.
b) The satellite is over the equator so the radio waves travel further through the atmosphere to reach northern Europe, so they become weaker. Hence a larger dish is needed to collect more radio waves.

Waves

ROUND UP

How much have you improved? Work out your improvement index on page 140.

1. a) Which of the following can be classified as (i) longitudinal waves (ii) transverse waves?

   water waves, radio waves, sound waves, waves on a rope [3]

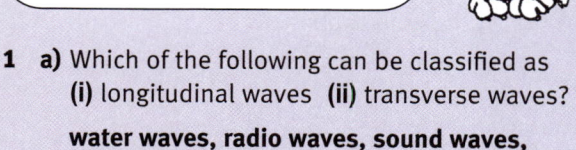

   b) State three differences between sound waves and light waves. [3]

2. Copy and complete each of these sketches, showing the wave after reflection. [4]

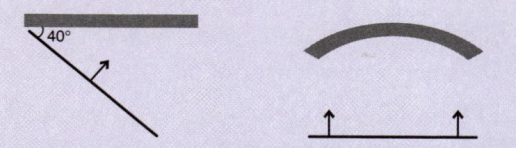

3. a) What is the name for the process that takes place when waves spread out after passing through a gap? [1]

   b) Does the spreading increase or decrease if
   (i) the gap is made narrower and the wavelength of the waves is not changed?
   (ii) the wavelength is made shorter and the gap width is not changed?
   (iii) the gap is made narrower and the wavelength is made longer? [3]

4. a) When light passes from air into glass, it slows down. What happens to its wavelength and its frequency? [2]

   b) The diagram shows plane waves about to cross a boundary between shallow and deep water. Copy and complete the diagram by showing the waves in the deep water as well as the shallow water. [2]

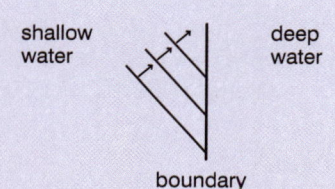

5. a) Sound travels at a speed of 1500 m/s in water. Calculate the wavelength in water of sound waves of frequency 3000 Hz. [1]

   b) Plane water waves of wavelength 0.2 m travel past five ducks spaced 0.3 m apart in a straight line. Each crest takes 3.0 s to pass from the mother duck at one end to the last duck at the other end. Calculate (i) the speed (ii) the frequency of the waves. [2]

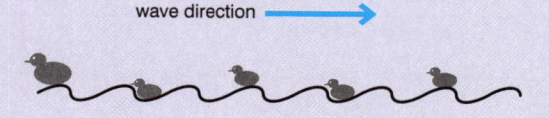

6. a) When sound waves pass through an open door, they spread out. What is the name for this process? [1]

   b) If the frequency of the sound waves is increased, what happens to the amount of spreading? [1]

7. a) A local radio station broadcasts at a frequency of 100 MHz. Calculate the wavelength of these radio waves, given that radio waves travel through air at a speed of 300 000 km/s. [1]

   b) The aerial of a portable radio is turned through 90°, causing the reception to become weaker. Explain why this happens. [3]

   c) A radio telescope consists of a large concave dish made from wire mesh with an aerial at its focal point. What is the purpose of the wire mesh? [1]

8. A boat travelling at constant speed produces bow waves as shown.

   How would the bow waves differ if the boat travelled a) faster b) slower? [2]

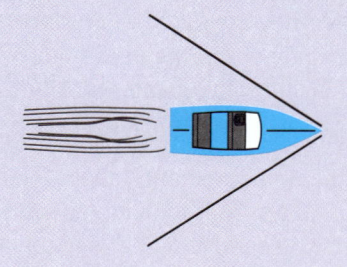

Chapter 5   Sound waves and seismic waves

PREVIEW

At the end of this topic you will be able to:
- describe how sound is produced and transmitted
- explain how pitch and loudness are related to frequency and amplitude
- describe reflection, refraction, diffraction and absorption of sound
- explain what ultrasound is and describe some uses of ultrasound
- explain how seismic waves are produced, measured and used.

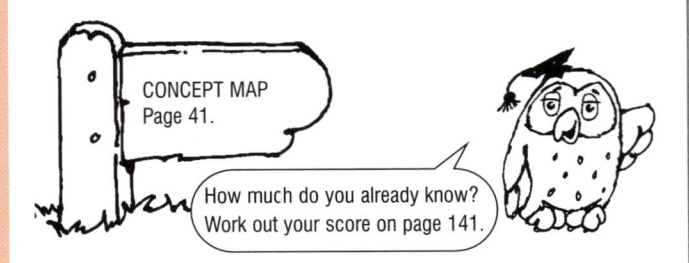

CONCEPT MAP Page 41.

How much do you already know? Work out your score on page 141.

Test yourself

1. a) Are sound waves longitudinal or transverse? [1]
   b) Are seismic waves longitudinal or transverse? [2]
2. What is special about the sound produced by a vibrating tuning fork? [1]
3. a) The pitch of a note produced by plucking a guitar string can be altered by changing the tension or changing the length of the vibrating section of the string. How does the pitch of the note change when the string is (i) tightened (ii) lengthened? [2]
   b) Two guitar strings of the same material have equal lengths but different thicknesses. They are tuned to produce notes of the same pitch when plucked. Which string is under the greater tension? [2]
4. What is an echo? [1]
5. How do the amplitude and the wavelength of the sound waves from a loudspeaker change if the sound is made a) louder at the same pitch b) quieter at higher pitch? [4]
6. A teacher is talking in a classroom with the door to the corridor open. The teacher's voice can be heard down the corridor even though the teacher cannot be seen from there. What property of sound is responsible for this? [1]
7. a) Which frequency **A** to **D** is nearest to the highest sound frequency that can be heard by the human ear? [1]

   A 200 Hz   B 2000 Hz   C 20 000 Hz
   D 200 000 Hz

   b) Which frequency **A** to **D** is nearest to the frequency at which the human ear is most sensitive? [1]

   c) A telephone circuit does not transmit frequencies above 4000 Hz. Explain how this affects voice signals. [1]
8. a) Outline how an ultrasonic depth gauge on a ship works. [5]
   b) State two other uses of ultrasonics. [2]
9. a) Ultrasonic waves of frequency 2 MHz in air travel at a speed of 340 m/s. Calculate the wavelength of these waves. [1]
   b) These waves travel faster in water than in air. On entering water from air, what change occurs in (i) the frequency (ii) the wavelength of the waves? [2]
10. a) What causes earthquakes? [2]
    b) Why are secondary (S) waves from an earthquake unable to travel through the Earth's centre to the opposite side of the Earth? [3]

5.1 Properties of sound

Sound waves are longitudinal. They are created by an object vibrating in a medium. The object pushes and pulls on the medium. The particles of the medium vibrate to and fro along the direction in which the sound travels.

Sound waves and seismic waves

Sound waves can be displayed using a microphone and an oscilloscope, as shown below.

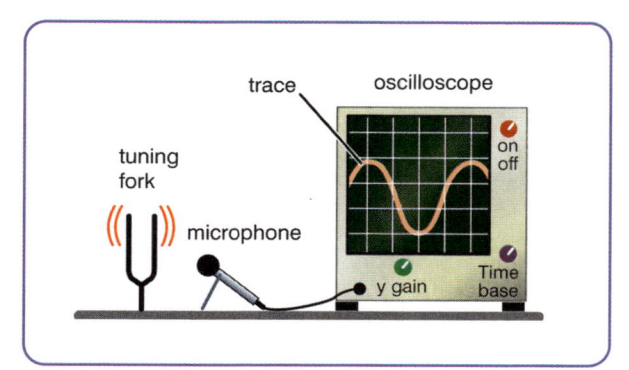

Displaying sound

The oscilloscope trace shows how the amplitude of the sound wave varies with time. The trace is usually referred to as the **waveform**. The trace on the screen is a transverse wave; the sound wave that creates the trace is a longitudinal wave.

★ If the sound is made louder, the trace becomes taller. The amplitude of a sound wave represents the volume.

★ If the sound is lowered in pitch, the trace is stretched out on the screen. The frequency of a sound wave represents the pitch.

★ Most sounds have more complicated waveforms than the pure waveform shown in the diagram.

Echoes

Sound is reflected by a hard surface such as a brick wall. **Echoes** are caused by sound reflections. First the original sound is heard, then an echo may be heard a little later due to reflection off the wall. The echo is delayed because the echo sound waves travel further than the direct sound waves.

Absorption of sound

Soft surfaces such as curtains absorb sound instead of reflecting it or transmitting it. This is why a curtained room sounds different from a bare room.

Refraction of sound

Like all waves, sound waves can be refracted. The speed of sound in air will change if the air temperature changes with height. Sound created on the ground may then be refracted, and may be heard a long way away from where it was produced.

Diffraction of sound

Sound waves spread through gaps and round obstacles. The sound from a car engine may be heard on the other side of a large building because of diffraction. The sound waves from the car engine pass round the edge of the building and spread round it on the other side.

Sound cannot travel through a vacuum

This fact is demonstrated by removing the air surrounding a ringing bell in a bell jar. The ringing bell can be heard before the air is pumped out. The sound of the bell fades away as the air is removed. If the air is allowed back into the bell jar, the sound returns.

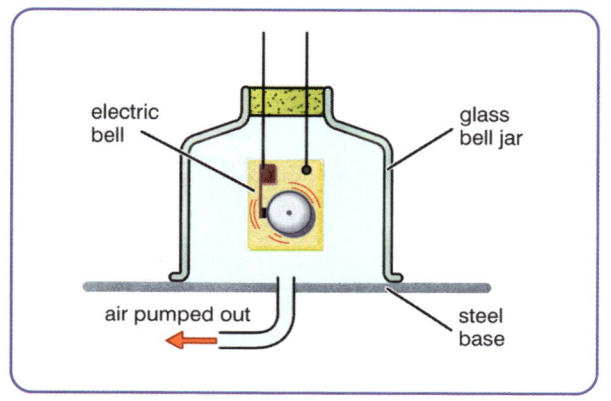

A soundless bell

Measuring the speed of sound

Two people stand a measured distance apart, at least 500 m. The starter makes a loud short sound, for example with a large gong, in view of the other person (the timer). The timer times the interval between observing the sound being created and hearing it. The speed of sound is calculated from the distance divided by the time taken.

To account for wind speed, the two people change roles and the experiment is repeated to give an average value.

Sound waves and seismic waves

5.2 Ultrasound

Hearing

The human ear is a remarkable organ. The loudest sounds your ears can withstand without damage are about one million million times more powerful than the faintest sound you can hear. Loudness levels are expressed in **decibels** (dB) where 0 dB is at the lower threshold of hearing and every 10 dB extra corresponds to ten times more power. The graph shows how the lower threshold of hearing varies with frequency.

★ The human ear is most sensitive at a frequency of about 3000 Hz.

★ The upper frequency limit for the human ear is about 20 000 Hz.

★ Hearing usually deteriorates with age – your upper frequency limit will decrease as you become older.

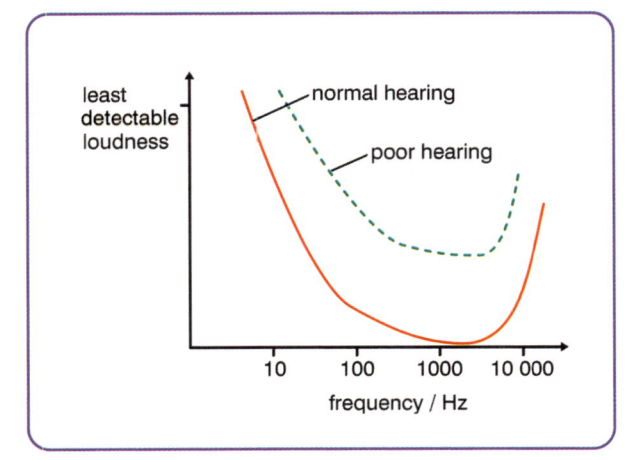

Hearing response

Ultrasound

Ultrasound is defined as sound at frequencies above the upper limit of the human ear. In other words, any sound waves of frequency above 20 kHz will be ultrasound.

Ultrasonic cleaning: dirt particles are removed from street lamps by immersing the lamp in an ultrasonic cleaning tank operating at 40 kHz. The ultrasonic waves in the water agitate the dirt particles which are then dispersed by the water.

Depth finding: the depth of the sea bed can be determined by sending ultrasonic pulses from a ship towards the sea bed, and timing how long the reflected pulses take to return to the ship. If the speed of sound c in water is known, the depth of the sea bed can be calculated from $\frac{1}{2}ct$, where t is the time taken for each pulse to travel to the sea bed and back.

Metal fatigue tests: cracks inside a metal weaken the metal, but cannot be seen from the outside. Such cracks can be detected using an ultrasonic probe. This sends ultrasonic waves into the metal and picks up reflections from internal boundaries within the metal.

Ultrasonic medical scanner: this is used to obtain images of organs within the body. It is also widely used to form images of unborn babies to monitor the health of the baby and the mother. An ultrasonic probe moved across the body surface directs ultrasonic waves into the human body. Internal boundaries partially reflect the ultrasonic waves, and the reflected waves are detected by the same probe, which is connected to a computer. The probe builds up an image of the reflecting boundaries inside the body. Unlike X-rays, ultrasonic waves do not cause ionisation, and are therefore thought to be harmless at low power.

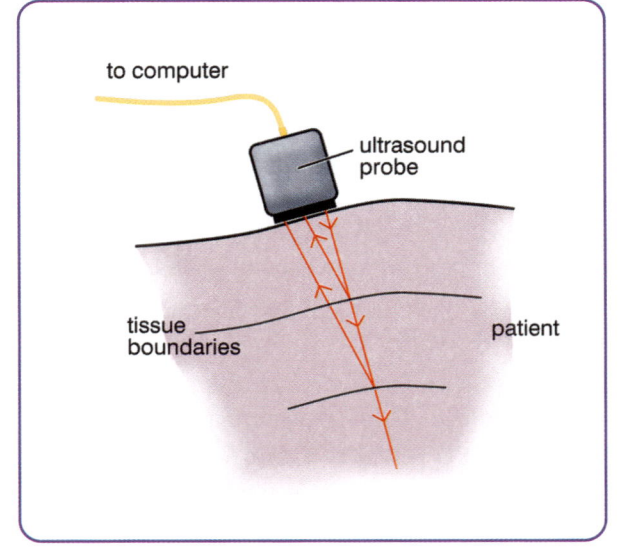

Ultrasonic scanner

Sound waves and seismic waves

5.3 Seismic waves

Inside the Earth

The Earth is thought to have formed about 4600 million years ago, originally in a molten state which gradually cooled and solidified. More dense materials such as iron sank to the centre when it was molten. The least dense material formed the Earth's crust.

Earthquakes

★ Earthquake belts occur where two plates press against each other or slide past each other. Stress builds up which is suddenly released when one plate gives way to the other. The crust shakes violently and seismic waves spread out through the Earth.

★ The point where the seismic waves originate from is called the **focus** of the earthquake. The nearest point on the surface directly above the focus is called the **epicentre**.

★ The energy released by an earthquake is measured on the **Richter scale** which is a 'times ten' scale. An earthquake that registers at a certain point on the Richter scale releases ten times as much energy as an earthquake that registers on the next point below.

Analysing seismic waves

An instrument called a **seismometer** is used to detect seismic waves.

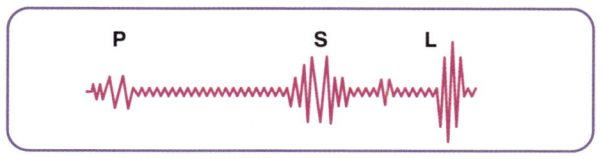

Recording of seismic waves made by a seismometer

★ **Primary (P)** waves cause the first tremors. These are longitudinal waves.

★ **Secondary (S)** waves arrive a few minutes later, causing more tremors. They travel more slowly than P waves. These are transverse waves.

★ **Long (L)** waves arrive last to cause the main shock. These travel along the crust only, making the surface move violently up and down as well as to and fro.

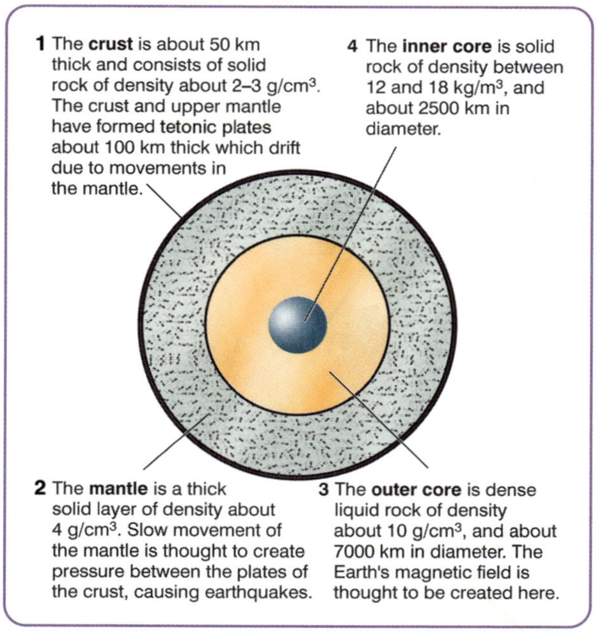

1 The **crust** is about 50 km thick and consists of solid rock of density about 2–3 g/cm³. The crust and upper mantle have formed tetonic plates about 100 km thick which drift due to movements in the mantle.

2 The **mantle** is a thick solid layer of density about 4 g/cm³. Slow movement of the mantle is thought to create pressure between the plates of the crust, causing earthquakes.

3 The **outer core** is dense liquid rock of density about 10 g/cm³, and about 7000 km in diameter. The Earth's magnetic field is thought to be created here.

4 The **inner core** is solid rock of density between 12 and 18 kg/m³, and about 2500 km in diameter.

The structure of the Earth

Continental drift is due to the gradual movement of tectonic plates.

Handy hint

P waves **P**ush and **P**ull.
S waves **S**hake **S**ide to **S**ide.
L waves go the **L**ong way round.

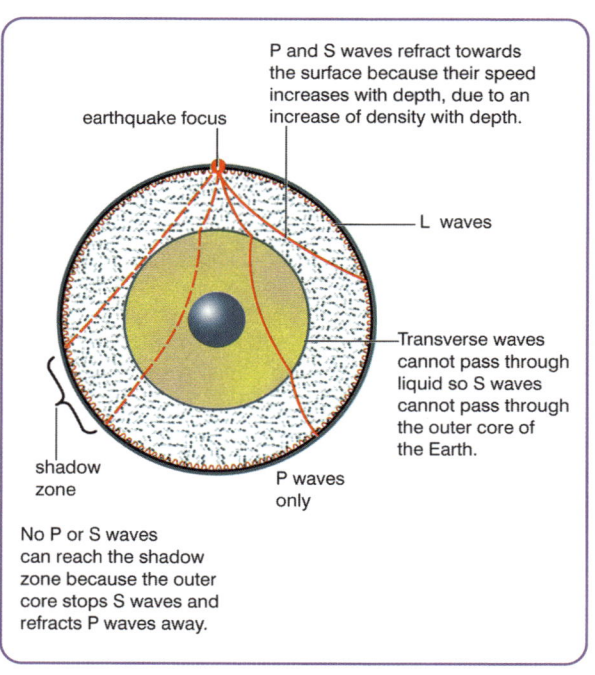

P and S waves refract towards the surface because their speed increases with depth, due to an increase of density with depth.

earthquake focus

L waves

Transverse waves cannot pass through liquid so S waves cannot pass through the outer core of the Earth.

shadow zone

P waves only

No P or S waves can reach the shadow zone because the outer core stops S waves and refracts P waves away.

Seismic waves inside the Earth

Sound waves and seismic waves

5.4 Resonance

On a swing

Higher and higher

A person on a swing moves to and fro, passing through the lowest point again and again. If given a single push, the swing oscillates with an amplitude that decreases with time.

If pushed at the right moment each time the swing is at its highest point, the person goes higher and higher. This is an example of **resonance**.

The swing is an example of an oscillating system. It can oscillate to and fro with its own **natural frequency of oscillation**. If such a system is repeatedly acted on by a force at the same frequency as its natural frequency, the system oscillates more and more.

A trampolinist uses resonance to reach great heights. She can bounce up and down with a natural frequency that depends on the springs of the trampoline and her mass. With training, she learns how to push on the trampoline at the right point in each rebound. As a result she bounces higher and higher.

Shake away

Any solid object that regains its shape after being distorted can be made to resonate. The ability to regain shape is called **elasticity**. The diagram shows a metal blade fixed at one end. If the free end is pushed then released, it vibrates up and down. The stiffer the blade is, the higher its natural frequency of vibration. If an electromagnet carrying an alternating current is placed near to the blade, the blade will resonate when the frequency of the alternating current is adjusted to equal the natural frequency of the blade.

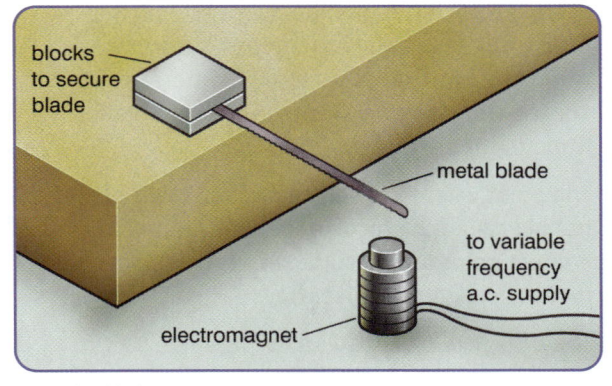

A vibrating blade

A vibrating metal panel in a washing machine resonates when the motor frequency is equal to the natural frequency of the panel. If the panel is not secure, it could break away from the machine frame.

The natural frequency of vibration of an object depends on:
- the **mass** of the object – the greater its mass, the lower will be its natural frequency
- the **size** of the object – the larger an object is, the longer it takes for vibrations to travel through it so the lower will be its natural frequency.

Bad vibrations – good vibrations

Very tall buildings and suspension bridges are known to sway. If they are subjected to seismic vibrations or wind vibrations of frequency equal to the natural frequency of the structure, resonance could occur and damage the structure.

Sound waves and seismic waves

The design of the structure must be such that its natural frequency is well outside the frequency range of the vibrations to which the structure is likely to be subjected.

Wind instruments use resonance to create musical notes. The column of air in the tubing of a wind instrument is made to vibrate when air is forced through the mouthpiece. If the vibrations from the mouthpiece are at the same frequency as the natural frequency of vibration of the air column, the air column resonates with sound. The diagram below shows how the air in an empty bottle can be made to resonate.

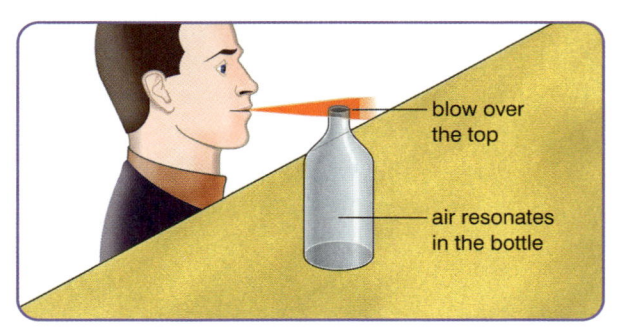

Resonance

★ In general, the bigger the instrument, the deeper the range of notes it can produce. This is because the range of sound wavelengths at which resonance occurs is of the same order of magnitude as the size of the instrument.

★ In some wind instruments like the trombone, making the air column longer causes resonance at a lower frequency. This is because the wavelength of sound at which resonance occurs needs to be longer if the air column is lengthened.

★ The wind organ has pipes of differing length. The longer the pipe, the deeper the note it can produce. The natural frequency of an organ pipe is higher the shorter its length.

Stringed instruments like the guitar produce sound by making the strings vibrate. The vibrations are transmitted to the hollow body of the instrument, causing it to resonate with sound. The shape of the body is important since it must respond evenly to a continuous range of frequencies – if not, it would buzz or screech even in the hands of an expert!

Questions

1. Explain the following observations.
   a) One of the metal panels of a car body vibrates noisily when the car is travelling at a certain speed.
   b) A guitar string vibrates when a second guitar string with the same natural frequency is plucked.
   c) An elephant produces a booming noise whereas a mouse squeaks.

2. a) When a violin bow is drawn across a violin string, a note of sound is produced. What would be the effect on the note of
      (i) shortening the string by holding it down with one finger near one end?
      (ii) varying the pressure on the string as the note is being produced?
   b) The bassoon and the flute are both wind instruments. The bassoon is a much bigger instrument than the flute. Explain why the range of frequencies from a bassoon is lower than the range of frequencies from a flute.

Answers

1. a) At a certain engine speed, the frequency of vibrations from the engine is equal to the natural frequency of the panel. This makes the panel resonate.
   b) The vibrations from the plucked string are at the same frequency as the natural frequency of the other string. The other string therefore resonates when the first string is plucked.
   c) For resonance inside a hollow cavity, the wavelength of sound is of the same order of magnitude as the length of the cavity. Sound produced by an elephant therefore has a longer wavelength and a lower frequency than sound produced by a mouse.

2. a) (i) The pitch of the note would be higher.
      (ii) The pitch and loudness of the note would vary.
   b) The bassoon resonates with sound of much longer wavelengths than a flute does. Therefore the range of frequencies of sound produced by a bassoon is deeper than that produced by a flute.

Sound waves and seismic waves

ROUND UP

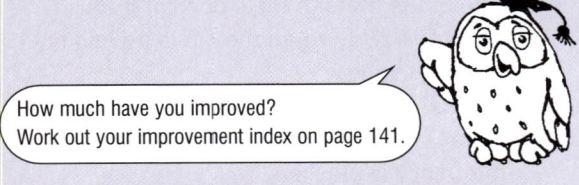

How much have you improved? Work out your improvement index on page 141.

1. The diagram shows a ship at sea near a cliff.

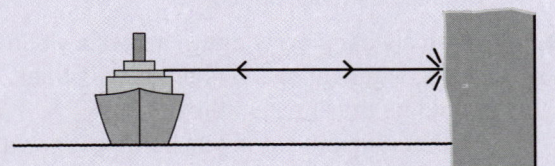

   An echo from the ship's siren is heard 5.0 s after the siren is sounded.

   a) Calculate the distance from the ship to the cliff. The speed of sound in air is 340 m/s. [1]

   b) If the ship was fog-bound, explain how the ship's captain could find out if the ship was moving towards or away from the cliffs. [2]

2. A loudspeaker connected to a signal generator is used to produce a continuous sound of constant pitch and loudness.

   a) Explain how the vibrating surface of the loudspeaker creates sound waves. [2]

   b) Why is a small loudspeaker likely to be able to produce sound waves of high frequency better than a large loudspeaker? [2]

3. The waveform of a note from a musical instrument is shown in the diagram below. Copy and draw on the diagram the waveform you would expect if the same instrument is

   a) played more quietly [2]

   b) played at a lower pitch. [1]

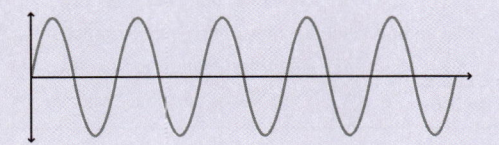

4. The speed of sound in air is 340 m/s.

   a) Calculate the frequency of sound waves of wavelength 0.10 m in air. [1]

   b) Calculate the wavelength of sound waves of frequency 5000 Hz in air. [1]

5. When indoors, noise from outside may be reduced by closing any open windows. How does this reduce the noise from outside? [2]

6. a) An ultrasonic cleaning tank operates at a frequency of 40 kHz. Calculate the wavelength of ultrasonic waves in water. The speed of sound waves in water is 1500 m/s. [1]

   b) When using an ultrasonic hospital scanner, a paste is applied to the body surface where the probe is used.

   (i) Explain why this is necessary. [2]
   (ii) Give two reasons why each reflected pulse is weaker than the pulse emitted by the probe. [2]

7. a) The diagram shows a cross-section of the Earth. The inner core is labelled A.

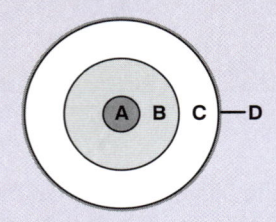

   (i) What are the parts labelled B, C and D? [3]
   (ii) State which of the parts A to D are molten and which are solid. [4]

   b) Why are earthquakes more common in certain parts of the world than in other parts? [1]

8. a) Are primary seismic waves longitudinal or transverse? [1]

   b) (i) Sketch and describe a typical seismic wave trace, labelling the P waves, the S waves and the L waves. [3]
   (ii) Why are S waves unable to travel through the Earth's core? [2]
   (iii) Why do P waves and S waves in the mantle curve towards the surface? [2]
   (iv) Copy the diagram above and use it to explain why shock waves from an earthquake can arrive without being preceded by tremors. [3]

Well done if you've improved. Don't worry if you haven't. Take a break and try again.

Sound waves and seismic waves

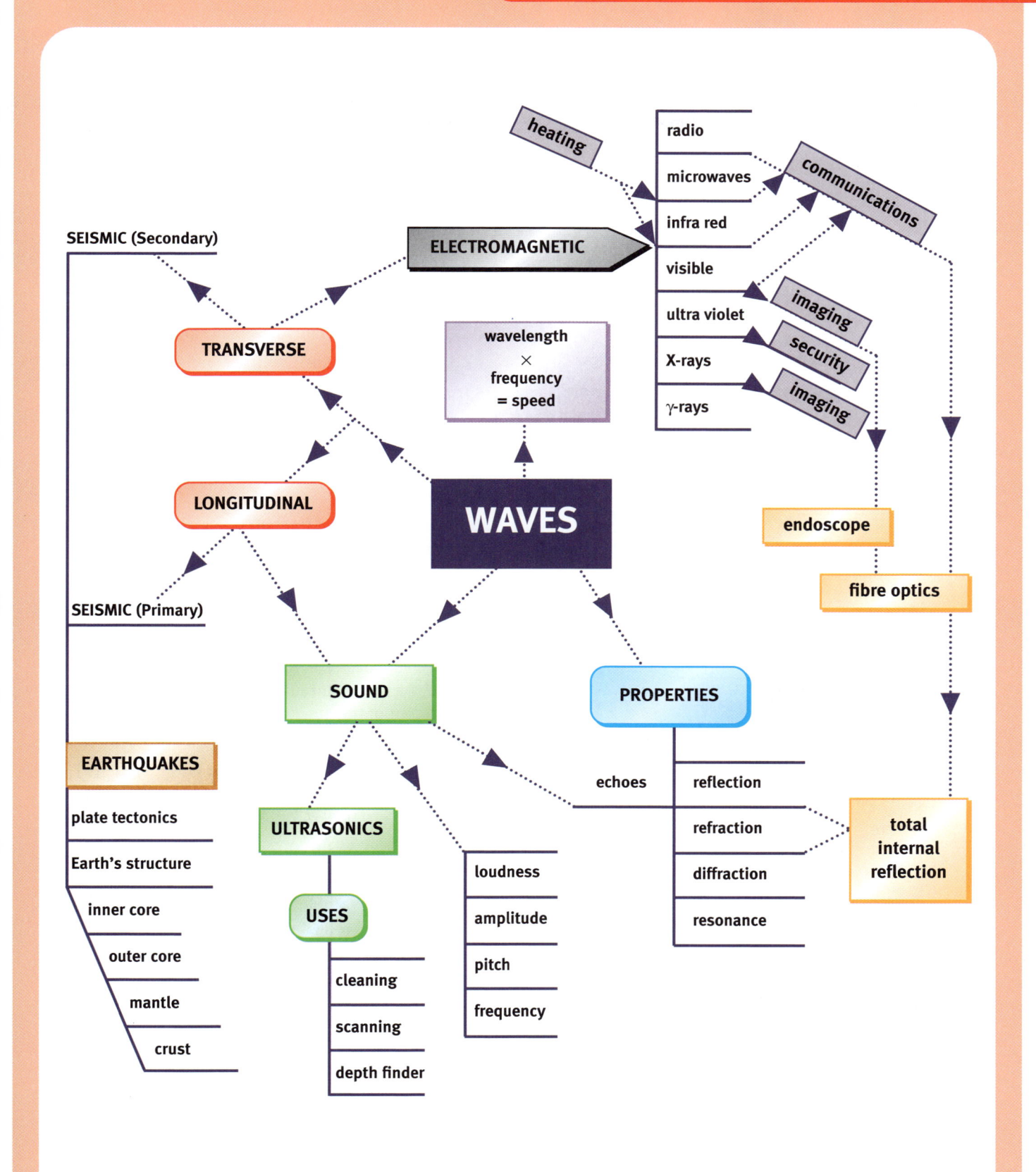

Concept map: waves

- **WAVES**
  - wavelength × frequency = speed
  - **ELECTROMAGNETIC**
    - radio — communications
    - microwaves — communications
    - infra red — heating, communications
    - visible — imaging
    - ultra violet — imaging
    - X-rays — security, imaging
    - γ-rays — imaging
  - **TRANSVERSE**
    - SEISMIC (Secondary)
  - **LONGITUDINAL**
    - SEISMIC (Primary)
  - **SOUND**
    - **ULTRASONICS**
      - **USES**
        - cleaning
        - scanning
        - depth finder
    - loudness
    - amplitude
    - pitch
    - frequency
  - **PROPERTIES**
    - echoes — reflection
    - refraction
    - diffraction
    - resonance
    - total internal reflection
      - endoscope
      - fibre optics
- **EARTHQUAKES**
  - plate tectonics
  - Earth's structure
    - inner core
    - outer core
    - mantle
    - crust

Chapter 6 — Light

PREVIEW

At the end of this topic you will be able to:

- state the law of reflection and explain what is meant by refraction of light
- describe image formation by a plane mirror and describe some uses of a plane mirror
- explain how total internal reflection can occur
- describe some applications of fibre optics
- explain how diffraction affects image detail
- describe how to split white light into a spectrum using a prism.

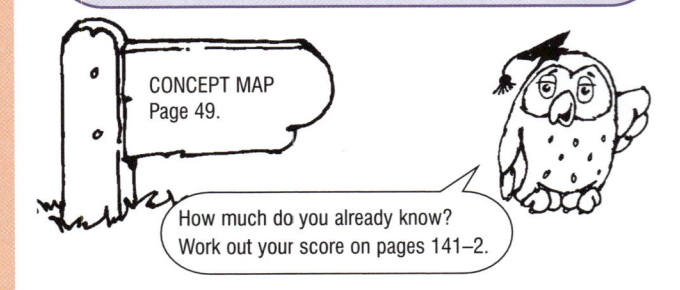

CONCEPT MAP Page 49.

How much do you already know? Work out your score on pages 141–2.

Test yourself

1. a) State the law of reflection at a plane mirror. [1]
   b) A person stands 0.6 m in front of a plane mirror and observes his own image. How far away is the image from the person? [1]

2. a) When a light ray passes from air into glass at a non-zero angle to the normal, does it bend towards or away from the normal? [1]
   b) A light ray passes from a pool of water into air, emerging at an angle of 30° to the vertical, as in the following diagram. Is the angle between the light ray in the water and the vertical more than, less than or equal to 30°? [1]

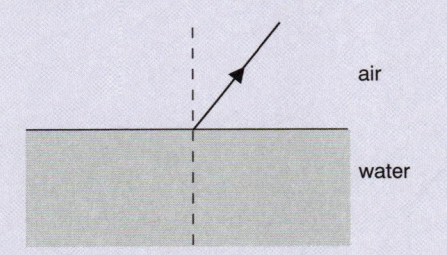

   c) In b), the angle between the light ray in the water and the vertical is increased until the refracted ray emerges along the water surface. What happens if this angle is made larger? [1]

3. State whether each of the following observations is due to reflection or refraction of light.
   (i) You look at yourself in a mirror.
   (ii) A river bed seen from the bank of the river appears much shallower than it really is.
   (iii) A piece of broken glass on the ground glints in sunlight. [3]

4. Why does a swimming pool appear shallower than it really is? [3]

5. When light travels from air into glass,
   a) does its speed increase or decrease?
   b) does its wavelength increase or decrease? [2]

6. State the colours of the visible spectrum. [1]

7. a) A beam of white light is split into a spectrum by passing it through a glass prism. Which colour of the spectrum is refracted least? [1]
   b) A surface that appears blue in white light will appear black in red light. Why? [3]

8. a) Explain what is meant by total internal reflection of light. [1]
   b) State one application of total internal reflection of light. [1]
   c) How does total internal reflection of light differ from reflection of light by a flat mirror? [2]

9. State two uses of fibre optics. [2]

10. a) Is the wavelength of red light less or more than the wavelength of blue light? [1]
    b) Why can you see more detail using a microscope with blue light instead of white light? [3]

Light

6.1 Reflection

The **law of reflection** states that the angle between the reflected ray and the normal is equal to the angle between the incident ray and the normal.

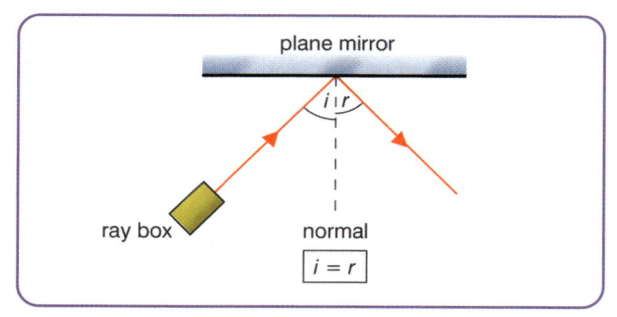

The law of reflection

The diagram above shows how this can be tested using a ray box and a plane mirror. Note that the normal is the line which is perpendicular to the mirror at the point where the light ray meets the mirror.

Mirror images

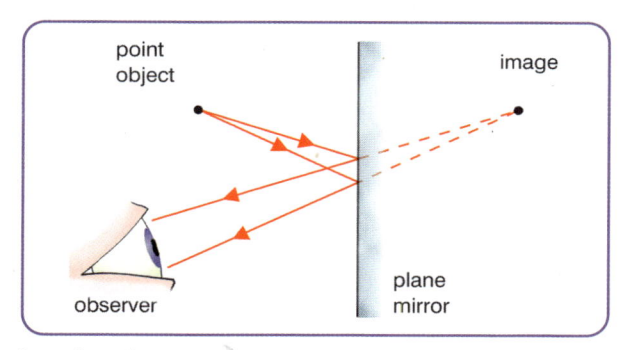

Image formation

The diagram above shows how a plane mirror forms an image. Note that the image of an object viewed by reflection using a plane mirror is:
- the same distance behind the mirror as the object is in front
- upright and the same size as the object
- virtual, which means it is formed where the reflected rays *appear* to come from
- laterally inverted, which means the image of a left-handed person is right-handed and vice versa. Try it if you don't believe it!

Uses of a plane mirror

1. A **wall mirror** needs to be at least half the height of the tallest person who uses it. It also needs to be mounted with its top edge level with the top of the head.

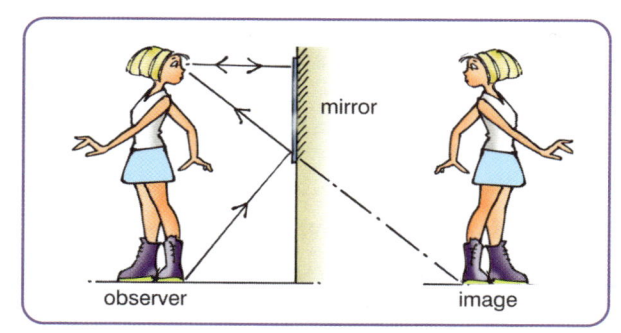

   Using a wall mirror

2. A **periscope** is useful for seeing over a crowd. It is also used in submarines to see above the surface when the submarine is under water.

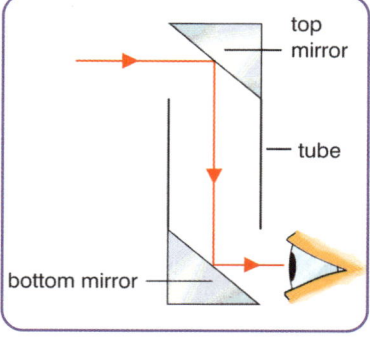

   Using a periscope

3. **Parallax errors** caused by incorrectly reading the position of a pointer on a scale can be eliminated using a plane mirror. The image of the pointer must be directly under the pointer when reading the scale.

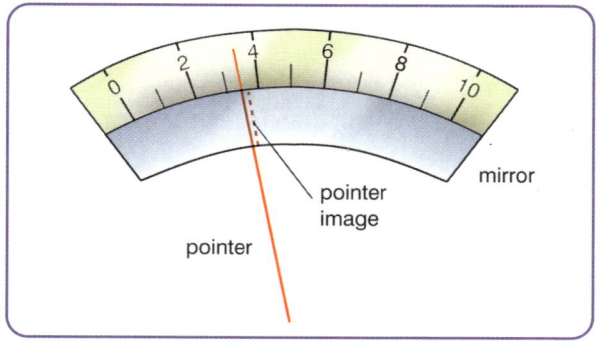

   Parallax errors

Note on rays and waves

A light ray shows the direction in which light travels. Light rays are usually drawn as straight lines, since diffraction is only significant where fine detail is needed. Ray diagrams describe how light is affected by mirrors and lenses.

Light

6.2 Refraction

Investigating refraction

★ If a light ray is directed at a glass block as shown, the light ray changes its direction when it enters the glass. It is closer to the normal in glass than in air. This is an example of the **refraction** of light. It occurs because light waves travel more slowly in glass than in air.

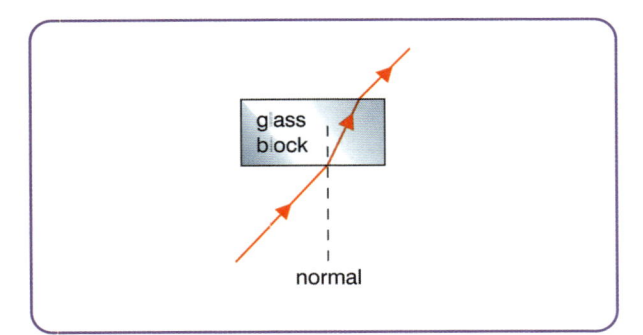

Refraction in a glass block

★ When a light ray passes from glass into air at a non-zero angle to the normal, it bends away from the normal. This happens because the light waves speed up when they pass from glass into air.

★ Refraction happens when light passes from one transparent medium into another. The light ray is always closer to the normal in the 'slower' medium.

Fact file

The speed of light through air is 300 000 km/s. Light travels more slowly in a transparent medium than in air. For example, its speed in glass is 200 000 km/s.

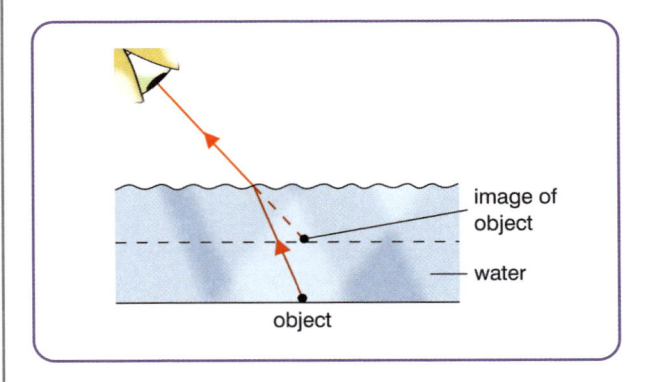

In deep water

A swimming pool appears shallower than it really is because light from the bottom of the pool is refracted away from the normal when it passes into air at the surface. Someone looking into the water from above sees an image of the bottom of the pool nearer the surface.

Questions

1 A light ray passes into and out of a glass block in air, as shown in the diagram on the left. Describe how its speed changes along this path.

2 Light travels more slowly in glass than in water and it travels more slowly in water than in air. In each of the following situations, a light ray travels across a boundary at non-normal incidence. State whether the light ray bends towards or away from the normal if it passes from:

a) glass to air

b) air to water

c) water to glass

d) glass to water.

Answers

1 When it passes from air into glass, its speed becomes less. When it passes from glass to air, its speed increases.

2 a) away b) towards c) towards d) away

How can you answer this if the author has not stated the speed of light in Water!

6.3 Fibre optics

Total internal reflection

This occurs when light in a transparent medium strikes the boundary at an angle of incidence greater than a **critical angle**. The light ray reflects internally just as if the boundary is a mirror.

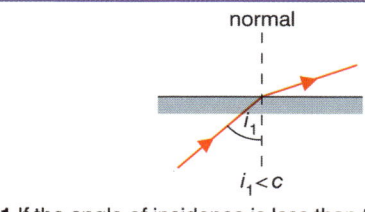

1 If the angle of incidence is less than the critical angle, the light ray bends away from the normal on leaving the glass.

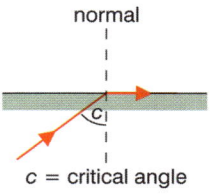

2 If the angle of incidence is equal to the critical angle, the light refracts along the boundary.

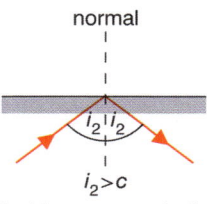

c = critical angle

3 If the angle of incidence exceeds the critical angle, the light ray is totally internally reflected.

Total internal reflection

Optical fibres

An optical fibre is a thin fibre of transparent flexible material. A light ray that enters the fibre at one end emerges at the other end, even if the fibre is curved round. This happens because the light ray is totally internally reflected at the fibre surface wherever it hits the boundary. Each light ray in the fibre travels along a straight line through the fibre between successive reflections. Provided the bends in the fibre are not too tight, light rays in the fibre do not emerge from its sides.

↳ a specification for minimum radius will be stated by the Manufacturers

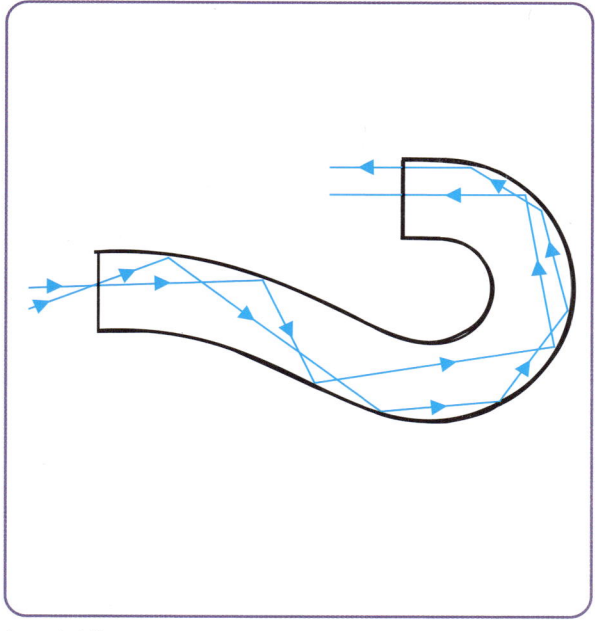

An optical fibre

Questions

1 The critical angle of glass in air is 47°. A light ray travelling in a glass block in air is incident on the boundary of the glass block. State whether the light ray is refracted or totally internally reflected if the angle of incidence in the glass is **a)** 40° **b)** 50°.

2 White light consists of all the colours of the spectrum. In glass, the speed of light decreases from red to blue. A ray of white light is directed into an optical fibre at one end. If the fibre is curved more and more, blue light is seen emerging from its sides where it bends.

 #

 a) Why does this happen?

 b) What colour emerges at the other end? Explain your answer.

Answers

1 **a)** Refracted **b)** Totally internally reflected
2 **a)** The critical angle is bigger for red light than for blue light. Therefore blue light emerges first when the fibre is bent.
 b) Yellow (white light minus blue light).

Thus the speed of light in a medium depends on its frequency/wavelength.

Light

Using optical fibres

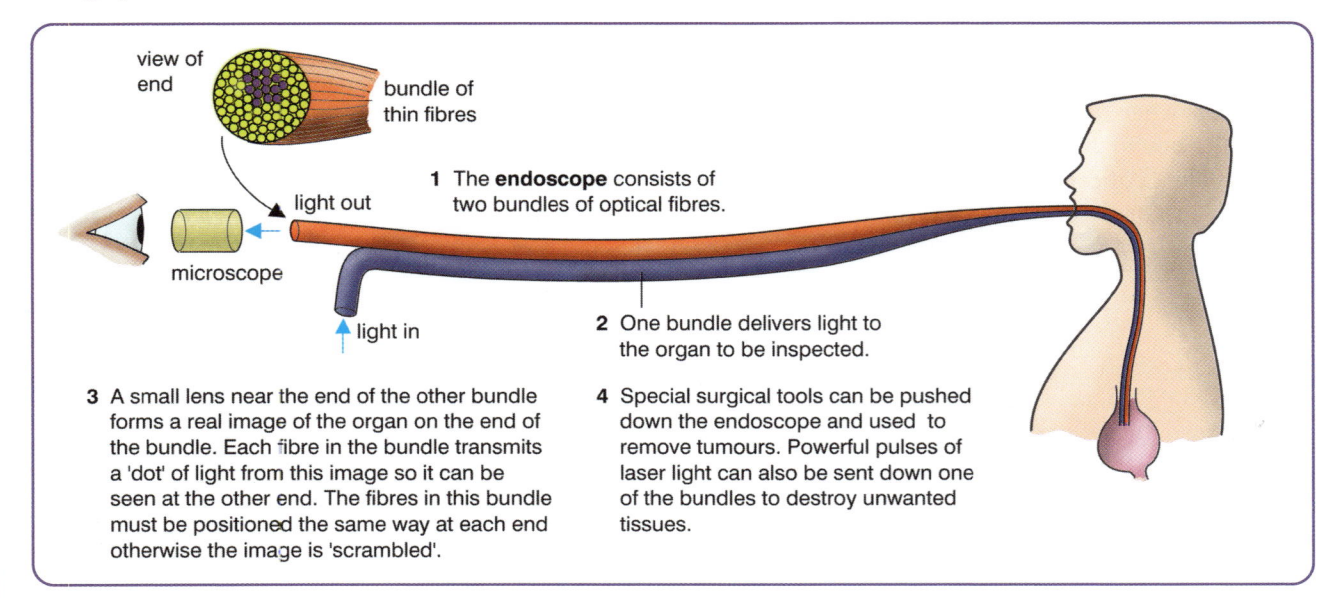

1. The **endoscope** consists of two bundles of optical fibres.
2. One bundle delivers light to the organ to be inspected.
3. A small lens near the end of the other bundle forms a real image of the organ on the end of the bundle. Each fibre in the bundle transmits a 'dot' of light from this image so it can be seen at the other end. The fibres in this bundle must be positioned the same way at each end otherwise the image is 'scrambled'.
4. Special surgical tools can be pushed down the endoscope and used to remove tumours. Powerful pulses of laser light can also be sent down one of the bundles to destroy unwanted tissues.

The endoscope

In communications, optical fibres are used to guide pulses of infrared light. Because the frequency of light is much higher than that of radio waves or microwaves, an infrared light beam can carry many more pulses per second than radio waves or microwaves. This means much more information can be carried using optical fibres than by other means.

In medicine, optical fibres are used in an **endoscope** to see inside the body, and to treat internal tumours. Use of an endoscope avoids the need to cut open the body and therefore shortens the post-operation recovery period.

Reflectors for road safety

The back surface of a cycle reflector consists of lots of triangles. Light rays falling directly on the reflector are totally internally reflected twice at this surface, so they are reflected back.

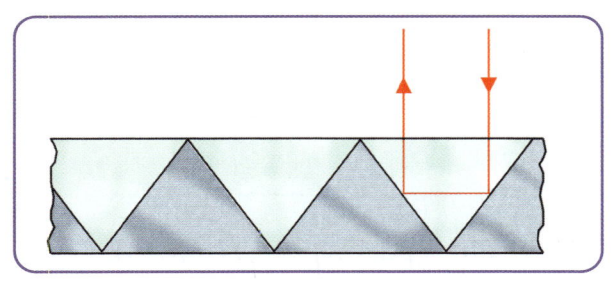

A reflector

6.4 Light and colour

The visible spectrum

This is produced by passing a beam of white light through a prism. Because the speed of light in glass decreases from red to blue, blue light is bent more than red light.

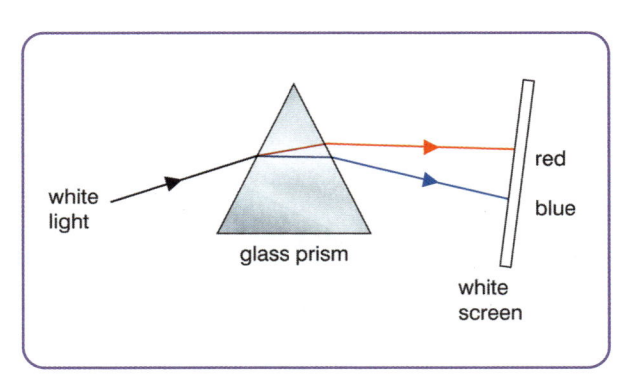

Producing a spectrum

★ Remember that **blue bends better than red**!

★ Also remember the colours of the spectrum (**R**ed **O**range **Y**ellow **G**reen **B**lue **I**ndigo **V**iolet) from a mnemonic, such as **R**ichard **O**f **Y**ork **G**ave **B**attle **I**n **V**ain, or remember Roy G Biv.

Handwritten notes:

$v = f\lambda \therefore \delta v = \delta(f\lambda)$

✗ i.e. the speed decreases in glass with increase of frequency.

'better' is a bad word. It is a value judgement.

✗ MORE!

Light

Colour and wavelength

★ Light is diffracted when it passes through a gap, because it consists of waves. The narrower the gap or the longer the wavelength, the greater the amount of diffraction (spreading).

★ For a gap of constant width, the spreading depends on the colour of the light. The closer the light is to the red part of the spectrum, the more it spreads.

★ It therefore follows that the wavelength of light increases across the spectrum from blue to red. The amount of spreading can be used to work out the wavelength of the light.

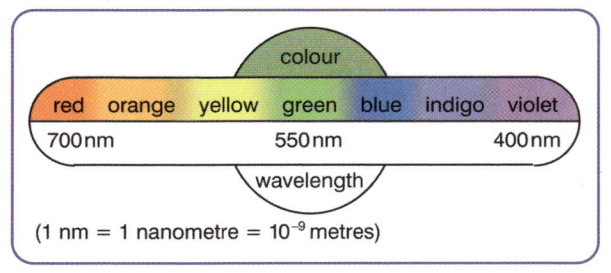

Colour and wavelength

(1 nm = 1 nanometre = 10^{-9} metres)

Diffraction at work

A **telescope** is used to magnify distant objects. It does not necessarily produce a detailed image.

★ Light from a point object entering the telescope is diffracted at the entrance and so an image 'spot' is formed.

★ If two point objects are too close, their image spots will merge and be seen as one spot.

★ The wider the objective lens of a telescope, the less diffraction it produces, so the greater the image detail that can be seen.

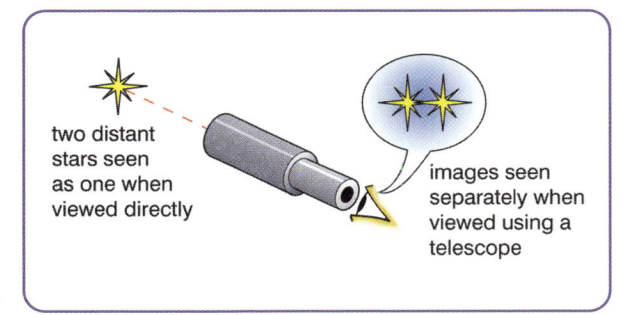

Using a telescope

A **microscope** is used to observe details of small objects.

★ Light from each point of an object under view spreads when it enters the microscope and forms an image spot.

★ The spreading is less for blue light than for any other colour. This is because blue light has a shorter wavelength than other colours of light.

★ Therefore two points that are very close together can be better distinguished in blue light than in any other colour. This is why more detail can be seen in an image if blue light is used instead of white light.

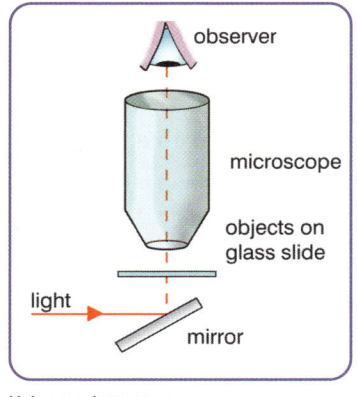

Using a microscope

Questions

Cheap cameras often produce images which are tinged in colours. The sketch below shows two rays of white light entering a convex lens at opposite edges. Each ray is split into coloured rays by the lens. The sketch shows the blue rays forming a point image on a colour film.

a) Describe what you would expect to see when the film is developed.

b) Which direction would you move the object to form a point image in red light?

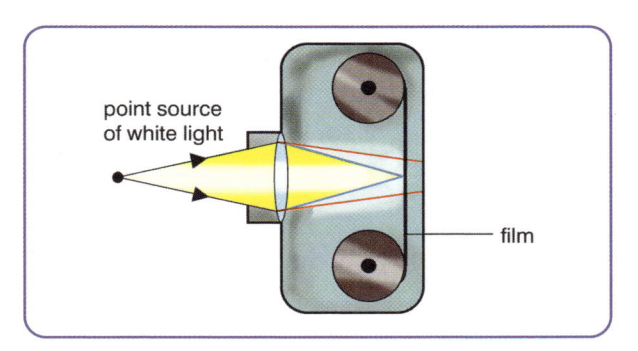

Answers

a) A point blue image surrounded by a reddish white disc.
b) Away from the lens.

47

Light

ROUND UP

How much have you improved? Work out your improvement index on page 142.

1 a) Complete the ray diagram to show where the image of point object O_1 is formed. [2]

b) Without drawing further rays on your diagram, mark the position where the image of point object O_2 is formed. [1]

c) Explain why the image of the arrow between O_1 and O_2 is the same length as the object. [2]

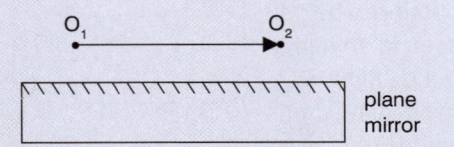

2 a) A student stands 1.0 m in front of a wall-mounted plane mirror. What is the distance from the student to her image? [1]

b) The student is 1.80 m tall. With the aid of a diagram, explain why the mirror needs to be at least 0.9 m in length if she is to be able to see a full-length image. [4]

c) State two further uses of a plane mirror. [2]

3 a) Explain with the aid of a diagram what is meant by total internal reflection of light. [2]

b) The diagram shows a light ray entering an optical fibre. Complete the diagram showing the path of the light ray after it enters the optical fibre. [2]

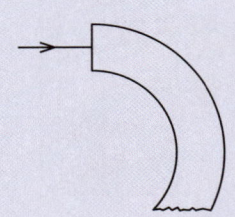

c) Why does an optical fibre lose light if it is bent too tightly? [1]

d) State two applications of fibre optics. [2]

4 Light travels more slowly in glass than in water and more slowly in water than in air. State whether or not a light ray incident on a boundary at a non-zero angle of incidence bends towards or away from the normal if it travels across the boundary from

(i) air to glass (ii) glass to air

(iii) glass to water. [3]

5 State whether reflection, refraction or diffraction takes place in each of the following situations.

(i) Light spreads out when it passes through a narrow gap.

(ii) Sunlight causes glare from a swimming pool.

(iii) Light passes along an optical fibre coiled round a tube.

(iv) An object viewed through a magnifying glass appears larger. [4]

6 Sketch a diagram to show how a glass prism can be used to split a ray of white light into a spectrum of colours.

Mark the order of the colours in the spectrum from red to blue. [3]

7 a) Blue light rays are refracted more by glass than red light rays. What does this statement tell you about the speed of blue light in glass compared with the speed of red light in glass? [1]

b) Explain why a microscope image is more detailed if it is observed using blue light than using white light. [3]

8 A military satellite is used to observe hostile troop movements. Explain why the satellite's camera must be fitted with a wide lens. [2]

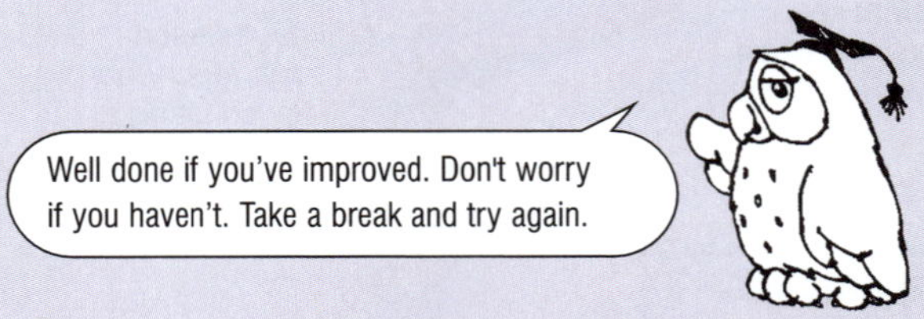

Well done if you've improved. Don't worry if you haven't. Take a break and try again.

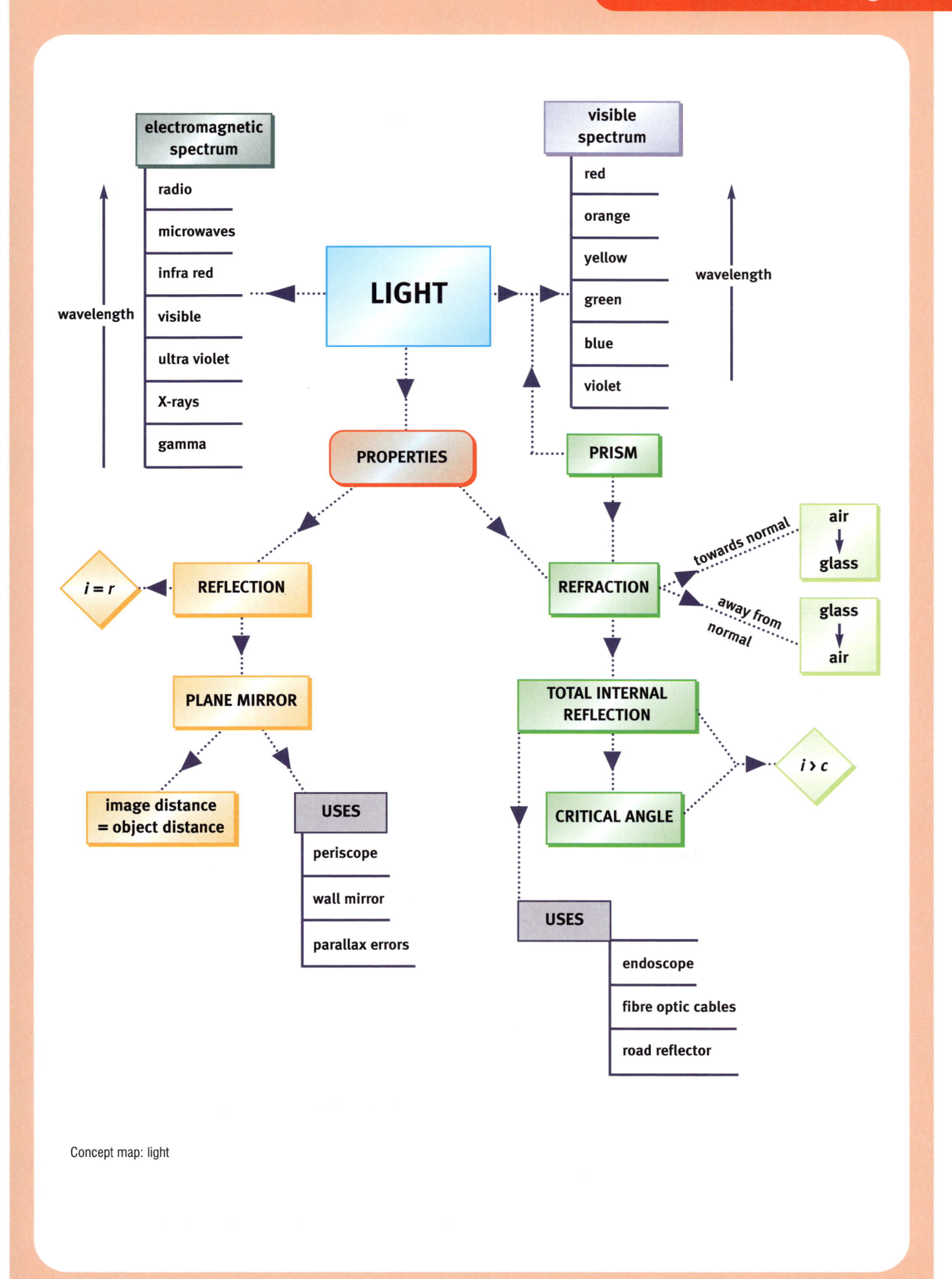

Light

Concept map: light

LIGHT

electromagnetic spectrum
- radio
- microwaves
- infra red
- visible
- ultra violet
- X-rays
- gamma

(wavelength)

visible spectrum
- red
- orange
- yellow
- green
- blue
- violet

(wavelength)

PROPERTIES

PRISM

REFLECTION
$i = r$

PLANE MIRROR
image distance = object distance

USES
- periscope
- wall mirror
- parallax errors

REFRACTION
- towards normal: air → glass
- away from normal: glass → air

TOTAL INTERNAL REFLECTION

CRITICAL ANGLE
$i > c$

USES
- endoscope
- fibre optic cables
- road reflector

Chapter 7   Optics

7.1 Waves and rays

PREVIEW

At the end of this topic you will be able to:
- describe and explain interference of light
- explain refraction and dispersion of light
- construct ray diagrams to describe image formation.

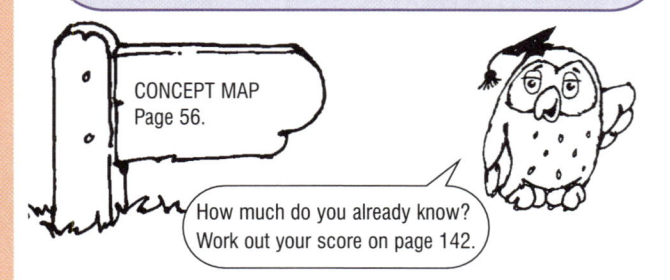

CONCEPT MAP Page 56.

How much do you already know? Work out your score on page 142.

Test yourself

1. When light passes through two closely spaced slits, a pattern of bright and dark fringes is seen.
   a) What is the name for this process?
   b) What happens to the pattern if one of the slits is blocked? [2]

2. a) Is the wavelength of red light longer or shorter than that of blue light?
   b) When light passes from air into water
      (i) does its speed increase or decrease?
      (ii) does its wavelength increase or decrease? *DECREASE* [3]

3. When white light passes through a prism, the light changes direction and is split into colours.
   What is the name for a) the change of direction b) the splitting into colours? [2]

4. A convex lens is used to form a clear image of a distant runner on a screen.
   a) Is the image (i) real or virtual (ii) upright or inverted?
   b) The runner moves towards the lens. To keep the runner's image in focus, should the screen be moved towards or away from the lens?
   c) Does the image become larger or smaller as the runner approaches the lens? [4]

The wave nature of light

If the light from a point source is observed through two closely spaced slits, a pattern of alternate bright and dark fringes is seen. Even though there are only two slits, lots of fringes may be visible. This is called an **interference pattern**, because the light from one slit:
- **cancels** the light from the other slit where the dark fringes are formed
- **reinforces** the light from the other slit where the bright fringes are formed.

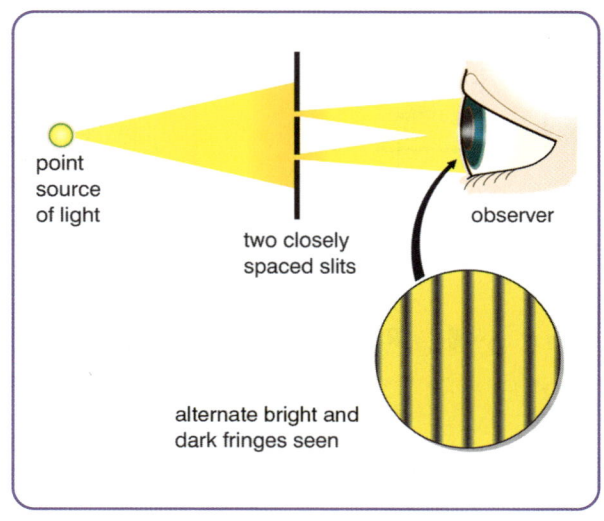

Observing interference of light

This type of pattern can be seen in a ripple tank where waves from two adjacent gaps overlap. The observation of an interference pattern using light is evidence that light consists of waves. The wavelength of light can be measured from interference experiments. The diagram below shows how the wavelength of light varies with its colour.

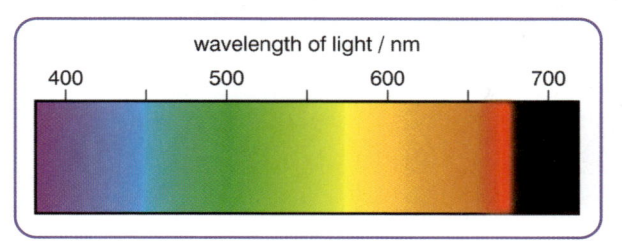

Colour and wavelength

$v = f\lambda$. When light travels from air into glass or water, v decreases, f is constant $\therefore \lambda$ decreases.

The visible spectrum barely covers one octave! It lies within 350–700 nm.

Optics

Explaining refraction

ie. Wavelength is reduced. But frequency is constant (ie colours do not change)

When light passes from air into a transparent medium, it slows down and its wavelength becomes smaller. Unless it is directed along the normal, it refracts towards the normal because the waves become closer as they pass from air into the medium.

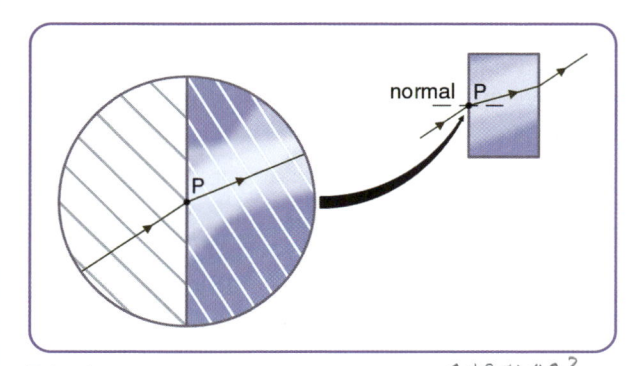

Refraction

refractive index of the medium = *average?* $\dfrac{\text{speed of light in a vacuum}}{\text{speed of light in the medium}}$

Note that the speed of light in air differs very little from the speed of light in a vacuum.

Explaining dispersion

A beam of white light is split into the colours of the spectrum when it is refracted by glass. This splitting into colours is called **dispersion.** It occurs because the speed of light in glass varies with the wavelength of the light. Blue light in glass travels more slowly than red light in glass. Therefore the refractive index of glass for blue light is larger than for red light.

Dispersion

$V = f\lambda$

$f = \dfrac{V}{\lambda}$ Thus if f is a constant, and if V is reduced, then λ is reduced

Lenses

Light changes direction on passing through a lens, unless it passes through the exact centre. The effect of a lens on light depends on the shape of the lens.

★ The position of the image formed by a lens depends on the object position.

★ The image of a point object is **real** if it can be formed on a screen. An image seen in a mirror or a magnifying glass cannot be formed on a screen. It is said to be **virtual**.

Key Point

The convex (or converging) lens

★ The **focal point** of a convex lens is the point where light rays parallel to the lens axis are brought to a focus.

★ A light ray directed at the lens through the focal point always emerges parallel to the lens axis.

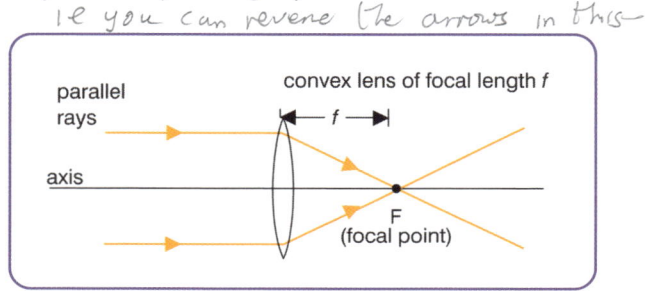

ie you can reverse the arrows in this

The convex lens — *diagram*

The concave (or diverging) lens

This makes a parallel beam of light spread out. The **focal point** is the point where light appears to diverge from. A concave lens can be used to widen a laser beam. It is also used to correct short sight.

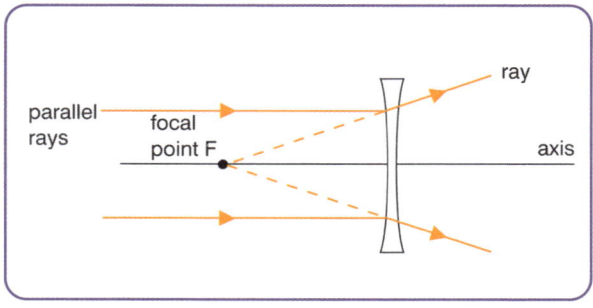

The concave lens

in air, f red = 430 Terahertz
= 430,000 GHz.

f violet = 720 THz
= 720,000 GHz.

Optics

Uses of a convex lens

1 The magnifying glass – the object must be between the lens and the focal point F to give an enlarged, upright and virtual image on the same side as the object.

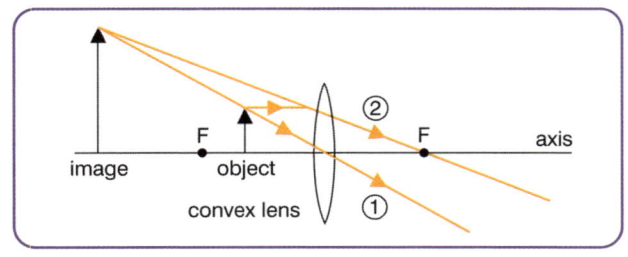

Magnifying glass

2 The projector lens – the slide transparency must be between F and 2F to give an enlarged real image beyond 2F on the other side of the lens. Note that the image is inverted.

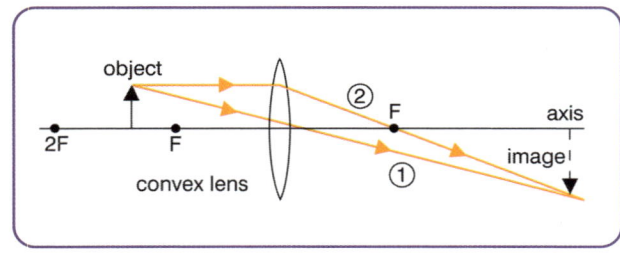

Projector

3 The camera lens – an object beyond 2F gives a real, inverted image on the other side of the lens between F and 2F.

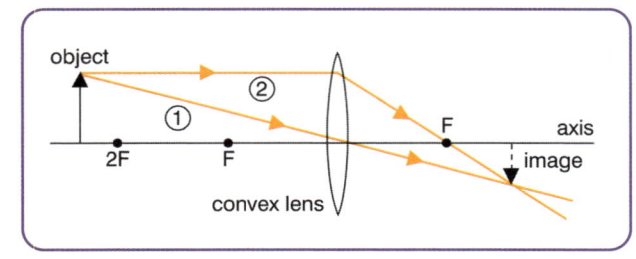

Camera

Note

Ray ① passes straight through the centre of the lens.

Ray ② passes through F.

Question

A convex lens is used to project an image of a slide on a screen. If the lens is moved closer to the slide, describe how the position and the size of the image change.

ROUND UP

How much have you improved? Work out your improvement index on page 143.

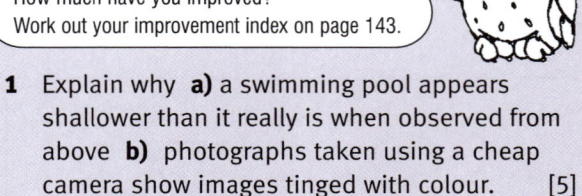

1. Explain why **a)** a swimming pool appears shallower than it really is when observed from above **b)** photographs taken using a cheap camera show images tinged with colour. [5]

2. **a)** Complete the ray diagrams below.
   b) For each diagram, state whether the image is real or virtual. [8]

   (i) object at $\frac{3}{2}$F

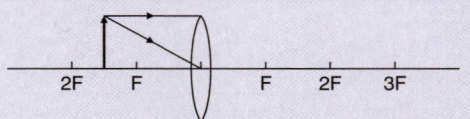

   (ii) object at 2F

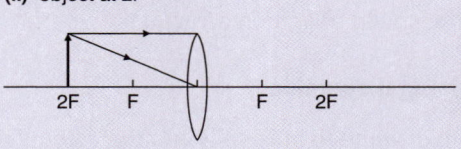

3. The refractive index of water is 1.33 and the refractive index of glass is 1.5. The speed of light in a vacuum is 3.0×10^8 m/s.

   a) Calculate the the speed of light in (i) water (ii) glass.

   b) The diagram shows a light ray in water incident on a boundary between water and glass. Complete the ray's path in the glass. [3]

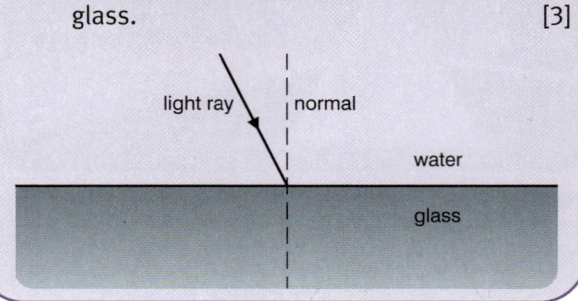

Answer

The image gets larger and further away from the projector.

Optics

7.2 The eye

PREVIEW

At the end of this topic you will be able to:

- draw a labelled diagram of the eye
- describe the functions of the main parts of the eye
- explain how the eye adjusts itself to see objects at different distances, and to changes of brightness
- describe the cause and correction of common sight defects, including short sight and long sight.

How much do you already know? Work out your score on page 143.

Test yourself

1. State the functions of a) the cornea b) the iris c) the retina. [4]

2. The near point of a normal adult eye is 25 cm away.
   a) What is meant by the term near point?
   b) When an object is observed at the near point, is the eye lens at its thickest or its thinnest?
   c) (i) Explain how the thickness of the eye lens is changed.
      (ii) Is the eye lens at its thickest or thinnest when the muscles of the eye are under most strain? [5]

3. What changes occur in the eye when
   a) you look up from reading a book and observe a distant object
   b) you walk into a very bright room from a dark room? [5]

4. a) What is meant by short sight?
   b) What type of lens is used to correct a short-sighted eye? [2]

The structure of the eye

1. The **cornea** is a tough curved transparent membrane over the front of the eye. It helps to focus light onto the retina.

2. The **eye lens** is a convex lens of variable thickness that focuses light to form a sharp image on the retina.

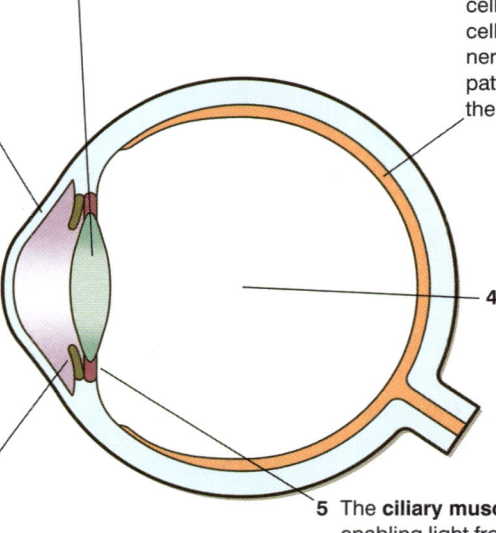

3. The **retina** is a layer of light-sensitive cells covering the inside of the back of the eye. When light falls on a retinal cell, an electrical impulse from the cell is transmitted to the brain via a nerve fibre. The brain interprets the pattern of impulses and recognises the image.

4. Transparent **fluids** fill the eyeball, keeping the internal structure under pressure and in place.

5. The **ciliary muscles** make the eye thinner or thicker, enabling light from objects at different distances to be focused on the retina. This process is called **accommodation**. The ciliary muscle fibres lie along the rim and therefore make the eye lens thicker when they tighten. This is what happens when you focus on a nearby object.

6. The **iris** controls the width of the pupil, which controls the entry of light into the eye. In bright light, the pupil automatically becomes narrow and therefore reduces the amount of light entering the eye. In dark conditions, the opposite happens.

The eye

Optics

Test your range of vision

The **near point** of the eye is the nearest point to the eye at which an object can be seen clearly, as shown below. The eye lens is at its thickest. Light from any object closer than the near point cannot be focused on the retina. For an average human adult eye, the near point is 25 cm from the eye. For a young person, the near point is usually closer than 25 cm. Test your own near point.

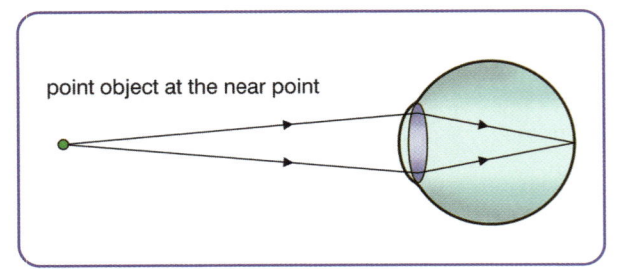

The near point

The **far point** of the eye is the furthest point from the eye at which an object can be seen clearly. The diagram below shows the eye viewing an object at the far point. For an average human eye, the far point is at infinity. Can you see distant objects clearly without the aid of spectacles or contact lenses?

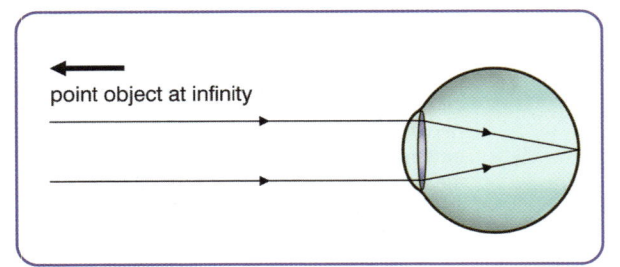

The far point

Correction of sight defects

★ **Long sight** occurs when a near object cannot be seen in focus. The near point is further from the eye than it ought to be. The eye lens is too weak, even at its thickest. It focuses light behind the retina. Long sight is corrected using a convex lens.

★ **Short sight** occurs when a distant object cannot be seen in focus. The far point is not at infinity. The eye lens is too powerful and focuses light in front of the retina. Short sight is corrected using a concave lens.

ROUND UP

How much have you improved? Work out your improvement index on page 143.

1. a) If the eye lens became cloudy, how would this affect what is seen?
   b) Why does a detached retina cause blurred vision? [3]

2. You can read a printed page held closer than your near point by observing the page through a pinhole in a card. Try this and explain why it is possible. [3]

3. a) Explain what is meant by short sight.
   b) What type of spectacle lens is used to correct short sight. [3]

4. a) An elderly person is unable to thread a piece of cotton through a needle without the aid of spectacles. What type of spectacle lens is needed?
   b) A student is unable to read a vehicle number plate 20 m away without spectacles. What type of lens is used in the spectacles? [2]

Well done if you've improved. Don't worry if you haven't. Take a break and try again.

7.3 Optical instruments

PREVIEW

At the end of this topic you will be able to:
- draw a labelled diagram of a simple camera and explain the function of each of its parts
- explain how a convex lens can be used to produce a magnified real image of a slide transparency
- draw a ray diagram to show how a convex lens may be used as a magnifying glass.

How much do you already know? Work out your score on page 144.

Test yourself

1. In a camera, what is the purpose of **a)** the shutter **b)** the aperture stop? [2]

2. A camera with a manually adjusted lens is used to take a close-up picture of a flower. The same camera is then to be used to photograph a distant object. What change must be made to the camera? [2]

3. A convex lens is used to form a clear image on a screen of a slide transparency.
   a) Is the image real or virtual?
   b) If the slide is moved closer to the lens, the image goes out of focus. To refocus it, should the screen be moved towards or away from the lens?
   c) Does the image become larger or smaller as a result of moving the lens and screen as described in **b)**? [3]

4. A printed page is observed with the aid of a magnifying glass. State whether the image of the print is **a)** real or virtual **b)** upright or inverted **c)** magnified or diminished. [3]

5. Draw a labelled diagram to show how a convex lens may be used as a magnifying glass. [2]

Looking back

Before you continue, re-read pages 51–2 to remind yourself how to construct a ray diagram for a convex lens.

Note in particular that:
- the image is real and inverted, provided the object is further away from the lens than the focal point F (for example, as in the camera and the projector)
- the image is magnified if the object is between F and 2F (for example, as in the projector but not the camera). Moving the object nearer F makes the image larger and further from the lens.
- the image is virtual, upright and on the same side of the lens as the object if the object lies between the lens and F (for example, as in the magnifying glass).

Inside a camera

The diagram below shows how a simple camera works. The film is coated with a thin layer of a light-sensitive chemical which is a compound of silver. Light causes tiny specks of metallic silver to form from the compound. The areas of the film exposed to light become dark. After the roll of film has been used, it is removed and developed. A digital camera has an array of light-sensitive cells called 'pixels' instead of a film.

1. The **shutter** opens and closes again when a photograph is taken.
2. The **aperture stop** is adjusted in width to control the amount of light entering the camera. The total exposure of the film is determined by the width of the aperture stop and the shutter speed.
3. The **lens position** is adjusted according to the object position in order to form a real image in focus on the film.
4. The camera body is lightproof so the film is only exposed to light when the shutter is opened.

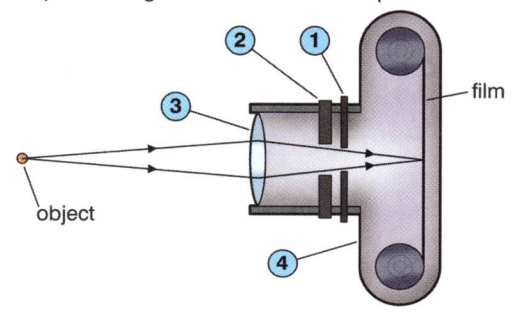

The camera

Optics

The magnifying glass

The diagram below shows a convex lens used as a magnifying glass. The image is virtual, upright and magnified. The lens is positioned so the image lies at the near point of the eye. If the lens is removed, the eye sees the object out of focus because it is closer than the near point.

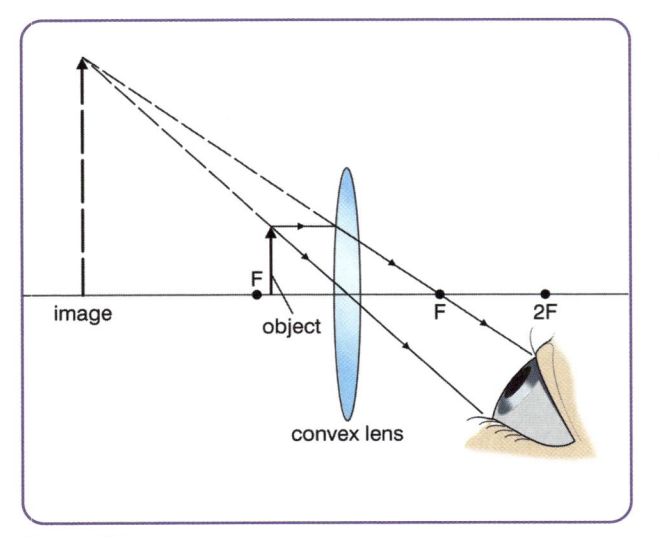

The magnifying glass

ROUND UP

How much have you improved? Work out your improvement index on page 144.

1. A slide projector is used to cast an image of a slide on a large movable screen. When it is set up, the image of the slide is in focus on the screen but it is too large for the screen. What changes need to be made to view the entire slide in focus on the screen? [3]

2. A convex lens is used as a magnifying glass to observe an insect. If the lens is moved closer to the insect, how does the image of the insect change? [2]

Well done if you've improved. Don't worry if you haven't. Take a break and try again.

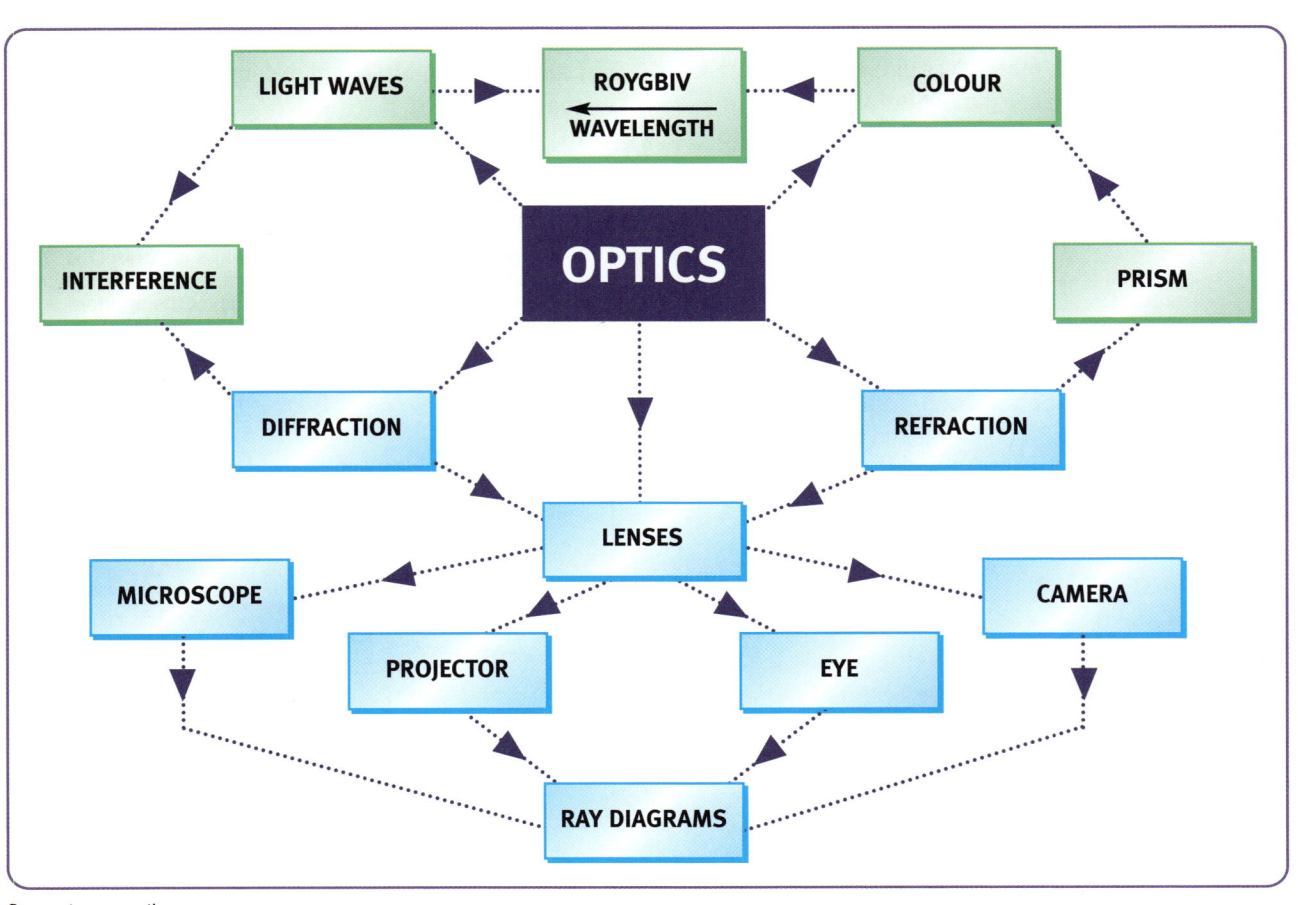

Concept map: optics

Electromagnetic spectrum — Chapter 8

PREVIEW

At the end of this topic you will be able to:
- state the six main bands of the electromagnetic spectrum in order of increasing wavelength
- outline the similarities and the main differences between the different bands
- describe some uses of electromagnetic waves in the home, in medicine and in communications
- relate uses of electromagnetic waves to their properties.

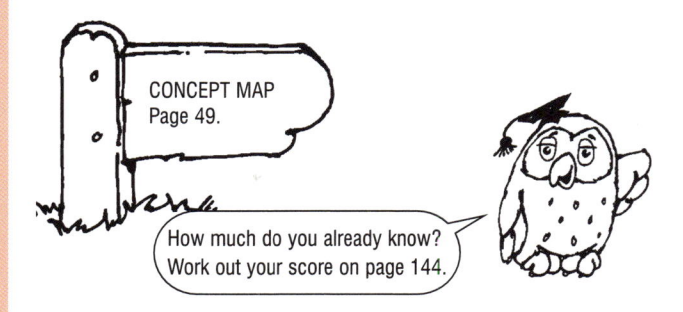

CONCEPT MAP Page 49.

How much do you already know? Work out your score on page 144.

Test yourself

1. Name the six main bands of the electromagnetic spectrum in order of increasing frequency. [6]
2. State one use for each of the main bands of the electromagnetic spectrum. [6]
3. Which two bands of the electromagnetic spectrum are not absorbed by the atmosphere? [2]
4. a) Which type(s) of electromagnetic radiation can cause ionisation? [2]
   b) Which type of electromagnetic radiation are you emitting at this very moment? [1]
   c) Which type of electromagnetic radiation causes sunburn? [1]
5. Name one type of electromagnetic radiation that can pass through a metal plate and one type that cannot. [2]
6. Which type of electromagnetic radiation is emitted when
   a) high-speed electrons are suddenly stopped? [1]
   b) a sunbed is used? [1]
7. a) A satellite broadcasts at a frequency of 10 GHz. What type of electromagnetic radiation is at this frequency? [1]
   b) Why is a satellite dish (i) concave (ii) made from metal? [2]
8. How does an invisible marker pen work? [3]
9. a) What type of electromagnetic radiation is detected by (i) a blackened thermometer (ii) a Geiger counter? [2]
   b) Which type(s) of electromagnetic radiation cannot be detected using photographic film? [1]
10. a) A fibre optic link uses electromagnetic radiation of wavelength 1000 nm. What part of the electromagnetic spectrum is this? [1]
    b) Which two types of electromagnetic radiation are emitted by a filament lamp? [1]

8.1 Using electromagnetic waves

All electromagnetic waves:
- do not need to be carried by a medium
- travel at the same speed of 300 000 km/s in a vacuum
- can be diffracted, refracted and reflected (although X-rays and gamma rays need special techniques)
- make charged particles vibrate
- are transverse waves and can be polarised.

Electromagnetic spectrum

INCREASING WAVELENGTH

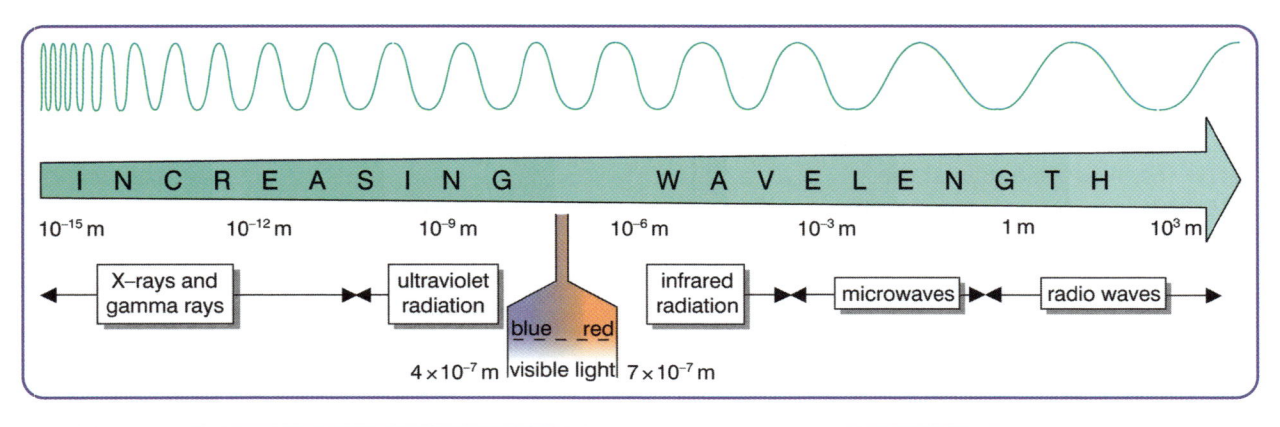

10^{-15} m 10^{-12} m 10^{-9} m 10^{-6} m 10^{-3} m   1 m 10^{3} m

X–rays and gamma rays ◄►◄ ultraviolet radiation ► visible light (blue 4×10^{-7} m — red 7×10^{-7} m) ◄ infrared radiation ►◄ microwaves ►◄ radio waves ►

	production	detection	absorption or reflection	uses
radio waves	transmitter aerial, Sun	receiver aerial	reflected by metal	communications
microwaves	microwave transmitter	microwave detector	reflected by metal	communications, heating,
infrared light	any object	blackened thermometer	reflected by shiny silvered surfaces, absorbed best by matt black surfaces	communications, heating, TV remote control handsets
visible light	glowing objects	eye, photographic film, electronic pixels	reflected by metal, absorbed by pigments	sight, communications
ultraviolet light	UV lamps, Sun	photocell, photographic film	absorbed by skin	security coding, sunbeds
X-rays and gamma rays	X-ray tube, radioactive isotopes	Geiger tube, photographic film	penetrates matter	medical

Electromagnetic waves at home

Microwave cookers: microwaves penetrate food and agitate water molecules within the food. This happens if the frequency is 2.5 GHz, so microwave cookers operate at this frequency. The oven case is metal, which reflects microwaves, so the oven does not heat up. All the electrical power supplied is used to heat the food.

Microwaves are also used for industrial heating, for example to dry wet fabrics after dyeing.

Infrared sensors: these are used for security purposes. **Passive** sensors detect infrared radiation emitted by intruders. **Active** sensors emit infrared rays and detect reflections from intruders. Infrared sensors fitted to TV cameras allow surveillance in the dark.

Halogen hobs: cookers fitted with transparent ceramic cooker rings use halogen lamp bulbs that emit mostly infrared radiation. Little energy is used to heat the ceramic plate, and when the cooker ring is switched off it cools much more rapidly than an ordinary cooker ring.

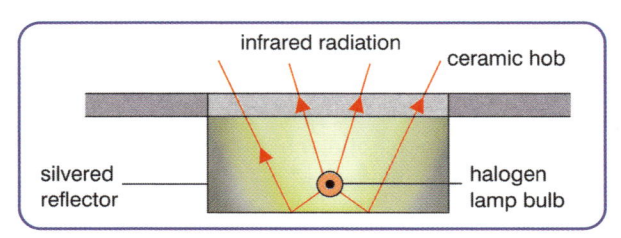

A halogen hob

UV-sensitive inks: these inks can only be seen using ultraviolet light. They are used for security marking.

Fluorescent lights: when one is switched on, ultraviolet light is produced in the tube. This radiation is absorbed by a fluorescent coating on the inside surface of the tube. As a result, this coating emits visible light, which illuminates the room.

Electromagnetic spectrum

8.2 Electromagnetic waves in medicine

A health warning

X-rays and gamma rays penetrate living tissues and so can be used in medicine to diagnose disorders and for treatment. These electromagnetic radiations are ionising, so excessive amounts will damage living cells. Great care is taken to ensure radiation doses given to patients are as low as possible and to ensure personnel are not exposed.

X-rays

These are produced in an **X-ray tube**. The X-ray beam consists of a continuous spread of wavelengths. The longer wavelengths are easily absorbed by tissues, unlike the shorter wavelengths which easily pass through tissues. A metal plate is placed in the path of the beam before the patient to remove longer wavelengths. This reduces absorption of X-rays by the patient.

X-ray photographs of internal organs are made with the aid of a suitable contrast medium. For example, a patient about to undergo a stomach X-ray may be given a barium meal in advance. Barium absorbs X-rays so the X-ray photograph shows a light image of the stomach on a darker background.

Personnel in a hospital X-ray department wear **film badges** to monitor their exposure to ionising radiations. If a film badge is over-exposed when it is developed, the wearer has been over-exposed too!

Gamma radiation

This is produced by radioactive isotopes. Gamma radiation is used at high doses to destroy unwanted tissue inside the body, and at low doses to 'image' internal organs.

★ **Treatment** – the use of gamma radiation from the radioactive isotope cobalt-60 is described on page 126. Read this section.

★ **Diagnosis** – the **gamma camera** is used with a suitable radioactive tracer to form an image of an internal organ. The tracer must emit gamma radiation and its half-life must be a suitable length. The tracer is given to the patient in advance, either by mouth or by injection.

Gamma radiation is also used to sterilise surgical instruments and to kill harmful bacteria in food.

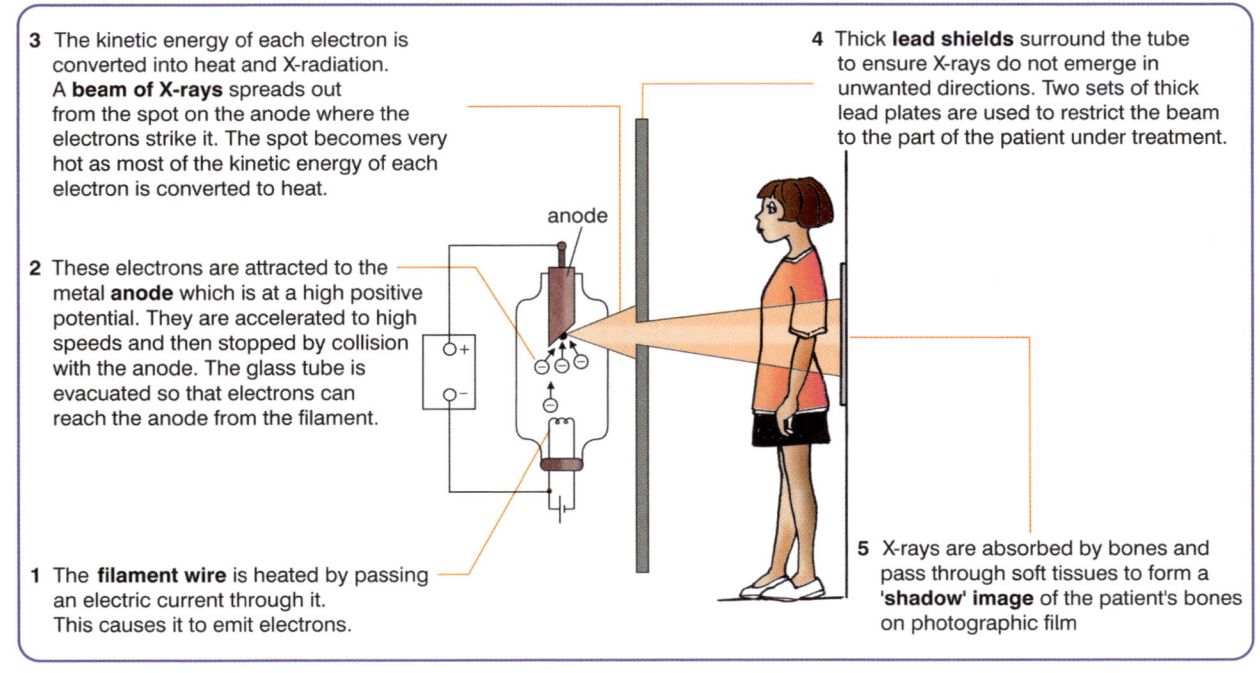

---

3. The kinetic energy of each electron is converted into heat and X-radiation. A **beam of X-rays** spreads out from the spot on the anode where the electrons strike it. The spot becomes very hot as most of the kinetic energy of each electron is converted to heat.

2. These electrons are attracted to the metal **anode** which is at a high positive potential. They are accelerated to high speeds and then stopped by collision with the anode. The glass tube is evacuated so that electrons can reach the anode from the filament.

1. The **filament wire** is heated by passing an electric current through it. This causes it to emit electrons.

4. Thick **lead shields** surround the tube to ensure X-rays do not emerge in unwanted directions. Two sets of thick lead plates are used to restrict the beam to the part of the patient under treatment.

5. X-rays are absorbed by bones and pass through soft tissues to form a **'shadow' image** of the patient's bones on photographic film

An X-ray tube in use

Electromagnetic spectrum

8.3 Communications

Radio waves, microwaves, infrared light and visible light are all used to carry information. The higher the frequency of the **carrier waves**, the more information can be carried. The information is carried by **modulating** the carrier wave:
- in **analogue form**, by modulating the amplitude (AM) or the frequency (FM) of the carrier wave
- in **digital form** as a stream of pulses.

The spread of frequencies in the signal determines the **bandwidth** of the carrier wave. Each carrier wave is allocated a frequency channel wide enough to transmit the bandwidth of the signal. For example, a channel width of 4000 Hz in telephone channels covers most of the audio range. A TV channel needs to be 8 MHz wide to carry all the information for TV pictures.

Electrical **noise** is created in the amplifiers used to boost weak signals, causing loss of information. Digital pulses can be 'cleaned up' to eliminate noise. This is one of the main reasons why digital communication is much more effective than analogue communication. Noise cannot be removed from an analogue signal as easily as it can be from a digital signal.

In addition, analogue signals can be distorted by amplifiers, which amplify different frequencies by different amounts, whereas digital regenerators always recreate a strong pulse from a weak pulse. One further advantage of digital transmission over analogue transmission is that more information can be carried.

Optical fibre communications

Optical fibres can carry pulses of infrared light hundreds of kilometres without interruption. The frequency of light is about 1 million times higher than the frequency of microwave radiation, so an optical fibre can carry much more information than a microwave beam or an electrical cable.

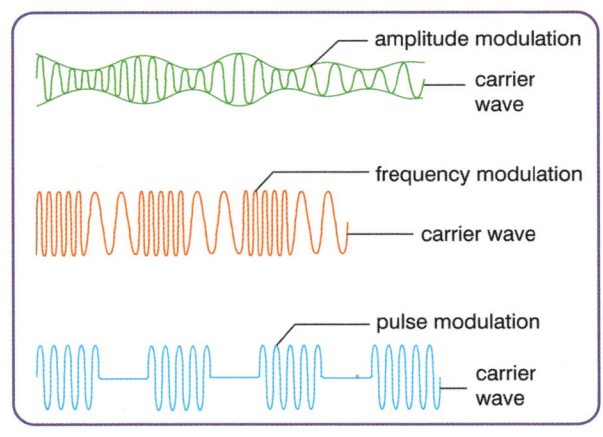

Amplitude modulation, frequency modulation and pulse modulation

Radio communications

★ Radio waves and microwaves create alternating voltages of the same frequency as the radiation itself when they are absorbed. This is why a receiver aerial picks up a signal from a transmitter.

★ Microwaves are used for satellite links because they pass straight through the atmosphere. They are also used for 'line of sight' links between communications towers because they do not spread out as much as radio waves do.

★ Radio waves of frequencies below 30 MHz reflect from the 'ionosphere', a layer of ionised gas in the upper atmosphere. Local radio and TV signals and mobile phone signals use frequencies well above 30 MHz.

Frequency bands

	frequency range	uses
long wave (LW)	up to 300 kHz	international AM radio
medium wave (MW)	300 kHz–3 MHz	AM radio
high frequency (HF)	3–30 MHz	AM radio
very high frequency (VHF)	30–300 MHz	FM radio
ultra high frequency (UHF)	300–3000 MHz	TV broadcasting, mobile phones
microwave	above 3000 MHz	satellite TV, global phone links
light	500 THz approx.	fibre optic communication links

Note: 1 MHz = 1 000 000 Hz
1 THz = 1 million MHz

Electromagnetic spectrum

Mobile phone links are only possible if the receiver is near a transmitter. A mobile phone signal is allocated a channel of bandwidth 25 kHz in the UHF band at a frequency of about 900 MHz. The transmitter is linked to the international phone network which uses undersea cable links, local microwave links and satellite links.

Satellite TV signals are carried by microwaves from a geostationary satellite. This orbits the Earth once every 24 hours round the equator, so stays in the same place above the Earth. A reflecting dish pointed towards the satellite focuses the microwaves on an aerial, which detects the signal and passes it on to a decoder.

Radio broadcasts at frequencies below 30 MHz travel long distances due to reflection from a layer of ionised gases in the upper atmosphere. Long wave broadcasts spread round the Earth because long wavelength radio waves follow the Earth's curvature.

Terrestrial TV signals are carried by radio waves in the UHF band range. Receiving aerials need to be in the line of sight of the transmitter. TV pictures from the other side of the world reach us via satellite links and ground stations.

Questions

1 a) Draw a diagram to show a wave that is modulated in **(i)** analogue form **(ii)** digital form.

b) State two advantages of digital transmission in comparison with analogue transmission.

c) What is meant by the bandwidth of a carrier wave?

2 a) What type of electromagnetic radiation is used for **(i)** optical fibre communications **(ii)** mobile phone communications **(iii)** satellite communications?

b) State two advantages of optical fibre communications in comparison with radio communications.

3 a) What is a geostationary orbit?

b) State one advantage and one disadvantage of putting a communications satellite in a geostationary orbit in comparison with putting it in a lower orbit.

Fact file

It is possible sometimes to pick up foreign radio stations on a radio receiver. If the atmospheric conditions are suitable, medium wave broadcasts from abroad can be picked up if they bounce between the ionosphere and the ground repeatedly. This happens best in summer at night when the ionosphere is most effective as a reflector. Long wave broadcasts from abroad can also be picked up sometimes but this is because they follow the Earth's curvature.

Answers

1 a) See the diagram on page 60 **b)** Noise and distortion are eliminated; more information can be carried **c)** It is the range of frequencies that can be carried.

2 a) (i) visible light or infrared radiation **(ii)** UHF radio waves **(iii)** microwaves.

b) it can carry more information, it is easier to maintain privacy.

3 a) An orbit in the same plane as the equator and in which a satellite remains at a fixed position relative to the ground.

b) Advantage: transmitters and receivers point in one direction only all the time; disadvantage: more energy is needed to put a satellite into a higher orbit so the launch rocket needs to be more powerful.

Electromagnetic spectrum

ROUND UP

How much have you improved? Work out your improvement index on pages 144–5.

1 a) List the six main bands of the electromagnetic spectrum in order of increasing wavelength. [6]
   b) (i) State two common properties of all electromagnetic waves. [2]
      (ii) List the types of electromagnetic waves that blacken photographic film. [3]
      (iii) List the types of electromagnetic waves that are used in communications. [4]

2 a) Microwave cookers operate at 2500 MHz and microwave satellites operate at about 10 000 MHz. Calculate the wavelength in air in each case. The speed of light in air is 300 000 km/s. [2]
   b) Food can be heated using a microwave oven or an ordinary oven. What are the advantages of using a microwave oven? [1]

3 a) Why is it possible to detect radio broadcasts from distant countries? [2]
   b) (i) What is it meant by the carrier frequency of a radio or TV broadcast? [1]
      (ii) Why is it necessary for TV transmitter stations in adjacent regions to broadcast at different carrier frequencies? [1]
   c) Why is it necessary to use a concave metal dish to detect electromagnetic waves from a satellite but not from a TV transmitter mast? [2]

4 a) A soap powder manufacturer decides to mix a substance into the powder which absorbs ultraviolet light and emits visible light as a result. Why would this make clothes washed in this powder seem very white in bright sunlight? [2]
   b) (i) Why is ultraviolet light harmful? [2]
      (ii) Why is it important to use protective skin cream if you are outdoors for a long time in summer? [2]

5 a) Why can an infrared TV camera see people and animals in darkness? [1]
   b) (i) What main type of electromagnetic radiation is emitted by a halogen lamp in a ceramic cooker hob? [1]
      (ii) Why does a ceramic hob heat food up more quickly than a conventional cooker ring does? [2]

6 a) In an X-ray tube, why is it essential to
      (i) make the anode positive relative to the filament?
      (ii) focus the electron beam onto a small spot of the anode? [3]
   b) (i) A photograph of a broken limb can be obtained using X-rays. What properties of X-rays are made use of in this process? [2]
      (ii) Before a stomach X-ray is taken, the patient is given a barium meal. Why? [2]

7 a) The diagram shows the waveform of two carrier waves with different frequencies. Identify the high frequency carrier wave and explain why it can carry more pulses than the low frequency carrier wave. [3]

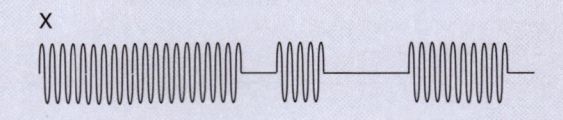

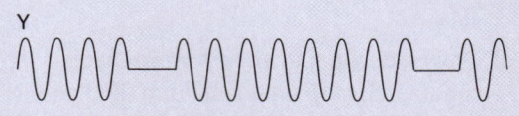

   b) Mobile phones operate at a frequency of about 900 MHz, each channel occupying a bandwidth of 25 kHz.
      (i) How many mobile phone channels can be carried in the frequency band from 900 to 925 MHz? [1]
      (ii) Terrestrial TV programmes are carried at lower frequencies and satellite TV is carried at higher frequencies. Why are no TV channels allocated to the frequency band from 900 to 925 MHz? [1]

8 A communications satellite must be in a geostationary orbit.
   a) What is meant by a geostationary orbit? [2]
   b) Why is it necessary for a communications satellite to be in such an orbit? [1]

Well done if you've improved. Don't worry if you haven't. Take a break and try again.

Force and motion — Chapter 9

PREVIEW

At the end of this topic you will be able to:

- define speed, velocity, acceleration, force, weight and work and state the unit of each quantity
- carry out calculations relating the above quantities to each other and to measurements of distance and time
- carry out calculations using the formulae for kinetic energy and potential energy
- sketch and interpret graphs of distance against time and speed against time
- describe the motion of a falling object with and without drag forces, including its energy changes.

CONCEPT MAP Page 85.

How much do you already know? Work out your score on page 145.

Test yourself

The acceleration of a freely falling object, $g = 10$ m/s².

1. A walker travelled a distance of 10 km in 2 hours. Calculate the walker's average speed in **a)** km/h **b)** m/s. [2]

2. **a)** What feature of a graph of speed against time gives the distance travelled? [1]
   b) What does the gradient of a distance against time graph represent? [1]

3. A 1000 kg car accelerates from rest to a speed of 10 m/s in 20 s. Calculate the acceleration of the car and the force needed to produce this acceleration. [2]

4. A car is travelling at a speed of 15 m/s when the driver sees a tree lying across the road ahead and is forced to brake. The graph shows how its speed changed with time.

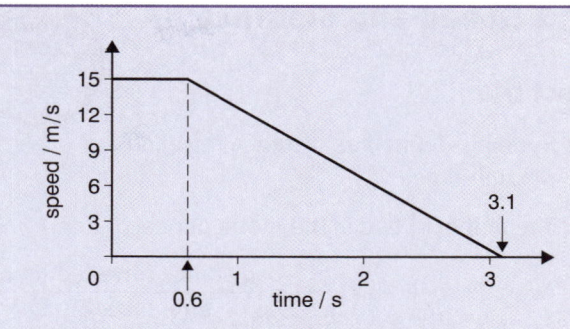

   a) If the driver's reaction time is 0.6 s, how far does the car travel before the driver applies the brakes? [1]
   b) The car takes 2.5 s to stop after the brakes are first applied. Calculate its deceleration. [1]
   c) (i) Use the graph to calculate the braking distance. [1]
   (ii) Hence calculate the total stopping distance. [1]

5. A lift of total mass 400 kg descends at a constant speed of 2 m/s.
   a) Calculate **(i)** its weight and its kinetic energy **(ii)** its loss of potential energy per second. [3]
   b) What happens to the potential energy lost by the lift? [3]

6. Explain why the shape of a vehicle affects its top speed. [3]

7. Why does a parachutist fall at constant speed? [3]

8. An aeroplane of total mass 8000 kg is in level flight at a constant speed of 60 m/s.

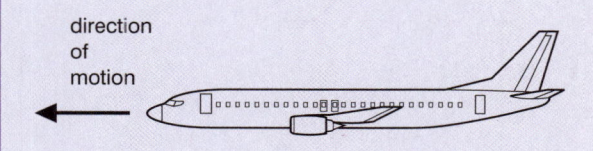

   direction of motion

   a) Calculate its weight and the lift force acting on the aeroplane. [2]
   b) The output power of its engines is 200 kW. Calculate **(i)** the distance it moves in 100 s **(ii)** the energy output from the engine in this time. [2]
   c) What happens to the energy supplied by the engine when the aeroplane is moving at constant speed in level flight? [1]

Force and motion

9.1 Speed and distance

Fact file

★ **Speed** is defined as distance travelled per unit time.

★ The **unit** of speed is the metre per second (m/s).

★ Average speed (in m/s) = $\dfrac{\text{distance travelled (in m)}}{\text{time taken (in s)}}$

★ **Velocity** is speed in a given direction.

Distance–time graphs for a moving object

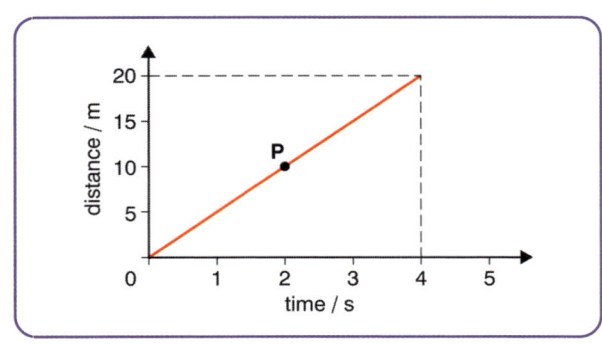

Constant speed

At **constant speed**, the distance travelled increases steadily with time as shown on the graph above.

1 The graph is a straight line with a constant gradient.
2 The steeper the line, the greater the speed.
3 The gradient of the graph is equal to the speed of the object.

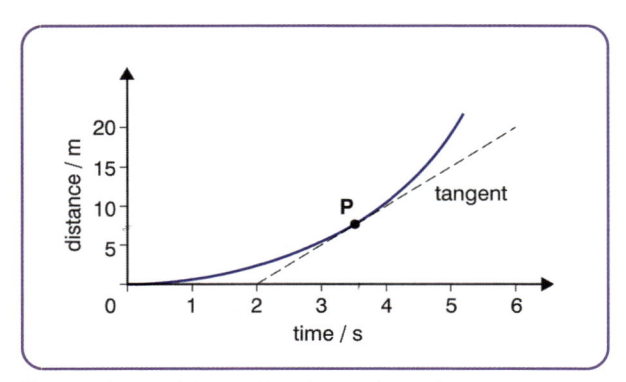

Distance–time graph for an object that accelerates from rest

At **changing speed**, the gradient of the line changes, as in the distance–time graph for an object that accelerates from rest.

1 The gradient changes with time.
2 The speed at any point is equal to the gradient of the tangent to the curve.
3 The speed is zero where the gradient is zero. This is at the origin 0 on the graph.

Questions

a) Determine the speed at point P on each graph.

b) On the second graph, how can you tell if the object is moving faster or slower after point P?

Speed and velocity

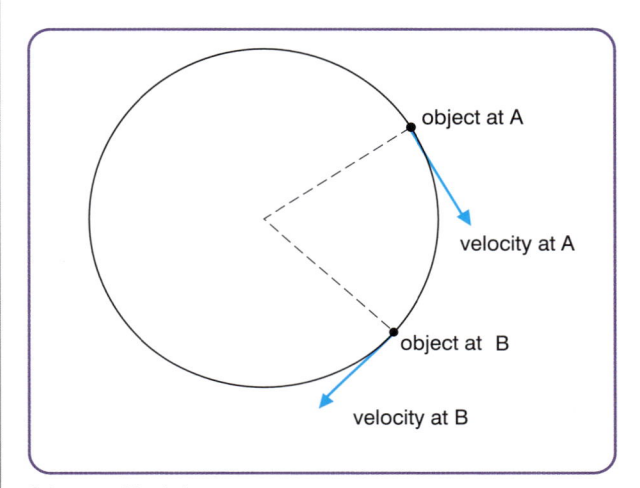

Going round in circles

Velocity is defined as speed in a given direction. An object moving round a circular path at a steady rate has a constant speed. However, it is continuously changing its direction so its velocity continually changes. Velocity is an example of a **vector** quantity, which is any quantity that has magnitude *and* direction. Other examples of vectors include acceleration, force and weight. Non-directional quantities such as speed, mass and energy are called **scalar** quantities.

Answers
a) 5 m/s, 5 m/s b) The gradient becomes steeper so the speed is increasing.

Thus the rotating object is constantly accelerating

Force and motion

9.2 Acceleration

Fact file

★ **Acceleration** is defined as change of velocity per unit time.

★ The **unit** of acceleration is the metre per second per second (m/s^2).

★ Acceleration is a vector quantity.

Constant acceleration

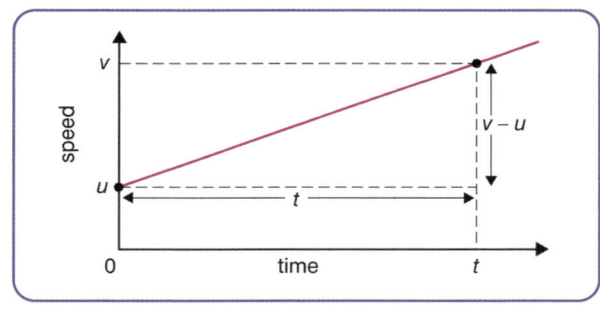

Velocity–time graph for constant acceleration

The graph shows how the speed changes with time for an object moving along a straight line at constant acceleration.

1. The gradient of the line is equal to the acceleration of the object.

2. The acceleration can be calculated using the equation

   $$\text{acceleration} = \frac{\text{change of velocity}}{\text{time taken}}$$

   If u represents the initial velocity and v represents the velocity at time t, the equation can be written as

   $$\text{acceleration } a = \frac{(v - u)}{t}$$

3. The distance moved s in time t can be calculated using the equation

   distance moved = average speed × time

   Since the average speed = $\frac{(u + v)}{2}$,

   this equation can be written as $s = \frac{(u + v)t}{2}$

4. The area under the line gives the distance travelled.

Note: deceleration *means decrease of velocity per unit time and has a negative value in a calculation.*

Maths workshop

The equation

$$a = \frac{(v - u)}{t}$$

can be rearranged to find v.

Step 1: multiply both sides of the equation by t to give $at = (v - u)$.

Step 2: Take u across to the other side to give $u + at = v$ or $v = u + at$.

Questions

The graph below shows how the speed of a train changed as it travelled between two stations.

a) Determine the acceleration and the distance moved in each of the three parts of the journey.

b) Hence calculate the average speed of the train.

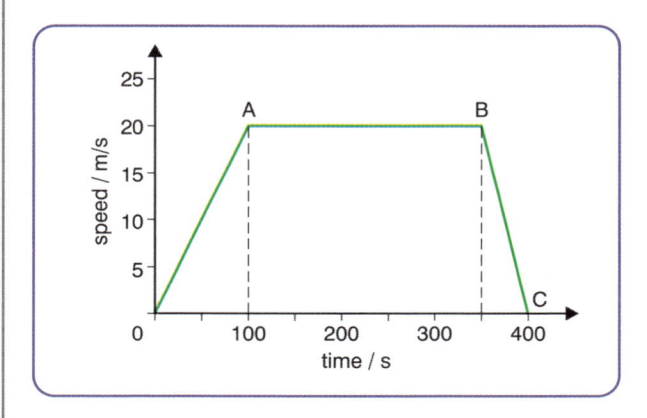

Acceleration due to gravity, g

The acceleration of an object falling freely is constant, equal to $10 \, m/s^2$. This means that an object falling freely increases its speed by $10 \, m/s$ every second – it accelerates at a constant rate.

Non-uniform acceleration

The acceleration can be determined at any point by drawing the tangent to the curve at that point and measuring the gradient of this line.

Answers
a) Acceleration = $0.2 \, m/s^2$; 0; $-0.4 \, m/s^2$
   Distance = 1000 m; 5000 m; 500 m
b) 16 m/s

Force and motion

9.3 On the road

Stopping distances

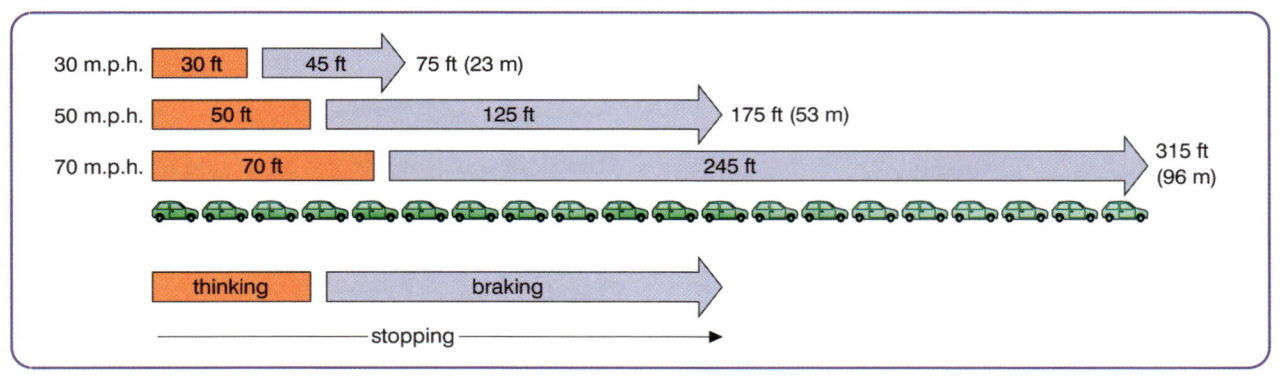

Shortest stopping distances of a car in good condition on a dry road for different speeds

★ **The thinking distance** is the distance travelled by the car in the time it takes the driver to react.

★ **The braking distance** is the distance travelled by the car from the point where the brakes are applied to where it comes to rest.

★ **The stopping distance** is the thinking distance added to the braking distance.

The graphs below show how each of these distances (in m) increases with speed (in m/s).

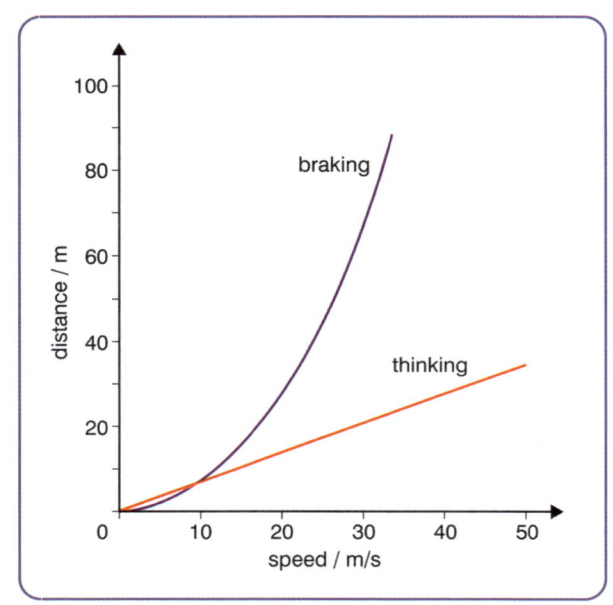

Distance–speed graphs for a braking car

1 **The thinking distance is proportional to the speed**. This is because the vehicle travels at constant speed during the reaction period before the brakes are applied. For constant speed, distance moved = speed × time. Prove for yourself from the graph that the reaction time for the data is 0.7 s. This is the average reaction time for a driver in an alert state of mind.

2 **The braking distance is proportional to the square of the speed**. This assumes the vehicle's deceleration is constant during braking.

Question

Determine the thinking distance and the stopping distance at a speed of 27 m/s (= 60 m.p.h.).

What affects the stopping distance?

1 **Reaction time**: the driver's reaction time depends on alertness.

2 **Road conditions**: when the brakes are applied, friction between the brakes and the wheels reduces the vehicle's speed, provided the tyres don't skid on the road. Skidding occurs if the braking force exceeds the grip (the maximum amount of friction possible) between the tyres and the road. Grip depends on the road conditions as well as the tyre condition.

Answer: thinking distance = 18 m, stopping distance = 55 m

Force and motion

9.4 Force and acceleration

Balanced forces

★ A **force** is anything that can change the velocity of an object.

★ If there is no force acting on an object, the object moves at constant velocity (constant speed without changing direction) or remains stationary.

★ If an object is acted on by two or more forces which balance each other out, the object either remains at rest or continues to move at constant velocity.

Changing velocity

The velocity of an object changes if the object is acted on by a force or by several forces which do not balance out. The combined effect of different forces acting on an object is called the **resultant force** on the object.

If an object is at rest or moving at constant velocity, the resultant force on it must be zero. This is known as **Newton's first law of motion**.

If an object's velocity is changing, the resultant force on it is not zero. Experiments show that the acceleration of an object is proportional to the resultant force on the object. This is known as **Newton's second law of motion** and it can be written as an equation:

$$\text{force} = \text{mass} \times \text{acceleration}$$
(in newtons, N) (in kg) (in m/s^2)

The unit of force is the **newton** (abbreviated N), equal to the force needed to give a 1 kg mass an acceleration of 1 m/s^2.

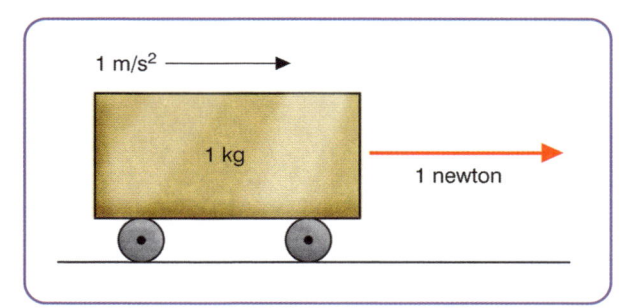

The newton

Weight

The **weight** of an object is the force of gravity on it. An object falling freely is acted on by gravity only. Since the acceleration due to gravity g is constant, then the force of gravity on an object (its weight) must be equal to its mass $\times g$.

$$\text{weight} = \text{mass} \times g$$
(in N)   (in kg) (in m/s^2)

Note that the unit of g may be written as N/kg or m/s^2 since 1 N = 1 kg m/s^2.

Terminal speed

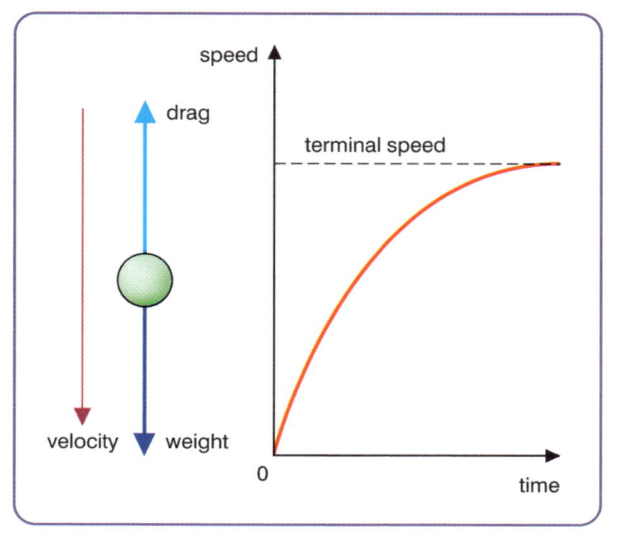

Terminal speed

When an object moves through a liquid or a gas, it experiences friction due to the liquid or gas, which opposes its motion. This resistance to its motion is called **drag**. The drag force increases with speed, and depends on the shape of the object and the substance the object is moving through.

★ An object released in air accelerates gradually until its speed is such that the drag force is equal and opposite to its weight. This speed is called the **terminal speed** (or terminal velocity).

★ A vehicle reaches its top speed when the drag force is equal and opposite to the engine force. The top speed can be increased by reshaping a vehicle to reduce the drag force on it.

Force and motion

Questions

A car of total mass 800 kg can accelerate from rest to a speed of 20 m/s in 20 s. Calculate
a) the acceleration of the car
b) the force producing this acceleration, assuming the drag force is negligible
c) the ratio of this force to the total weight of the car. Assume $g = 10 \text{ m/s}^2$.

9.5 Work and energy

At work

Fact file

★ A force does **work** on an object when it moves the object in the direction of the force.

★ **Work done** = force × distance moved in the direction of the force.

★ **Energy** is the capacity to do work.

★ The unit of work and of energy is the **joule** (J), which is equal to the work done when a force of 1 N moves its point of application through a distance of 1 m.

★ **Power** is defined as rate of transfer of energy. The unit of power is the **watt** (W), which is equal to 1 J/s.

Gaining height

Gravitational potential energy

If a mass m is moved through a height h, its

change of gravitational potential energy = mgh,

where g is the acceleration due to gravity. This is because the force of gravity on the object (its weight) is mg.

1. Any object at rest is acted on by a support force which is equal and opposite to its weight.

2. If the object is raised, the work done by the support force is mgh (equal to force × distance). This is therefore the gain of potential energy of the object.

3. If the object is lowered, the work done by gravity is mgh (equal to force × distance). This is therefore the decrease of potential energy of the object.

Kinetic energy

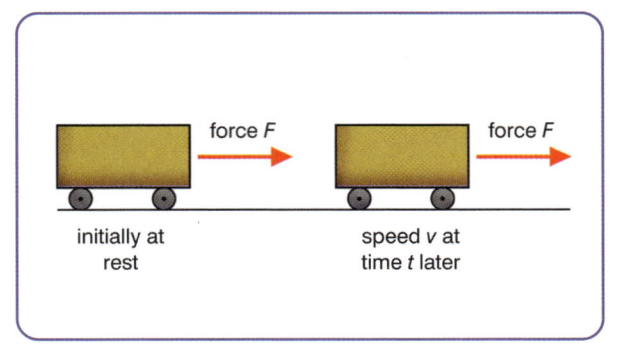

Kinetic energy

For a mass m moving at speed v, its

kinetic energy = $\frac{1}{2}mv^2$.

This can be proved by considering a constant force F acting on an object of mass m, initially at rest, for time t. From pages 65 and 67 and above,

1. its distance moved $s = \dfrac{vt}{2}$ where v is its speed at time t

2. its acceleration $a = \dfrac{v}{t}$

   hence $F = ma = \dfrac{mv}{t}$

3. Hence the work done = $Fs = \dfrac{mv}{t} \times \dfrac{vt}{2} = \frac{1}{2}mv^2$

   which is therefore the kinetic energy of the object.

Answers a) 1 m/s² b) 800 N c) 0.1

Force and motion

Questions

Set out your answers clearly. In an examination, if you slip up on a calculation, you will only lose one mark if you have shown clearly that you understand the principles involved. Where necessary, assume $g = 10 \text{ m/s}^2$.

1. A tennis ball of mass 0.20 kg is released from rest at a height of 2.0 m above a concrete floor. It rebounds to a height of 1.5 m.

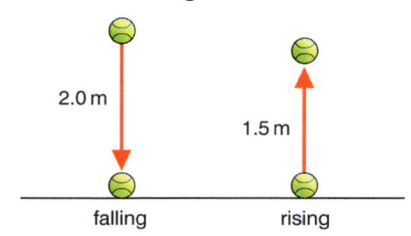

   a) Calculate its kinetic energy and speed just before impact.
   b) Calculate its kinetic energy and speed just after impact.
   c) Calculate its loss of energy between release and its maximum height after rebounding.

2. A fairground train of total mass 600 kg descended a total height of 50 m into a dip after it went over the highest point on the track. Calculate

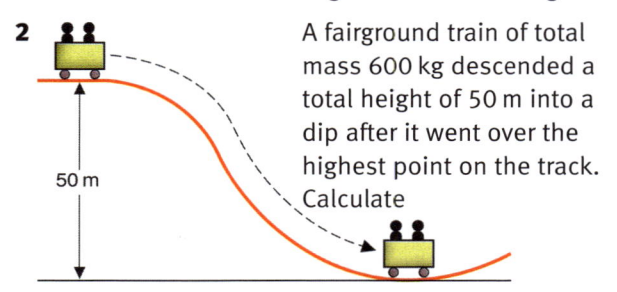

   a) its loss of potential energy in this descent
   b) its kinetic energy and speed at the bottom of the dip, assuming air resistance was negligible and its kinetic energy at the highest point was zero.

3. An aeroplane of mass 600 kg takes off from rest in 50 s over a distance of 1500 m.

   a) Calculate (i) its speed when it lifts off
      (ii) its acceleration during take-off
      (iii) the force needed to produce this acceleration.
   b) Why is the engine force greater than the force calculated in a) (iii)?

4. A hot air balloon and its occupants have a total weight of 5000 N. It is descending at a constant speed of 0.5 m/s.

   a) What is the total upward force on it during this descent?
   b) Calculate its kinetic energy.
   c) Calculate its loss of height and loss of potential energy in 1 minute.
   d) Explain why it does not gain kinetic energy.

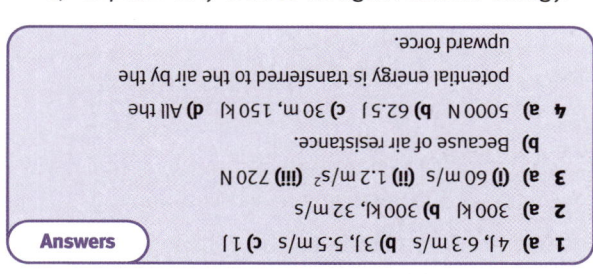

Answers

1 a) 4 J, 6.3 m/s b) 3 J, 5.5 m/s c) 1 J
2 a) 300 kJ b) 300 kJ, 32 m/s
3 a) (i) 60 m/s (ii) 1.2 m/s² (iii) 720 N
  b) Because of air resistance.
4 a) 5000 N b) 62.5 J c) 30 m, 150 kJ d) All the potential energy is transferred to the air by the upward force.

ROUND UP

continues on page 70

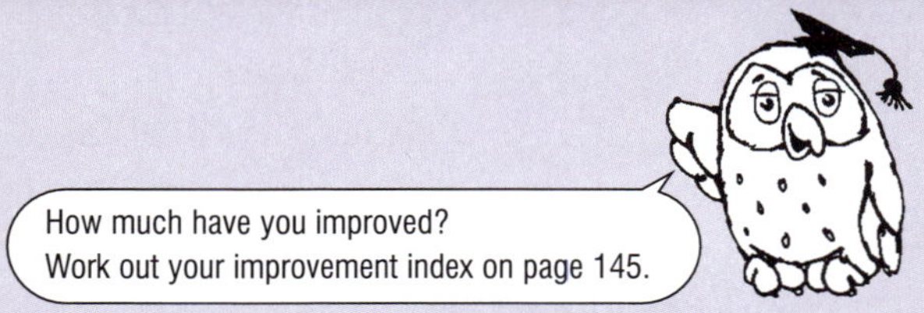

How much have you improved? Work out your improvement index on page 145.

The acceleration of a freely falling object, $g = 10 \text{ m/s}^2$.

1. a) A walker leaves a car park and walks at a steady speed of 1.2 m/s for 1 hour. How far did the walker travel in this time in
   (i) metres (ii) kilometres? [2]

   b) A runner leaves the same car park 40 minutes after the walker and catches up with the walker at a distance of 4 km from the car park. What was the runner's speed? [1]

2. The graph shows the progress of two cyclists in a 10 km road race.

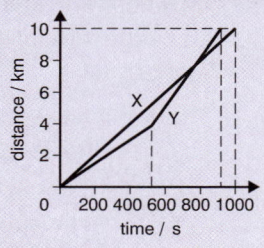

   a) One cyclist X maintained a constant speed throughout. What can you deduce from the graph about the speed of the other cyclist Y? [4]

   b) (i) From the graph, calculate the speed of X. [1]
      (ii) From the graph, calculate the speed of Y when Y overtook X. [1]

Force and motion

ROUND UP
continued

3 a) Explain the difference between speed and velocity. [2]

b) A police car joins a motorway and travels north at a constant speed of 30 m/s for 5 minutes. It then leaves the motorway at a motorway junction, rejoins it immediately and travels south in the opposite direction for 20 minutes at a steady speed of 20 m/s to the scene of an accident.

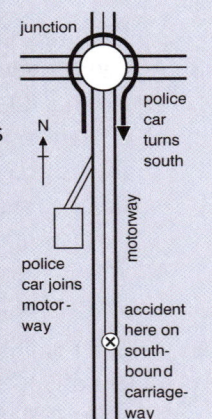

  (i) How far did the police car travel in each direction? [2]

  (ii) How far from the point where the police car first joined the motorway was the scene of the accident? [1]

4 A vehicle of mass 700 kg accelerates steadily from rest to a speed of 8 m/s in a time of 5 s. The graph shows how the speed of the vehicle increased with time.

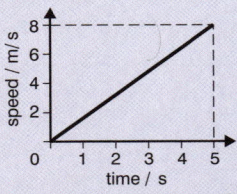

a) Calculate the acceleration of the vehicle and the distance travelled in this time. [2]

b) What force acting on the vehicle is necessary to produce this acceleration? [1]

5 a) A ball of mass 0.2 kg is thrown directly upwards with an initial speed of 25 m/s. Calculate how long it took to reach its highest point. [1]

b) The graph shows how its vertical position changed after it left the thrower's hand.

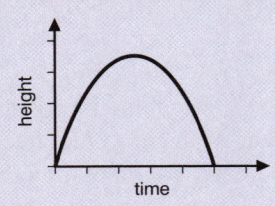

  (i) What was its initial kinetic energy? [1]
  (ii) Calculate its maximum gain of potential energy. [1]
  (iii) Calculate its maximum gain of height. [1]

6 a) An athlete runs a distance of 100 m in a time of 10.5 s. Calculate the athlete's average speed over this distance. [1]

b) The athlete's mass is 60 kg. Calculate the athlete's kinetic energy at the speed calculated in **a)**. [1]

c) If all the kinetic energy calculated in **b)** could be converted into potential energy by the athlete, what height gain would be possible? [1]

d) A pole vaulter is capable of jumping considerably higher. Discuss how this is achieved. [1]

7 A train of total mass 30 000 kg is travelling at a constant speed of 10 m/s when its brakes are applied, bringing it to rest with a constant deceleration in 50 s.

a) Sketch a graph to show how the speed of the train changed with time. [2]

b) Calculate **(i)** the distance moved by the train in this time **(ii)** its deceleration. [2]

c) Hence calculate the force of the brakes on the train. [1]

d) Calculate the ratio of the braking force to the train's weight. [1]

8 a) Explain why a moving car skids if the brakes are applied too hard. [1]

b) Explain why the stopping distance of a car travelling at a certain speed is greater if the road surface is wet. [4]

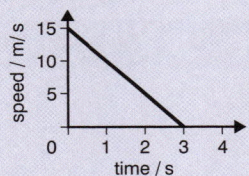

c) The graph shows how the speed of a car of mass 1200 kg on a dry road decreases with time when it stops safely in the shortest possible distance. The car is initially moving at a speed of 15 m/s. Calculate **(i)** the braking distance **(ii)** the deceleration of the car and the braking force. [3]

d) On a wet road, the braking force is reduced by half. Calculate the time it would take to brake safely from a speed of 15 m/s on a wet road and determine the braking distance in this condition. [2]

Forces in balance — Chapter 10

PREVIEW

At the end of this topic you will be able to:

- identify the forces acting on a body in equilibrium
- explain what is meant by centre of gravity
- describe the use of levers as force multipliers *
- state and use Hooke's law and describe elastic and plastic behaviour *
- carry out simple pressure and density calculations *
- describe pressure applications, including hydrostatic pressure and hydraulics *

*Not needed for AQA, EDEXCEL and OCR specifications.

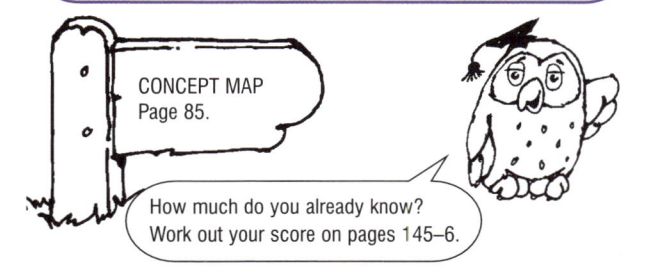

CONCEPT MAP Page 85.

How much do you already know? Work out your score on pages 145–6.

Test yourself

1. What forces are acting on your body at the moment? [2]

2. State whether each of the following is in stable, unstable or neutral equilibrium
   a) a ball at rest on the floor
   b) a child sitting on a fence
   c) a coat hanger hanging from a rail. [3]

3. The diagram shows a person pushing a wheelbarrow containing sand. The total weight of the wheelbarrow and its contents is 800 N.

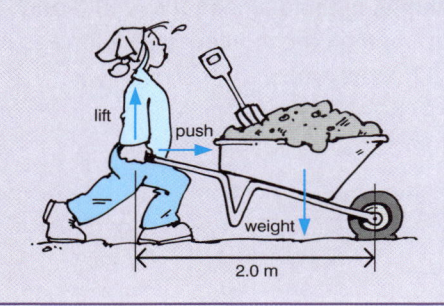

   a) Estimate how far the centre of gravity of the wheelbarrow is from the handle. [1]
   b) Explain why the force needed to lift the wheelbarrow is much less than 800 N. [2]
   c) The wheelbarrow contains 0.020 m^3 of sand. The density of the sand is 2500 kg/m^3. Calculate the mass of sand in the wheelbarrow. [1]

4. a) (i) Explain why a sharp knife cuts more easily than a blunt knife. [1]
      (ii) Explain why a suction cap pushed onto a smooth vertical tile doesn't fall off. [2]
   b) A spade has a rectangular blade which measures 25 cm × 20 cm. It is used to flatten a mound of earth. Each impact of the blade's flat surface on the mound creates a force of 300 N. Calculate the pressure due to this force. [2]

5. a) What is meant by elastic behaviour? [1]
   b) What is meant by plastic behaviour? [1]

6. A steel spring stretches by 4 cm when it is stretched by a 1 N force applied at either end.
   a) What is the extension of the spring when it is stretched by a force of 5 N? [1]
   b) How much force is needed to extend the spring by 10 cm? [1]

7. A spanner is used to unscrew a wheel nut on a bicycle. Why is it easier to do this using a long spanner rather than a short spanner? [2]

8. A metre rule is pivoted on a knife edge at its centre with a 1.0 N weight on a thread suspended from the 10 cm mark of the rule. The rule is then balanced by suspending an object of unknown weight W at its 65 cm mark. The arrangement is shown in the diagram below. Calculate
   a) the moment of the 1.0 N weight about the pivot [1]
   b) the weight W of the unknown object. [2]

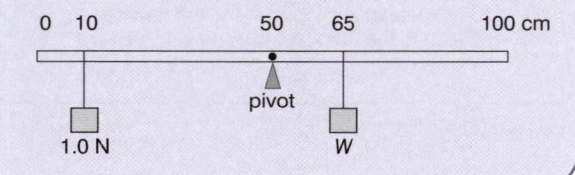

Forces in balance

10.1 Equilibrium

Fact file

★ Different types of force include **weight** (the force of gravity), **tension** (forces that stretch), **compression** (forces that squeeze), **twisting forces**, **electrical forces** and **magnetic forces**.

★ The unit of force is the newton (N). Note that 10 N is the weight of a mass of 1 kg at the Earth's surface.

★ The centre of gravity of an object is the point where its weight may be considered to act.

Balanced forces

An object at rest is said to be in **equilibrium**. The forces acting on an object at rest balance each other out. If an object is acted on by two forces only, the object will be in equilibrium if the two forces are:
1. equal to each other, **and**
2. acting on the object along the same line in opposite directions.

Some examples of objects in equilibrium are shown in the diagram below.

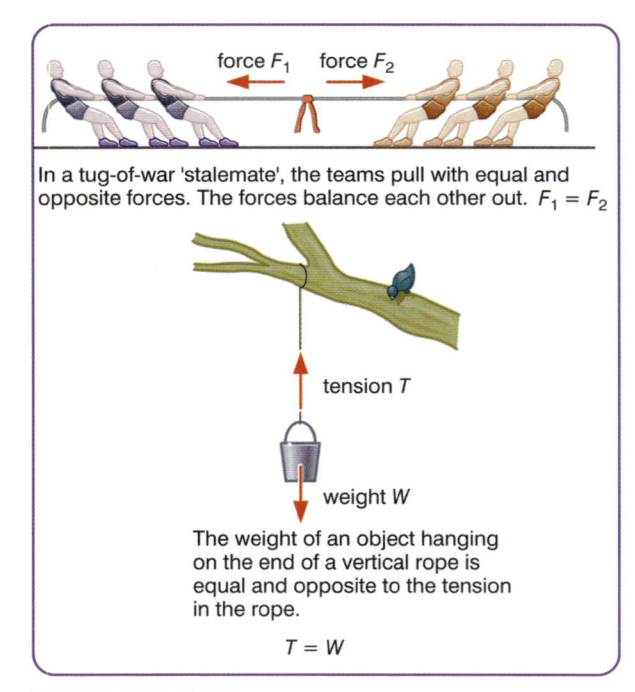

In a tug-of-war 'stalemate', the teams pull with equal and opposite forces. The forces balance each other out. $F_1 = F_2$

The weight of an object hanging on the end of a vertical rope is equal and opposite to the tension in the rope.
$T = W$

Equal and opposite forces

Stability

If an object at equilibrium is displaced slightly and then released, it is said to be:
- in **stable equilibrium** if it returns to equilibrium
- in **neutral equilibrium** if it stays at its new position
- in **unstable equilibrium** if it moves away from the point where it was in equilibrium.

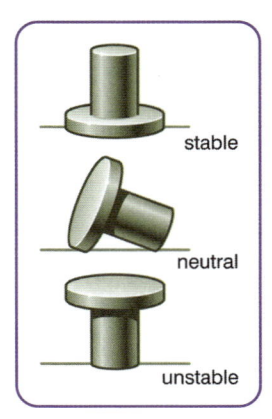

Turning effects

A force acting on an object can have a turning effect on the object. For example, the diagram below shows a force acting on a spanner that is used to turn a nut. The turning effect of such a force depends on the size of the force and its perpendicular distance from the line of action of the force to the nut.

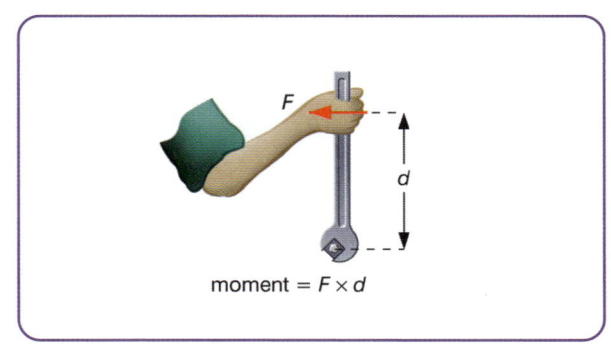

moment = $F \times d$

Turning a nut

★ The **moment** of a force about a point is defined as the force × the perpendicular distance from the line of action of the force to the pivot.

For example, in the diagram, if $F = 40$ N and $d = 0.20$ m, then the moment of the force is 8 N m (= 40 N × 0.20 m).

Forces in balance

★ For any object in equilibrium, the moments of the forces about the same point balance each other out. This is known as the **principle of moments**. Two examples are shown in the diagram below.

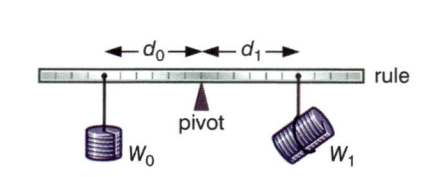

The unknown weight W_1 can be measured by adjusting its distance from the pivot until the rule is balanced. The moment of W_1 = the moment of the known weight W_0.

$$W_0 d_0 = W_1 d_1$$

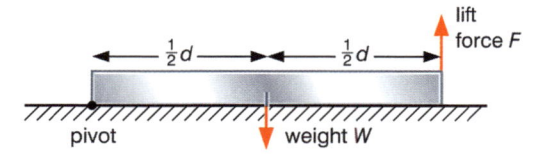

The force F required to lift the concrete post at one end is half the weight W. This is because the moment of this force about the pivot must be at least equal to the moment of the weight about the pivot.

$$Fd = \tfrac{1}{2}dW$$

Equal and opposite moments

Tilting and toppling

The diagram shows a tall cupboard tilted on one side. It will topple if released because the perpendicular from its centre of gravity to the ground falls outside its base. This means its weight tries to turn it anticlockwise about the edge which acts as the pivot. A force F as shown is necessary to provide an equal and opposite moment.

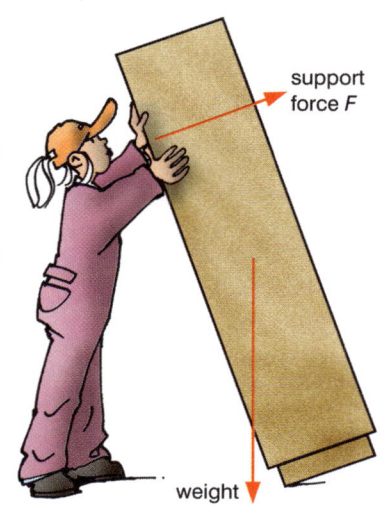

Action and reaction

Whenever two objects interact, they exert equal and opposite forces on each other. For example, if you lean on a wall with a certain force, you experience an equal and opposite force from the wall. The same rule applies when two objects collide; they push on each other with an equal and opposite force.

Questions

1 A spanner of length 0.3 m is used to turn a nut by applying a force of 50 N to the free end of the spanner. Calculate the moment of this force.

2 In the top diagram above, a ruler pivoted at its centre supports two weights W_0 and W_1. The rule is horizontal. If W_0 = 1.5 N, d_0 = 0.20 m and d_1 = 0.30 m, calculate
   a) the moment of W_0 about the pivot
   b) the unknown weight W_1.

3 A plank of weight 200 N rests horizontally on two bricks, one at either end as shown.
   a) What force does the plank exert on each brick?
   b) What force is necessary to lift the plank at one end?

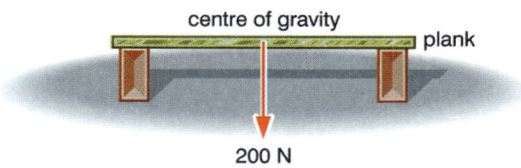

Answers

1 15 N m
2 a) 0.30 N m b) 1.0 N
3 a) 100 N b) 100 N

Forces in balance

10.2 Strength of solids

Solids and strength

★ **Stiffness** is the ability to withstand being stretched or bent.

★ **Toughness** is the ability to withstand fracture.

★ **Strength** is a measure of how much force is needed to break an object.

★ **Brittleness** is a measure of how easily an object snaps.

Hooke's law

This law states that **the extension of a spiral spring is proportional to the force used to stretch it**. The diagram shows how Hooke's law may be tested, and a graph of some typical results for a steel spring. Note that the extension is the change of length from its unstretched length.

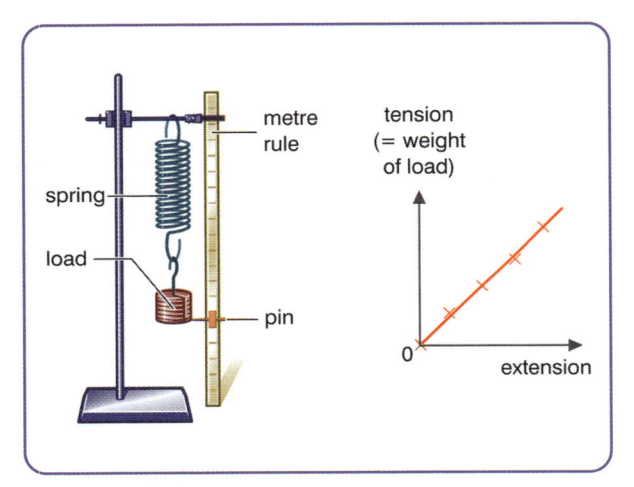

Hooke's law

Hooke's law may be written in the form $T = ke$ where T is the tension in the spring, e is the extension of the spring and k is a constant. This is the equation for the line in the graph. The line is straight and it passes through the origin because the tension is proportional to the extension. Its gradient is equal to the spring constant k. Note that the equation $T = ke$ may be rearranged to give

$$e = \frac{T}{k} \text{ or } k = \frac{T}{e}$$

Elastic and plastic behaviour

★ **Elastic behaviour** is the ability of a solid to regain its shape when the external forces are removed. The atoms return to their original positions when the external forces are removed.

★ The **elastic limit** of a solid is the limit of its ability to regain its shape. Beyond its elastic limit, it deforms permanently.

★ **Plastic behaviour** occurs when the shape of a solid is permanently changed by external forces. The atoms are pulled out of position permanently.

The graphs below show how the extension of different objects under tension increases with the external force.

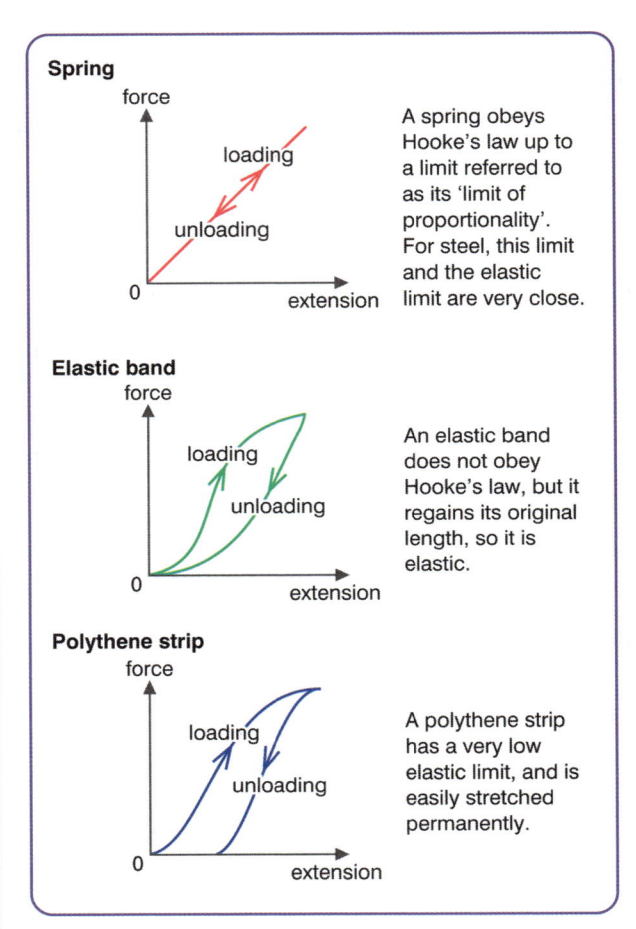

Spring: A spring obeys Hooke's law up to a limit referred to as its 'limit of proportionality'. For steel, this limit and the elastic limit are very close.

Elastic band: An elastic band does not obey Hooke's law, but it regains its original length, so it is elastic.

Polythene strip: A polythene strip has a very low elastic limit, and is easily stretched permanently.

Stretching materials

Forces in balance

10.3 Pressure and its measurement

Fact file

★ **Pressure** is defined as force per unit area acting normally on a surface.

★ The unit of pressure is the **pascal** (Pa), equal to 1 N/m².

★ Density = $\dfrac{\text{mass}}{\text{volume}}$

★ The unit of density is the kilogram per cubic metre (kg/m³).

★ The pressure p due to a force F acting normally on an area A may be calculated from the equation

$$p = \dfrac{F}{A}$$

★ Note that an area of 1 m² is equal to 10 000 cm² (= 100 cm × 100 cm).

Therefore a force of 1 N acting on an area of 1 cm² gives a pressure of 10 kPa (= 10 000 Pa).

Pressure points

The larger the area of surface over which a force acts, the smaller the pressure. The smaller the area, the greater the pressure.

Question

Calculate the pressure in kPa exerted by a 60 kg person standing on the floor if the total area of contact between the person's feet and the floor is 100 cm². Assume g = 10 N/kg.

Pressure in a liquid

The pressure in a liquid:
- acts equally in all directions
- increases with depth
- is the same at all points at the same depth
- depends on the density of the liquid.

Floating and sinking

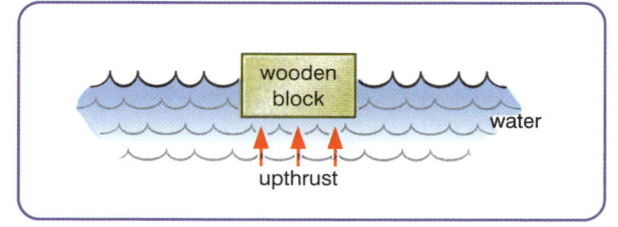

A floating object

An **upthrust** acts on any object in a fluid. This is because the pressure of the fluid is greater on the bottom of the object than on the top. If an object is slowly lowered into a liquid, the upthrust on it increases gradually. The object will:
- **float** if the upthrust becomes large enough to support its weight
- **sink** if the upthrust is not enough to support its weight.

The U-tube manometer

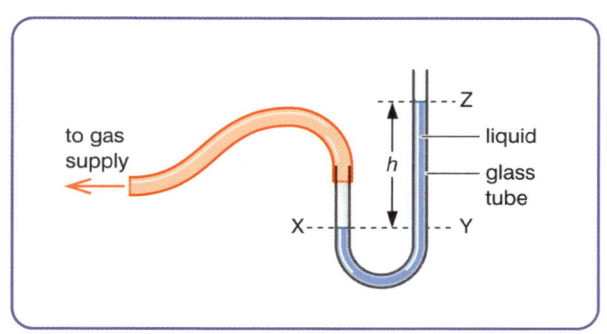

The U-tube manometer

This device is used to measure gas pressure.

★ The pressure at X is due to the gas supply.

★ The pressure at Y is caused by atmospheric pressure at Z + the pressure of the liquid column YZ.

★ The pressure at Y = the pressure at X since they are on the same level.

★ Therefore the gas supply pressure = the pressure due to YZ + atmospheric pressure.

★ Hence the height of column YZ is a measure of how much the gas supply pressure exceeds atmospheric pressure (the 'excess' gas pressure).

Answer 60 kPa

Forces in balance

10.4 Hydraulics

Vehicle brakes

A brake system exerts a large braking force on the wheels as a result of a much smaller force being applied to the foot pedal.

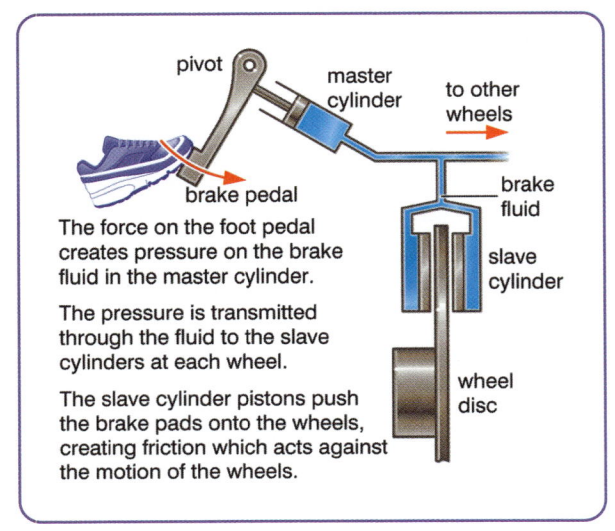

The force on the foot pedal creates pressure on the brake fluid in the master cylinder.

The pressure is transmitted through the fluid to the slave cylinders at each wheel.

The slave cylinder pistons push the brake pads onto the wheels, creating friction which acts against the motion of the wheels.

Disc brakes

Using the pressure equation

1. The pressure exerted on the fluid is given by the equation $p = \dfrac{F_1}{A_1}$ where F_1 is the force on the master cylinder and A_1 is the area of the master cylinder.

2. This pressure is transmitted to the slave cylinders without loss. This assumes no air in the brake system.

3. The force exerted by each slave cylinder $F_2 = pA_2$, where A_2 is the area of each slave cylinder.

4. Hence $F_2 = \dfrac{F_1 A_2}{A_1}$.

   Since A_2 is much larger than A_1, then it follows that F_2 is much larger than F_1.

Questions

A brake system has a master cylinder of area 5 cm² and each slave cylinder has an area of 100 cm². A force of 20 N is applied to the master cylinder.

a) Calculate (i) the pressure in the system in pascals (ii) the force exerted by each slave piston.

b) Why is it important not to allow any air into the brake system?

More hydraulic machines

A hydraulic car jack is used to raise a car wheel off the ground. The car jack handle is a lever which multiplies the effort applied to it. The lever force is then magnified further by the hydraulic cylinders which contain oil. The force of the slave cylinder on the vehicle is enough to raise the vehicle at that point.

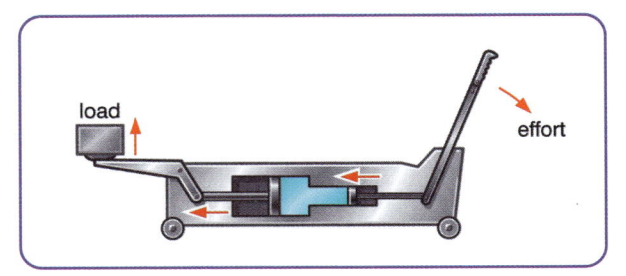

A hydraulic car jack

A hydraulic press is capable of exerting enough force to stamp metals into shape. The effort is applied to a lever which acts on the master piston. The pressure in the oil is then transmitted to the much wider slave cylinders which then exert a much greater force on the object to be stamped.

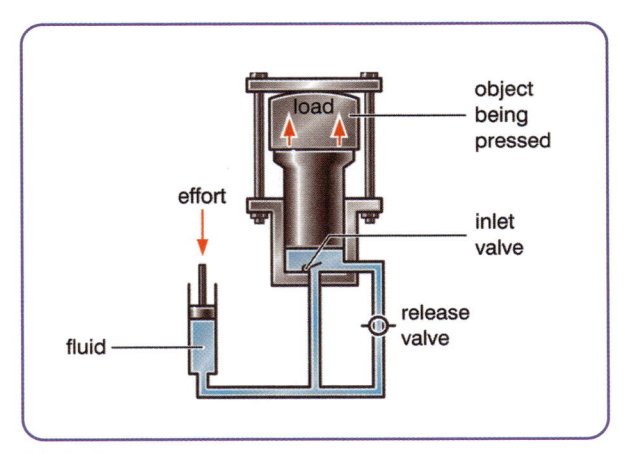

A hydraulic press

Answers

a) (i) 40 000 Pa (ii) 400 N
b) Unlike a liquid, air can be compressed. Therefore the pressure would not be transmitted to the slave cylinders.

Forces in balance

ROUND UP

How much have you improved? Work out your improvement index on page 146.

1 a) Why do the rear wheels of a tractor need to be much larger than the wheels of a van of equal weight? [2]

b) With the aid of a diagram, explain why the shape of a bowling alley pin makes it easy to knock over. [2]

2 a) Calculate the pressure exerted by a person of weight 600 N when she is

(i) standing on both feet, with an area of contact between each foot and the floor of 0.0015 m^2. [1]

(ii) sitting on a chair, with a total area of contact on the chair of 0.10 m^2. [1]

b) Calculate the total area of contact between the tyres of a bicycle and the ground if the air pressure in each tyre is 150 kPa and the total weight of the bicycle and cyclist is 600 N. [1]

3 A student proposes to replace a steel spring in a spring balance with an elastic band. She tests the stiffness of the elastic band and the spring in separate experiments. The graphs show her results.

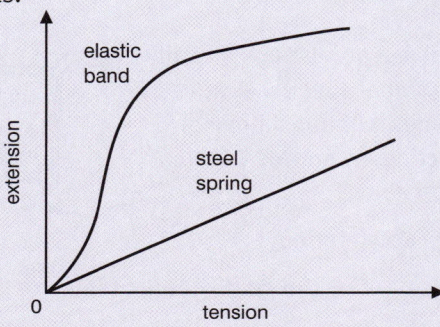

a) Use these results to compare the stiffness of the elastic band and the steel spring. [2]

b) Would the elastic band be satisfactory in place of the steel spring? Give a reason for your answer. [2]

4 a) In an experiment to compare the densities of salt water and pure water, the following measurements were made.

(1) mass of an empty measuring cylinder = 120 g

(2) mass of this measuring cylinder containing 100 cm^3 of pure water = 220 g

(3) mass of this measuring cylinder containing 100 cm^3 of salt water = 228 g

Use these measurements to calculate the density of pure water and of salt water in
(i) g/cm^3 (ii) kg/m^3. [4]

b) Why do objects float more easily in salt water than in pure water? [3]

5 The diagram shows a metre rule in equilibrium in a horizontal position. The rule is pivoted at its midpoint and it supports two weights W_1 and W_2 at distances d_1 and d_2 from the pivot. The following table shows four incomplete sets of measurements taken with different weights. Calculate each missing measurement. [4]

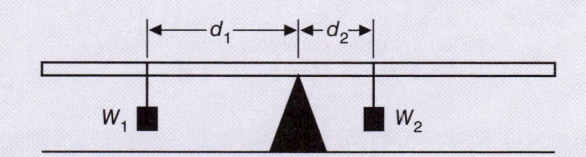

	W_1 / N	W_2 / N	d_1 / m	d_2 / m
set 1	3.2	1.6	0.2	?
set 2	?	1.5	0.4	0.3
set 3	2.5	?	0.4	0.1
set 4	4.5	3.2	?	0.27

6 A steel spring of length 300 mm was used to measure the weight of an object. With the spring hanging vertically from a fixed point, its length was measured when it supported different known weights. Then its length was measured when it supported the unknown weight W. The measurements are given below.

weight / N	0	1	2	3	4
spring length / mm	300	340	382	419	461

Spring length for the unknown weight = 376 mm

a) Plot a graph of weight (vertical axis) against the extension of the spring. [4]

b) Use your graph to determine the unknown weight W. [1]

Chapter 11 — Additional mechanics

11.1 Dynamics equations and graphs

PREVIEW

At the end of this topic you will be able to:
- **interpret graphs of distance versus time and velocity versus time**
- **use the dynamics equations for constant acceleration**
- **describe the motion of a projectile.**

CONCEPT MAP Page 85.

How much do you already know? Work out your score on page 146.

Test yourself

Where necessary, assume $g = 10$ N/kg.

1. A car travelling at 30 m/s brakes to a halt at a set of traffic lights. The graph shows how its speed changes as it approaches the lights.

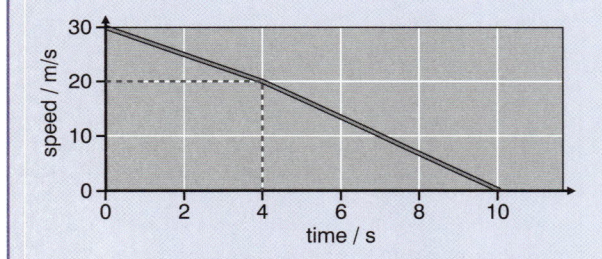

   a) Describe how its speed changes as it approaches the lights.

   b) Calculate the acceleration and the distance travelled by the car in (i) the first 4 s (ii) the last 6 s of the braking motion. [6]

2. An object released from the top of a tall tower took 3 s to fall to the ground. Ignoring the effect of air resistance

   a) calculate its speed just before it hit the ground

   b) sketch a graph to show how the speed of the object changed with time as it fell

   c) determine the distance fallen by the object. [5]

3. The speed of an aircraft decreased uniformly from 60 m/s, when its wheels touched down, to rest 40 s later.

   a) Sketch a graph to show how its speed decreased from the moment its wheels touched the ground to the time when it came to rest.

   b) Calculate (i) the deceleration of the aircraft (ii) the distance it took to stop on the ground.

   c) If its mass was 40 000 kg, calculate the force needed to stop it. [6]

Graphs and equations

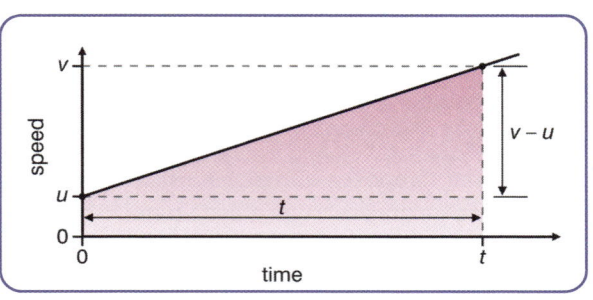

Constant acceleration

An object accelerates steadily from initial speed u to speed v in time t without change of direction, as shown in the graph above.

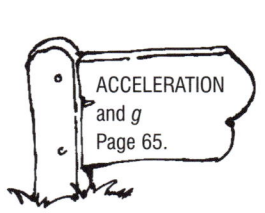

ACCELERATION and g Page 65.

★ Its **acceleration**

$$a = \frac{v - u}{t} = \text{the gradient of the line}$$

★ The **distance** it moves

$$s = \frac{(u + v)t}{2} = \text{the area under the line above the time axis.}$$

Rearranging the first equation gives $v = u + at$.

Substitute $u + at$ for v in the second equation.

$$s = \frac{[u + (u + at)]t}{2} = \frac{2ut + at^2}{2}$$

hence $s = ut + \frac{1}{2}at^2$

78

Additional mechanics

A timeless equation

The two equations $s = \frac{(u+v)t}{2}$ and $a = \frac{v-u}{t}$

may be combined as follows to eliminate t

$$as = \frac{(u+v)t}{2} \times \frac{(v-u)}{t} = \frac{v^2 - u^2}{2}$$

Rearranging this equation gives

$v^2 = u^2 + 2as$

Worked example

An aeroplane accelerates on take-off from rest to a speed of 80 m/s in a distance of 2000 m before it loses contact with the ground. Calculate
a) its acceleration
b) the time taken to reach its take-off speed.

Solution

$u = 0$, $s = 2000$ m, $v = 80$ m/s

a) To calculate a, rearrange $v^2 = u^2 + 2as$ to give
$$a = \frac{v^2 - u^2}{2s} = \frac{80^2 - 0^2}{2 \times 2000} = \mathbf{1.6\ m/s^2}$$

b) To calculate t, rearrange $v = u + at$ to give
$$t = \frac{v-u}{a} = \frac{80}{1.6} = \mathbf{50\ s}$$

Projectiles

An object in free fall with horizontal motion falls at the same rate as if it had no horizontal motion.

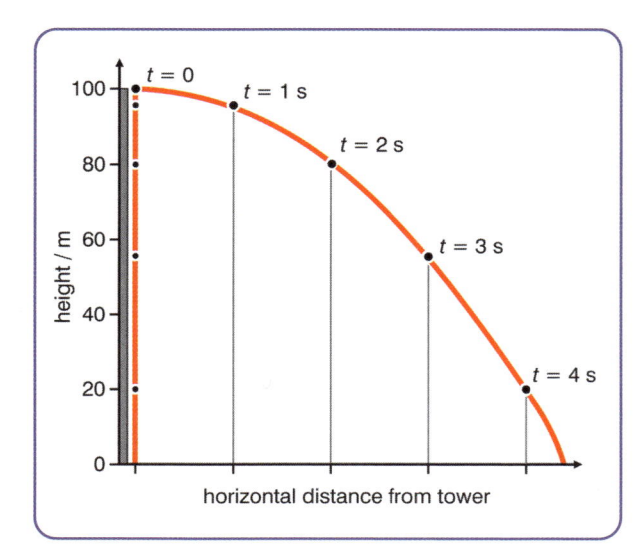

Projectiles

★ Its vertical motion is at constant acceleration, g.

★ Its horizontal motion is at constant speed.

The diagram at the bottom-left shows the position at one-second intervals of a ball thrown horizontally from the top of a tall tower. Assuming air resistance is negligible, the ball moves equal distances horizontally each second because gravity does not alter its horizontal motion. However, its vertical motion is the same as if it had been released from rest.

ROUND UP

How much have you improved?
Work out your improvement index on page 146.

Where necessary, assume $g = 10\ m/s^2$.

1. A ball thrown vertically upwards returns to the thrower 2.5 s later.
   a) (i) How long does it take to reach maximum height?
      (ii) What is its speed at maximum height?
   b) Calculate (i) its speed of projection
      (ii) its maximum height. [6]

2. A heavy ball is dropped from a height of 1.5 m above soft earth.
   a) Calculate the speed of the ball just before impact with the ground.
   b) The ball creates a hollow in the ground of depth 20 mm without rebounding. Calculate its acceleration on hitting the ground. [4]

3. A vehicle in a collision came to rest after producing skid marks of length 65 m. Subsequent tests on the tyres proved that skidding could only produce a deceleration of 7 m/s². Calculate the initial speed of the vehicle in a) m/s b) miles per hour.
   (5 miles = 8 kilometres) [3]

Well done if you've improved. Don't worry if you haven't. Take a break and try again.

Additional mechanics

11.2 Force and momentum

PREVIEW

At the end of this topic you will be able to:

- define momentum and relate change of momentum to force
- explain why an impact force is reduced if the contact time is increased
- use the principle of conservation of momentum to analyse collisions and explosions
- apply the principle of conservation of momentum to explain how a rocket engine and a jet engine work.

How much do you already know? Work out your score on page 147.

Test yourself

1. Calculate the momentum and the kinetic energy of an athlete of mass 60 kg running at a speed of 8 m/s. [2]

2. A vehicle of mass 600 kg accelerates from rest to a speed of 20 m/s in a time of 5 s. Calculate
   a) the gain of momentum of the vehicle
   b) the gain of momentum per second as it accelerates
   c) the force needed to produce this acceleration. [3]

3. A railway truck of mass 2000 kg travelling at a speed of 5 m/s collides with another truck of mass 3000 kg, which is initially stationary. The two trucks couple together as a result of the collision, as shown in the diagram. Calculate
   a) the speed of the two trucks after the collision
   b) the loss of kinetic energy as a result of the collision. [7]

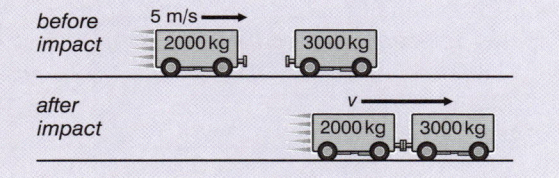

   before impact: 2000 kg at 5 m/s, 3000 kg
   after impact: 2000 kg + 3000 kg at v

4. The engines of a rocket burn fuel at a rate of 2000 kg/s, ejecting the combustion products at a speed of 1600 m/s. Calculate
   a) (i) the momentum loss from the rocket each second
      (ii) the force produced by the rocket engine.
   b) the maximum mass of the rocket on the launch pad if its engines are to produce an initial upward acceleration of 8.0 m/s^2. [5]

Newton's second law

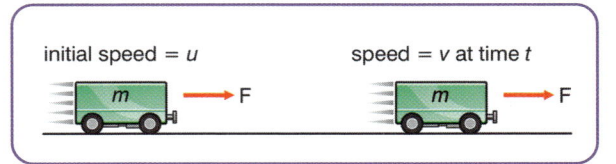

initial speed = u, mass m, force F speed = v at time t, mass m, force F

Force and motion

The momentum of a moving object is defined as its mass multiplied by its velocity. When an object is acted on by unbalanced forces, the momentum of the object is changed.

Consider an object of mass m acted on by a force F which increases its speed from initial speed u to speed v in time t without change of direction.

★ Its acceleration: $a = \dfrac{(v - u)}{t}$

★ The force necessary to produce this acceleration:

$$F = ma = \dfrac{m(v-u)}{t} = \dfrac{(mv - mu)}{t}$$

Since mv is the momentum at time t and mu is the initial momentum, then $(mv - mu)$ is the change of momentum of the object. Therefore

$$\text{force } F = \dfrac{\text{change of momentum}}{\text{time taken}}$$

This is a general form of Newton's second law.

The **impulse** of a force F acting on an object for time t is equal to Ft. This is equal to the change of momentum.

Worked example

In a crash test, an unoccupied vehicle of mass 800 kg travelling at a speed of 25 m/s is made to collide with a brick wall. The time taken for the impact was found to be 0.080 s. Calculate
a) the loss of momentum   b) the impact force.

Solution

a) Initial momentum = $800 \times 25 = 20\,000$ kg m/s,
final momentum = 0
Change of momentum
= final momentum – initial momentum
= **–20 000 kg m/s**

b) Force = change of momentum / time taken
= –20 000/0.080
= **–250 000 N**
(The minus sign shows that the force is in the opposite direction to the initial velocity.)

Conservation of momentum

For a system of bodies that interact with each other, the **total momentum is unchanged** provided no external force acts on the system. This is known as the **principle of conservation of momentum**.

In a **collision** between two bodies, equal and opposite forces act at the point of contact. The two bodies therefore experience equal and opposite changes of momentum. In other words, one of the two bodies gains momentum and the other body loses momentum. The total momentum is unchanged.

**The total momentum before the collision
= the total momentum after the collision**

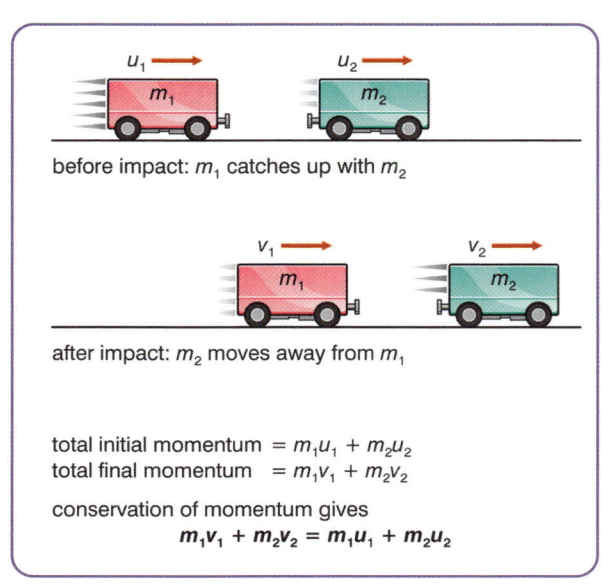

before impact: m_1 catches up with m_2

after impact: m_2 moves away from m_1

total initial momentum = $m_1 u_1 + m_2 u_2$
total final momentum = $m_1 v_1 + m_2 v_2$
conservation of momentum gives
$$m_1 v_1 + m_2 v_2 = m_1 u_1 + m_2 u_2$$

Conservation of momentum in a collision

In an **explosion,** in which two bodies fly apart after being initially stationary, the two bodies carry away equal and opposite momentum. Momentum is a vector quantity so the total final momentum is zero, the same as the total initial momentum. In other words, the total momentum is unchanged.

**The total momentum before the explosion
= the total momentum after the explosion = 0**

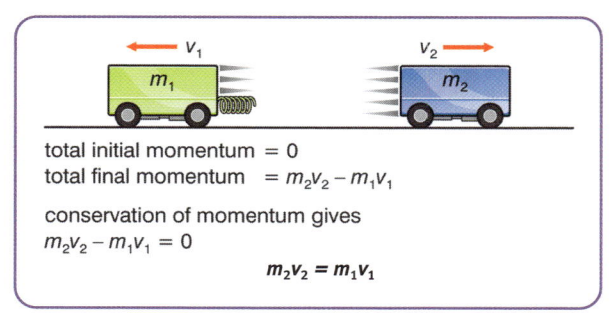

total initial momentum = 0
total final momentum = $m_2 v_2 - m_1 v_1$

conservation of momentum gives
$m_2 v_2 - m_1 v_1 = 0$
$$m_2 v_2 = m_1 v_1$$

Conservation of momentum in an explosion

Worked example

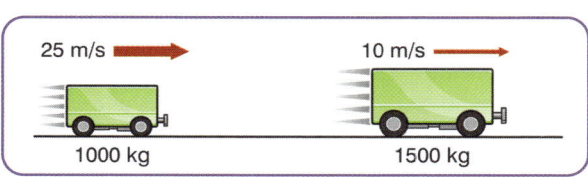

A vehicle of mass 1000 kg travelling at a speed of 25 m/s collides with a vehicle of mass 1500 kg moving at a speed of 10 m/s in the same direction. The two vehicles lock together on impact. Find the speed of the two vehicles immediately after impact.

Solution

Total initial momentum = $(1000 \times 25) + (1500 \times 10)$
= 40 000 kg m/s

Total final momentum = $(1000 + 1500)v$
where v is the speed immediately after impact of the two vehicles.

Using the principle of conservation of momentum therefore gives $2500v = 40\,000$

hence $v = 40\,000/2500 = $ **16 m/s**

Note

If the second vehicle had been moving in the opposite *direction, the total momentum would have been 10 000 kg m/s (= 25 000 – 15 000) giving a final speed of* **4 m/s**.

Additional mechanics

Jets and rockets

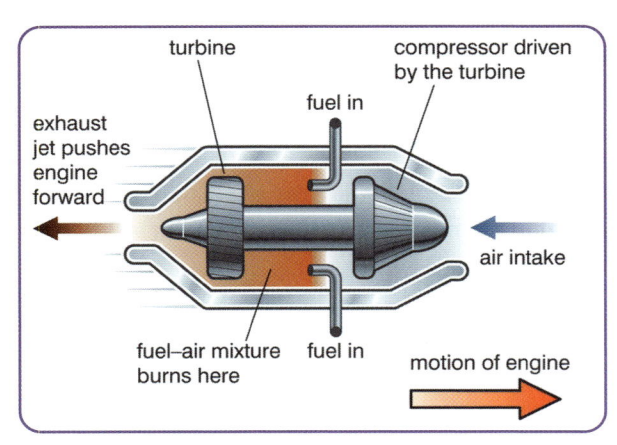

The jet engine

In a **jet engine**, the fuel is mixed with air drawn into the engine by a compressor. The fuel mixture is burned in the combustion chamber to produce hot gases which are ejected at high speed. The thrust force is equal and opposite to the momentum per second carried away by the hot gases.

In a **rocket engine**, the fuel is mixed with oxygen from an on-board liquid oxygen tank and then burned in the combustion chamber.

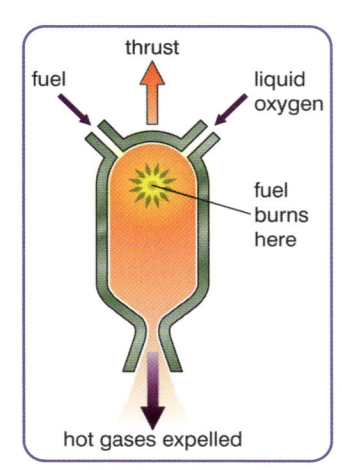

The rocket engine

Worked example

A 250 tonne rocket, to be launched vertically, is designed to burn 225 tonnes of fuel in 100 seconds, ejecting hot gases at a speed of 1500 m/s. Calculate
a) the momentum loss per second from the rocket
b) the thrust force produced by its engines
c) the initial acceleration of the rocket.
(1 tonne = 1000 kg)

Solution

a) Mass loss per second
= 225 000 kg/100 s = 2250 kg/s
Momentum loss per second
= 2250 × 1500 = **3.4 × 10⁶ kg m/s²**
b) Thrust force = change of momentum per second = **3.4 × 10⁶ N**
c) Resultant force = thrust force − weight
= 3.4 × 10⁶ − 2.5 × 10⁶
= 0.9 × 10⁶ N
Initial acceleration = resultant force/initial mass
= 0.9 × 10⁶ / 2.5 × 10⁵
= **3.6 m/s²**

ROUND UP

How much have you improved? Work out your improvement index on page 147.

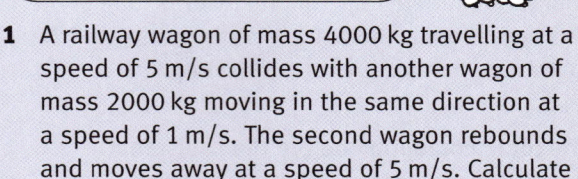

1 A railway wagon of mass 4000 kg travelling at a speed of 5 m/s collides with another wagon of mass 2000 kg moving in the same direction at a speed of 1 m/s. The second wagon rebounds and moves away at a speed of 5 m/s. Calculate
   a) the total initial momentum of the two wagons
   b) the velocity of the first wagon immediately after the impact. [5]

2 Repeat question **1** with the 2000 kg wagon initially moving in the opposite direction to the 4000 kg wagon. [5]

3 A student of mass 50 kg jumps off a stationary skateboard of mass 5 kg.
   a) Explain why the skateboard recoils.
   b) If the skateboard recoils at a speed of 8 m/s, calculate the student's speed. [5]

Well done if you've improved. Don't worry if you haven't. Take a break and try again.

Additional mechanics

11.3 More about forces

PREVIEW

At the end of this topic you will be able to:
- explain what is meant by a vector quantity and what is meant by a scalar quantity
- use the parallelogram rule to add two vectors together
- explain the difference between speed and velocity
- use a formula to calculate the centripetal acceleration of a satellite in a circular orbit.

How much do you already know? Work out your score on page 147.

Test yourself

1. State two examples of a) vector quantities b) scalar quantities. [4]

2. A barge is pulled along a river at steady speed by means of a steel cable from a tug boat. The tension in the cable is 8000 N.
   a) What is the magnitude of the drag force of the water on the barge?
   b) What is the resultant force on the barge just after the cable is released? [2]

3. A point object X is acted on by a force of 4.0 N and a force of 3.0 N acting in opposite directions. What single additional force is necessary to keep X in equilibrium? [2]

4. If the direction of the 3.0 N force in question 3 is changed so it is at right angles to the direction of the 4.0 N force, as in the diagram, what single force would now be necessary to keep X in equilibrium? [2]

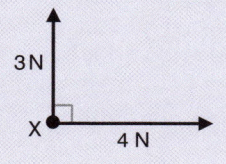

5. A satellite in a circular orbit passes directly overhead. At the instant it is overhead, what is the direction of a) its acceleration b) its velocity? [2]

6. A satellite is in a geostationary orbit of radius 42 000 km above the Earth.
   a) How long does it take to go round the Earth once?
   b) What is the significance of a geostationary orbit?
   c) What is the speed of the satellite? [3]

Vectors and scalars

★ A **vector** is any physical quantity that has a direction as well as a magnitude. Examples of vectors include velocity, acceleration, force, weight and momentum.

★ A **scalar** is any physical quantity that has a magnitude but no direction. Examples of scalars include speed, mass and energy.

★ A **vector** may be represented by an arrow pointing in the appropriate direction. The length of the arrow is proportional to the magnitude of the vector. For example, the diagram shows a point object X acted on by a force of 8.0 N in a direction due east.

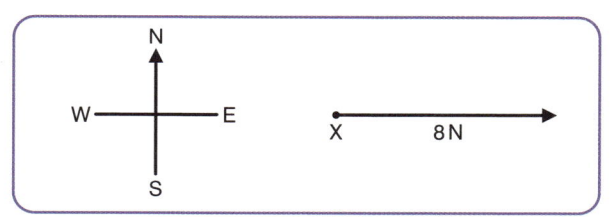

Representing vectors

★ The **parallelogram rule** may be used to add together two vectors. The vectors are drawn to form adjacent sides of a parallelogram. The combined effect of the two vectors, called the **resultant** R, is the diagonal of the parallelogram between the two vectors, as shown here.

The parallelogram rule

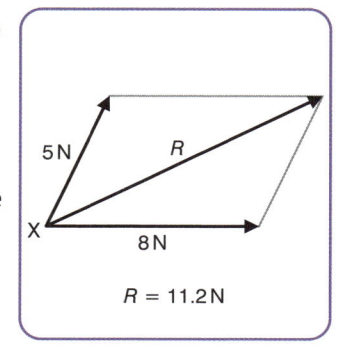

★ For a point object in equilibrium acted on by three forces, the resultant of any two of the forces is equal and opposite to the third force.

83

Additional mechanics

Circular motion

The diagram below shows a snapshot of an object moving at steady speed v on a circular path of radius r.

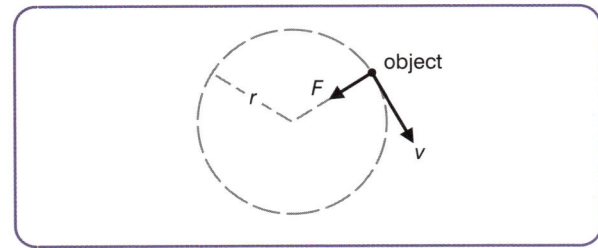

Circular motion

★ Its **speed** $v = 2\pi r/t$, where t is the time it takes to go round once.

★ Its **velocity** is at a tangent to the path. In other words, its velocity is in a direction at right angles to the radius. As the object progresses round the circle, the direction of its velocity continually changes.

★ The **centripetal force** F on the object is directed towards the centre of the circle. The force changes the direction of the velocity, making the object move round on a circular path. Because the force is at right angles to its direction of motion, no work is done by this force so the kinetic energy of the object remains constant.

★ The **centripetal acceleration** a of the object is towards the centre. The magnitude of the centripetal acceleration $a = v^2/r$.

Satellites

The centripetal force on a satellite in orbit about a planet is due to the force of gravitational attraction between the satellite and the planet. The force of gravity between any two objects decreases with increased separation. Consequently, the greater the radius of orbit of a satellite, the smaller its speed and the longer it takes to go round.

A **geostationary satellite** orbits the Earth from west to east above the equator once every 24 hours. This means that it remains above the same point on the equator. It can therefore be used to relay radio signals between any points on the Earth which can send signals directly to the satellite. To be in a geostationary orbit, a satellite must be put into an orbit of radius 42 000 km. If it is any lower, it will orbit the Earth in less than 24 hours; if it is any higher, it will take more than 24 hours to orbit the Earth.

ROUND UP

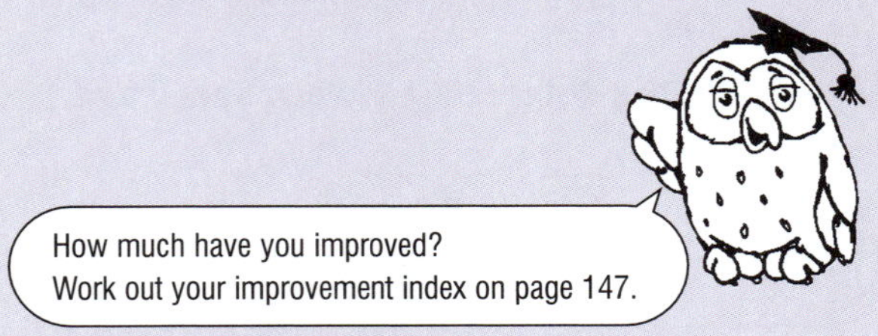

How much have you improved? Work out your improvement index on page 147.

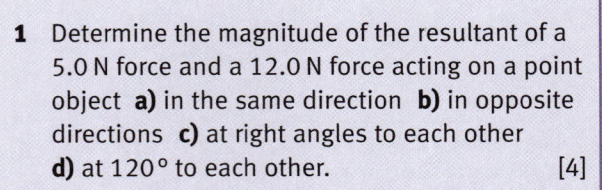

1 Determine the magnitude of the resultant of a 5.0 N force and a 12.0 N force acting on a point object **a)** in the same direction **b)** in opposite directions **c)** at right angles to each other **d)** at 120° to each other. [4]

2 A parachutist is descending vertically at a steady speed of 8 m/s when she is caught in a steady cross-wind of speed 10 m/s acting horizontally.
   a) Calculate the resultant velocity of the parachutist in this wind.
   b) If she is 200 m above the ground when the wind first catches her, how far downwind would the wind carry her? [4]

3 A satellite is in a circular orbit of radius 6600 km, just above the Earth's atmosphere. At this low height, the centripetal acceleration is the same as the acceleration of free fall g at the surface (10 m/s^2).
   a) Use the equation for centipetal acceleration ($a = $ speed^2/radius) to calculate the speed of the satellite.
   b) Hence calculate the time taken by the satellite for each orbit. [5]

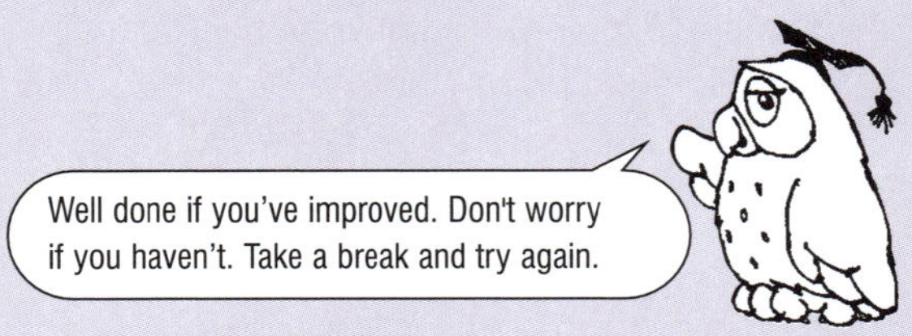

Well done if you've improved. Don't worry if you haven't. Take a break and try again.

Additional mechanics

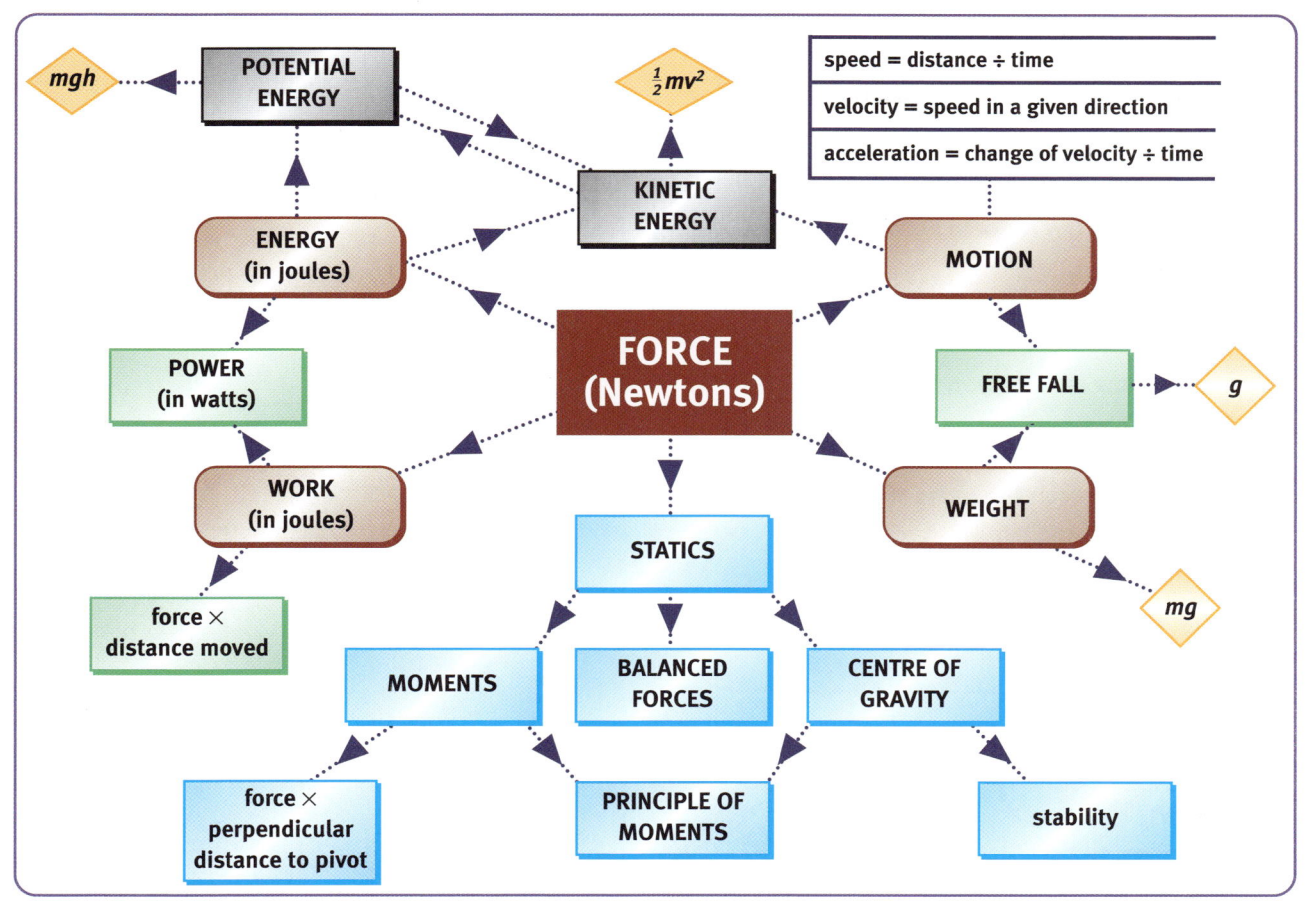

Concept map: force

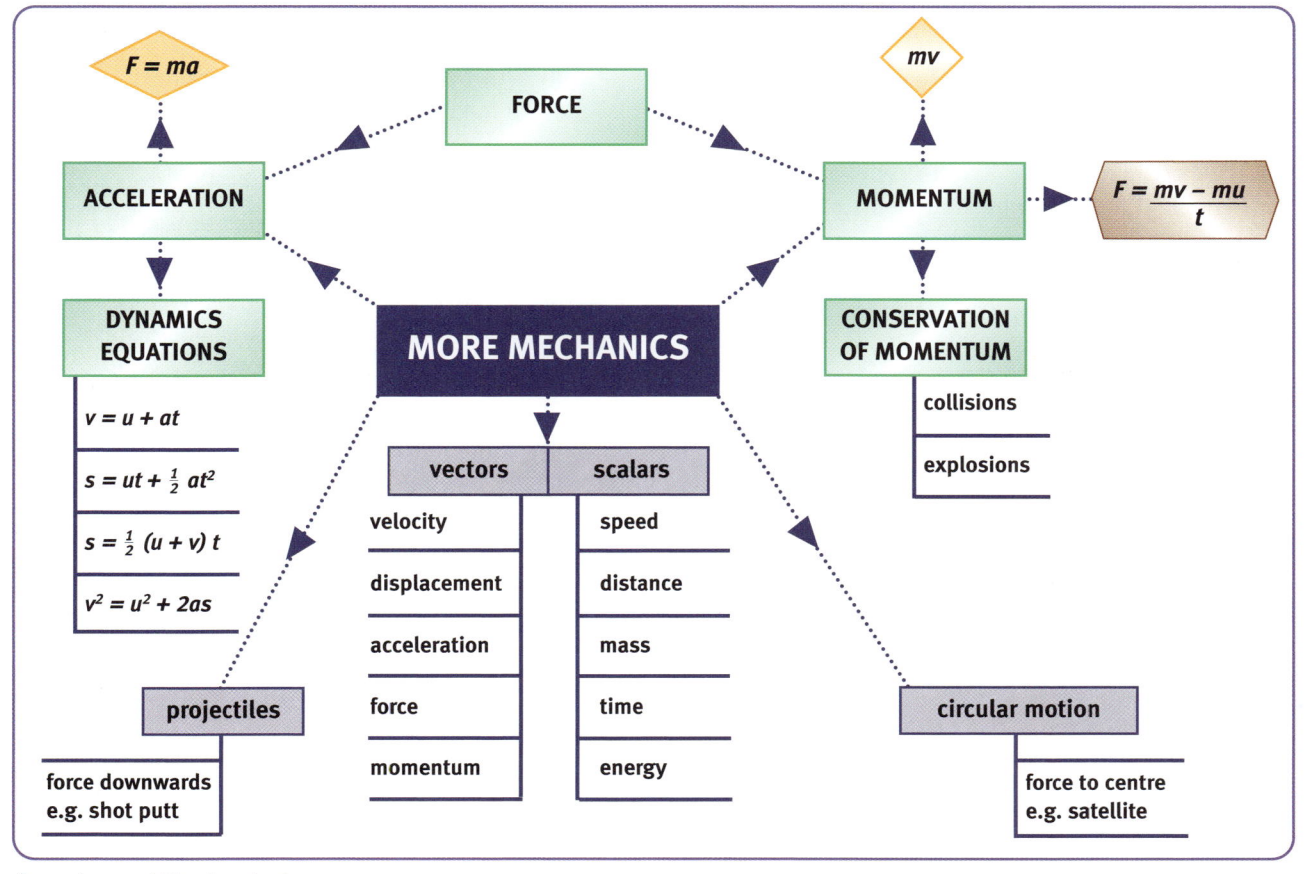

- **POTENTIAL ENERGY** — mgh
- **KINETIC ENERGY** — $\frac{1}{2}mv^2$
- **ENERGY (in joules)**
- **POWER (in watts)**
- **WORK (in joules)** — force × distance moved
- **MOTION**
  - speed = distance ÷ time
  - velocity = speed in a given direction
  - acceleration = change of velocity ÷ time
- **FREE FALL** — g
- **WEIGHT** — mg
- **FORCE (Newtons)**
- **STATICS**
  - **MOMENTS** — force × perpendicular distance to pivot
  - **BALANCED FORCES** — PRINCIPLE OF MOMENTS
  - **CENTRE OF GRAVITY** — stability

Concept map: additional mechanics

- **FORCE**
- **ACCELERATION** — $F = ma$
- **DYNAMICS EQUATIONS**
  - $v = u + at$
  - $s = ut + \frac{1}{2}at^2$
  - $s = \frac{1}{2}(u + v)t$
  - $v^2 = u^2 + 2as$
- **MOMENTUM** — mv — $F = \dfrac{mv - mu}{t}$
- **CONSERVATION OF MOMENTUM**
  - collisions
  - explosions
- **MORE MECHANICS**

vectors	scalars
velocity	speed
displacement	distance
acceleration	mass
force	time
momentum	energy

- **projectiles** — force downwards e.g. shot putt
- **circular motion** — force to centre e.g. satellite

85

Chapter 12   Electric charge

PREVIEW

At the end of this topic you will be able to:
- explain how objects become charged
- describe the law of force between charged objects
- describe some of the uses and some of the dangers associated with charged objects
- explain how earthing works and why it is necessary
- recall that an electric current is a flow of charge, and recall the units of current and charge
- describe examples of electrolysis
- explain how electricity is conducted by a metal and by an electrolyte.

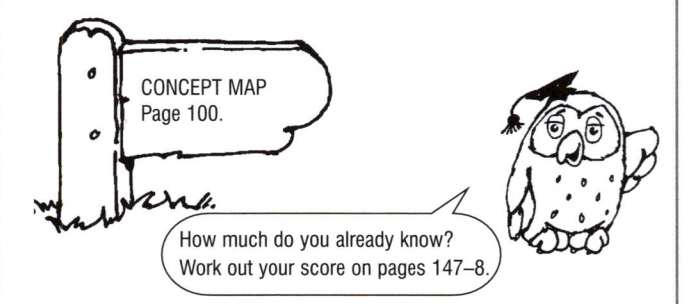

CONCEPT MAP Page 100.

How much do you already know? Work out your score on pages 147–8.

Test yourself

1. Two charged objects X and Y repel each other. Which of the following statements could be true?
   - A   X is positive and Y is negative.
   - B   X is positive and Y is positive.
   - C   X is negative and Y is negative. [2]

2. a) When a polythene rod is charged by rubbing it with a dry cloth, it becomes negatively charged. This happens because
   - A   electrons transfer from the rod to the cloth
   - B   protons transfer from the rod to the cloth
   - C   electrons transfer from the cloth to the rod
   - D   protons transfer from the cloth to the rod. [1]

   b) A negatively charged rod is touched on a metal sphere which is insulated. As a result, electrons transfer
   - A to earth   B to the sphere
   - C to the rod   D from the sphere. [1]

3. a) Why does a metal conduct electric charge? [2]

   b) Why is an electrical insulator unable to conduct electric charge? [2]

4. The diagram shows a gold leaf electroscope. When a charged rod is held above the cap of the electroscope, the electroscope leaf rises. Explain why this happens. [4]

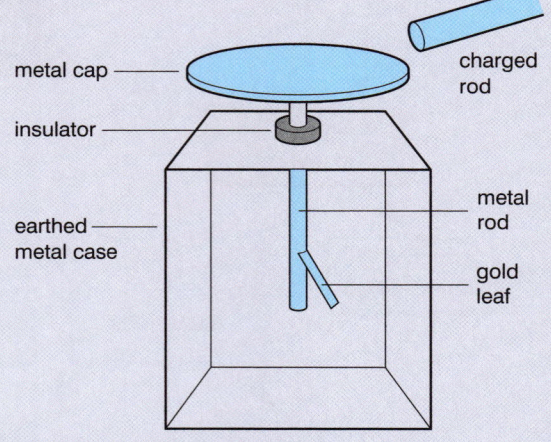

The gold leaf electroscope

5. In a photocopier, an image is formed on the surface of an electrically charged plate or drum.
   - (i) What happens to the charge where the image is bright?
   - (ii) Why do particles of the toner powder stick to the plate where the image is dark? [2]

6. A road tanker is used to deliver heating oil from a refinery to homes and offices. When oil is being pumped from the road tanker, the outlet pipe must be earthed. Why is this necessary? [2]

7. State two applications of static electricity. [2]

8. In a copper-plating experiment, a current of 0.2 A is passed through the electrolytic cell for 30 minutes exactly. How much charge passes through the cell in this time? [2]

9. When current is passed through an electrolytic cell, chlorine gas bubbles off at the anode and hydrogen gas at the cathode. Explain why this happens. [3]

10. State two applications of electrolysis. [2]

Electric charge

12.1 Electrostatics

Atomic structure

★ An atom consists of a nucleus surrounded by electrons. The nucleus is made up of neutrons and protons. Most of the mass of an atom is carried by the nucleus. A proton and an electron carry equal and opposite charge. A neutron is uncharged.

★ An uncharged atom has equal numbers of electrons and protons. Removing one or more electrons from an uncharged atom makes the atom into a positive ion. Adding one or more electrons to an uncharged atom makes the atom into a negative ion.

The law of force between charged objects

Any two charged objects exert a force on each other. This type of force is called an **electrostatic force**. The greater the distance between two charged objects, the weaker the electrostatic force between them.

- **Like charges repel; unlike charges attract.**

Conductors and insulators

1 In an **insulator**, all the electrons are firmly attached to atoms.

2 In a **conductor**, such as a metal, some electrons have broken away from the atoms. These electrons move about freely inside the conductor.

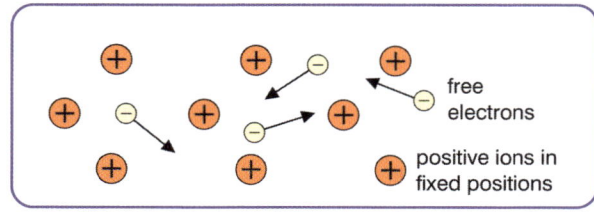

Inside a metal

Charging by friction

★ Certain insulators can be charged by rubbing with a dry cloth.

★ This happens as a result of the transfer of electrons to or from the surface atoms of the insulator.

★ Insulators that lose electrons to the cloth become positively charged (e.g. pers**P**ex; **P** for positive!).

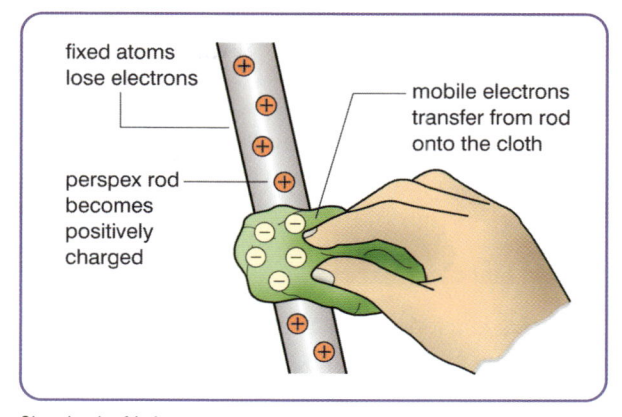

Charging by friction

★ Insulators that gain electrons from the cloth become negatively charged (e.g. polythe**N**e; **N** for negative!).

Charging an insulated metal object by direct contact

An uncharged insulated metal object can be charged by direct contact with a charged insulator.

1 **To make the metal object positive**, a positively charged rod is touched on the object. Free electrons in the metal transfer onto the positive rod, where they become trapped by the surface atoms. As a result, the metal object becomes positively charged and the rod becomes less positive.

2 **To make the metal object negative**, a negatively charged rod is touched on the object. Electrons from the rod's surface atoms transfer to the metal. As a result, the metal object becomes negatively charged and the rod becomes less negative.

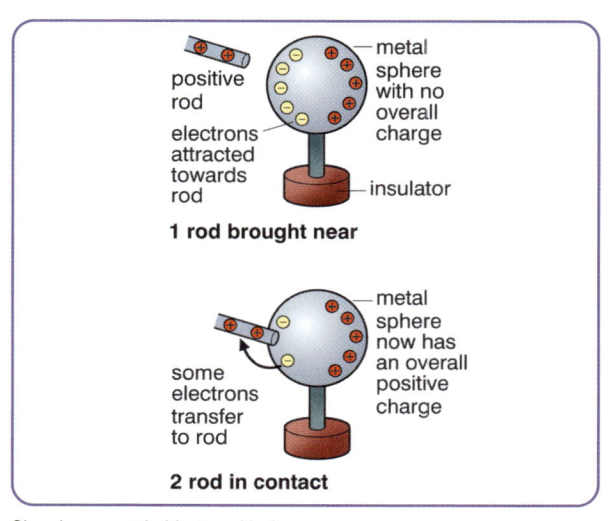

Charging a metal object positively

Electric charge

Earthing

A charged metal object can be discharged by connecting it to the earth with a wire. Electrons transfer between the object and the earth so the object loses its charge. This process is called **earthing**.

The gold leaf electroscope

This device is used to detect charge, and to determine whether the charge is positive or negative. If a charged object is touched on the cap of the electroscope, electron transfer makes the electroscope charged.

★ **If the charge on the object is negative**, the electroscope gains electrons. The leaf and the stem of the electroscope both become negative so the leaf rises as it is repelled from the stem.

★ **If the charge on the object is positive**, the electroscope loses electrons. The leaf and the stem of the electroscope both become positive so the leaf rises as it is repelled from the stem.

The diagram below shows the use of an electroscope to detect whether an object is positively or negatively charged.

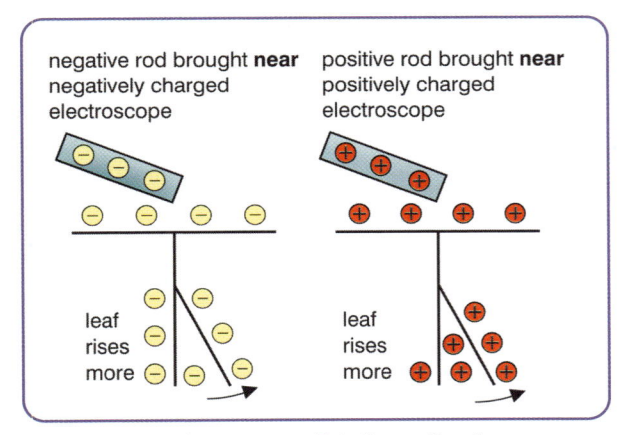

Detecting negative charge   Detecting positive charge

Electrostatic hazards

In an operating theatre, a tiny spark could make an anaesthetic gas leak explode. Such a spark could be generated if charge builds up on an insulated metal object. All metal objects, and the theatre floor itself, must therefore be earthed.

Pipe flow: powders and non-conducting fluids being pumped out of a metal pipe charge the pipe up, unless it is earthed. This occurs because of friction between the metal and the powder or fluid. If the pipe is not earthed, charge builds up on it until a spark jumps from the pipe to earth. If the powder or the fluid is flammable, a disaster could follow! Earthing the pipe prevents the pipe becoming charged.

Computer damage: expensive computer chips need to be handled with care since they are damaged by static electricity. Anyone handling a computer chip should not touch the pins of the chip, otherwise the pins will become charged if a charged object is nearby. This process, known as **charging by induction**, is explained in the diagram below.

Charging without direct contact

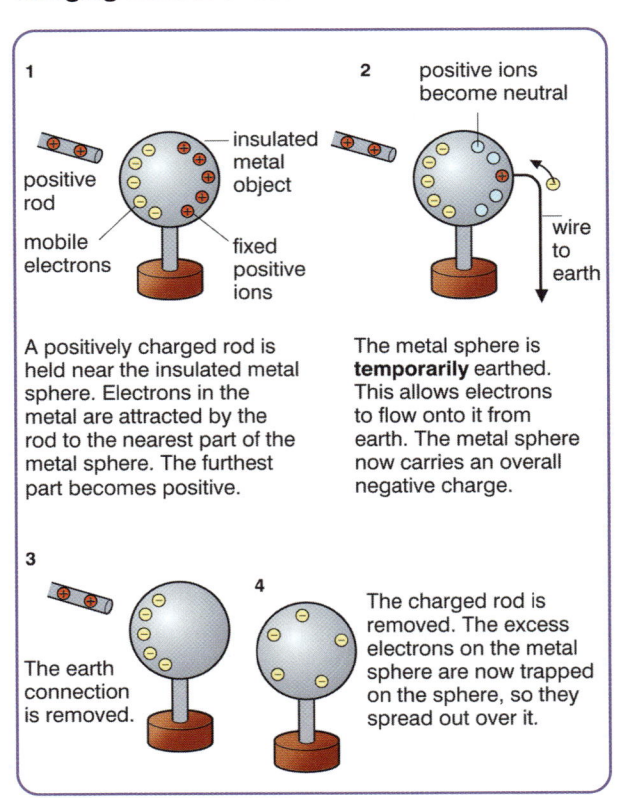

1. A positively charged rod is held near the insulated metal sphere. Electrons in the metal are attracted by the rod to the nearest part of the metal sphere. The furthest part becomes positive.

2. The metal sphere is **temporarily** earthed. This allows electrons to flow onto it from earth. The metal sphere now carries an overall negative charge.

3. The earth connection is removed.

4. The charged rod is removed. The excess electrons on the metal sphere are now trapped on the sphere, so they spread out over it.

Charging by induction

Electric charge

12.2 Electrostatics at work

Electrostatics is used in a wide range of devices. In addition, safety measures are necessary to eliminate static electricity as a hazard in a wide range of situations.

The electrostatic paint spray

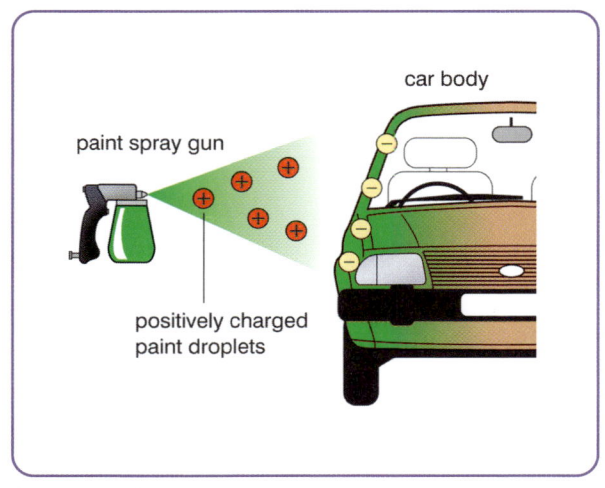

Electrostatic paint spray

A fixed potential difference is maintained between the paint spray nozzle and the metal panel to be painted. The paint droplets in the spray become charged when they are forced out of the spray gun. They are then attracted onto the metal panel to form an even layer of paint on the panel.

The electrostatic precipitator

The ash and dust from coal burned at a power station is prevented from entering the atmosphere by an electrostatic precipitator in the chimney. The dust particles touch the charged wire grid of the precipitator and become charged. The particles are then attracted on to the earthed metal tube surrounding the grid.

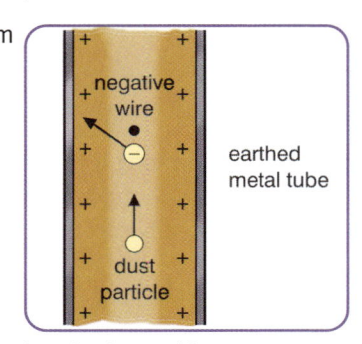

Attracting dust particles

The photocopier

When a photocopier is used:
- a copying plate or drum is charged electrostatically with a uniform layer of charge across its surface
- an image of the page to be copied is projected onto the copying plate
- charge leaks away from the areas of the plate where the image is bright. This is because the plate surface is made of material that conducts electricity when it is illuminated
- black 'toner' powder applied to the surface sticks to the charged areas of the surface because the powder particles are electrostatically attracted to it
- the powder is transferred onto a sheet of white paper pressed against the surface
- heating the paper makes the black powder melt, stick to the paper and dry to form a copy of the original page.

Handy hint

The process can be summarised as:

charge plate, project image, leak charge, apply powder, press paper and heat.

The inkjet printer

This is used to print characters on paper. Each character is formed from closely spaced tiny ink dots. Each character is represented by a digital signal from a computer linked to the printer. The signal is a string of 1s and 0s which control the direction of tiny droplets of ink forced out of a fine nozzle onto a sheet of paper.

★ The droplets are charged electrically when they are forced out of the nozzle.

★ Each droplet then passes between two metal plates. A voltage can be applied to these plates to make one plate positive and the other one negative. This causes each droplet to be deflected because it experiences an electrostatic force towards the plate with the opposite charge as it passes between the plates.

★ The deflection of each droplet depends on the size and the direction of the voltage applied to the plates. This voltage therefore determines where the ink dot produced by each droplet appears on the paper.

Electric charge

12.3 Current and charge

Fact file

★ An **electric current** is a flow of electric charge.

★ The unit of electric current is the **ampere** (A); the unit of electric charge is the **coulomb** (C).

★ **Electrons** are responsible for the flow of charge through a **metal** when it conducts electricity.

★ **Positive and negative ions** are responsible for the flow of charge through an **electrolyte** when it conducts electricity.

Steady currents

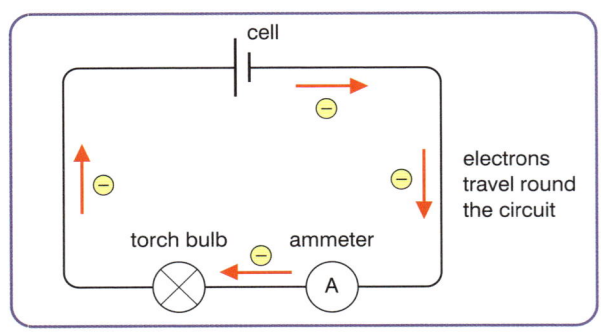

A steady current

The diagram above shows a simple electric circuit in which a cell is connected in series with an ammeter and a torch bulb.

★ **The current in this circuit is constant**. This means that charge passes through each component at a steady rate. Electrons pass through each component at a steady rate.

★ **The current through each component is the same**. Equal amounts of charge pass through each component in a set period of time. The number of electrons per second passing through each component is the same.

Equation for charge flow

★ **One coulomb of charge** is defined as the amount of charge passing a point in a circuit in one second when the current is one ampere.

★ **The charge passing a point in a circuit** that is carrying a steady current is calculated as follows:

charge passed = current × time taken
    (in C)   (in A)   (in s)

At a junction

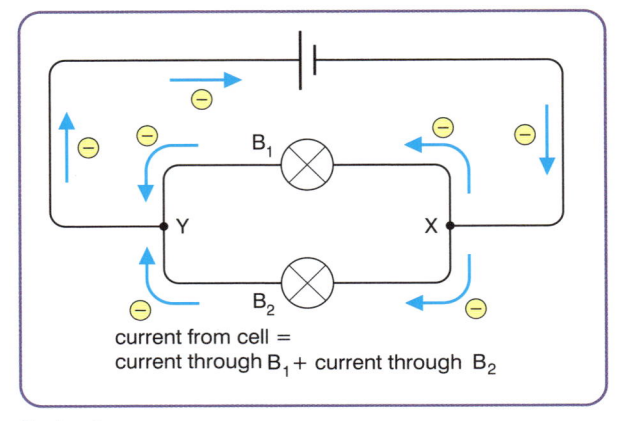

current from cell =
current through B_1 + current through B_2

At a junction

In this circuit, two torch bulbs B_1 and B_2 are in parallel with each other. Each electron from the cell passes through one of the torch bulbs and then returns to the positive terminal of the cell. The flow of electrons from the cell divides at junction X and recombines at junction Y.

The charge flow per second from the cell = charge flow per second through B_1 + charge flow per second through B_2. Since charge flow per second is current, it follows that cell current = current through B_1 + current through B_2.

In other words, at a junction in a circuit,

the total current entering the junction is equal to the total current leaving the junction.

Questions

a) Calculate the charge that flows through a torch bulb carrying a steady current of 0.25 A in

(i) 1 minute

(ii) 5 minutes.

b) Calculate how long it takes for a charge of 100 C to pass through a torch bulb that is carrying a steady current of 0.2 A.

Answers
a) (i) 15 C (ii) 75 C
b) 500 s

Electric charge

12.4 Electrolysis

Electrolytic conduction

This occurs when a substance is decomposed by an electric current passing through it. Decomposition does not happen when an electric current passes through a wire – the chemical composition of the wire is unaffected by the electric current. In comparison, the passage of an electric current through sodium chloride solution causes a gas to bubble off at each electrode. In an electrolytic cell:
- the **electrolyte** is the conducting liquid
- the **anode** is the positive electrode
- the **cathode** is the negative electrode.

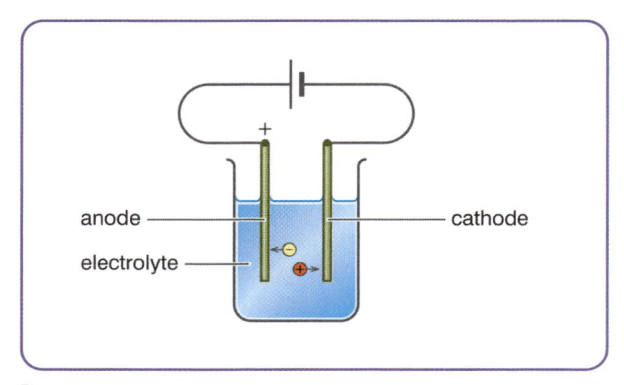

Electrolysis

In an electrolyte

An electrolyte is a liquid which contains positive and negative ions. For example, in sodium chloride solution, the positive ions are hydrogen ions (H^+) and sodium ions (Na^+). The negative ions are chloride ions (Cl^-) and hydroxide ions (OH^-).

The positive ions are attracted to the cathode because they carry the opposite charge. Where there is more than one type of positive ion, the ion that attracts an electron most easily off the cathode is discharged. In sodium chloride solution, hydrogen gas bubbles off the cathode because the hydrogen ions are more easily discharged than the sodium ions.

The negative ions are attracted to the anode. The ion that gives up an electron most easily is discharged at the anode. In sodium chloride solution, chlorine gas bubbles off at the anode.

Copper-plating

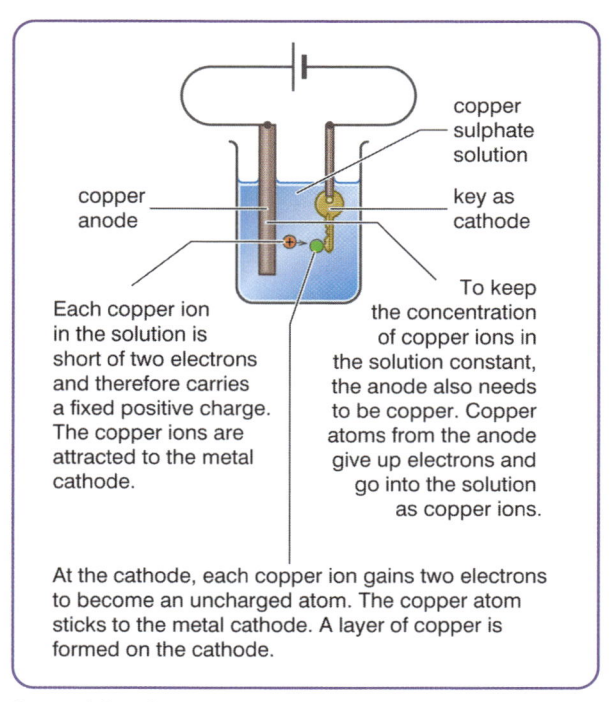

Each copper ion in the solution is short of two electrons and therefore carries a fixed positive charge. The copper ions are attracted to the metal cathode.

To keep the concentration of copper ions in the solution constant, the anode also needs to be copper. Copper atoms from the anode give up electrons and go into the solution as copper ions.

At the cathode, each copper ion gains two electrons to become an uncharged atom. The copper atom sticks to the metal cathode. A layer of copper is formed on the cathode.

Copper-plating a key

A metal object can be copper-plated by making the object the cathode in an electrolytic cell containing copper sulphate solution.

Each copper atom deposited on the cathode adds the same mass and gains the same amount of charge (2 electrons). The mass of copper deposited is therefore proportional to the charge flow through the cell. Hence the mass deposited is proportional to the **current** and the **time taken**.

Questions

In a copper-plating experiment, a metal key was used as the cathode. Its initial mass was 25.25 g. After being used for 30 minutes as the cathode with a steady current of 0.25 A, its mass had increased to 25.40 g. Calculate

a) the amount of charge needed to deposit 1 g of copper

b) the mass of copper that would be deposited by a current of 0.1 A for exactly 3 hours.

Answers: a) 3000 C b) 0.36 g

Electric charge

ROUND UP

How much have you improved?
Work out your improvement index on page 148.

1 An insulated metal object M can become charged without making direct contact with a charged object O. The diagram shows how one stage in this process could happen. The complete sequence of actions including the stage shown in the diagram are listed below in the wrong order.

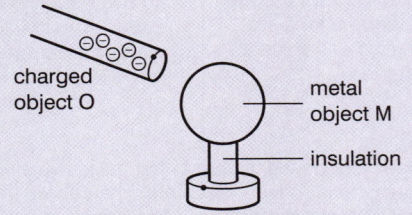

(i) The earth connection to the metal object M is removed.
(ii) The charged body O is brought near the metal object M.
(iii) The charged body O is removed.
(iv) The metal object M is earthed.

a) Rewrite the list in the correct order. [4]
b) What type of charge is left on the metal object M if the charged body O carries a negative charge? [1]
c) Does the total charge on the charged object O alter as a result of M being charged in this way? [1]

2 A gold leaf electroscope is charged by direct contact with a positively charged rod, as shown.

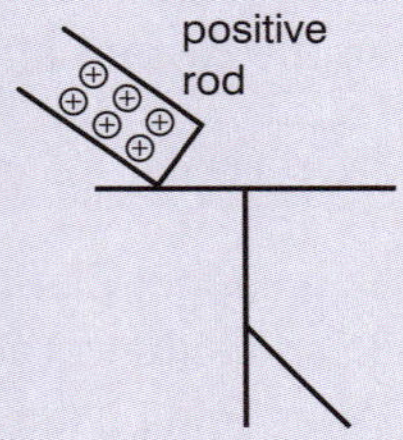

a) Explain in terms of electrons why the leaf rises when the electroscope is charged in this way. [3]
b) Explain why the leaf remains in the position shown when the charged rod is removed. [1]
c) Explain how the electroscope could be charged negatively using a positively charged rod. [4]
d) Describe how the electroscope could be used to determine the type of charge on a charged object. [3]

3 a) In dry weather, the metal body of a car becomes charged when the car is in motion on a dry road. If the car is not fitted with a trailing conductor,
(i) explain why someone who touches the car when it stops would receive a shock [2]
(ii) explain why the car driver would receive a shock on getting out of the car after it stops. [2]
b) Why does the metal body of a car not become charged
(i) if a trailing conductor is fitted to the car? [1]
(ii) in wet weather? [2]

4 In an electroplating experiment, a layer of copper was being deposited on a metal plate. The initial mass of the plate was measured at 64.50 g. The current was maintained at 0.1 A for 30 minutes, then the plate was carefully dried and reweighed at 64.56 g. It was then reconnected and the current was increased to 0.30 A for a further 60 minutes.
a) Calculate the charge passed through the cell in each of the two parts of the experiment. [2]
b) Calculate the increase in mass of the plate in the first part of the experiment. [1]
c) Hence calculate the increase in mass in the second part of the experiment. [1]
d) What steady current would have given the same total increase in mass in a total time of 1 hour? [1]

5 a) (i) A photocopier sometimes produces copies on which the print is too light. State and explain one reason why this can happen.
(ii) Explain why a photocopy is sometimes smudged when it emerges from the photocopier. [4]
b) In an ink jet printer, an ink droplet is deflected to a certain point on the paper when a certain voltage is applied. How would the deflection change if the voltage is
(i) changed to zero? (ii) reversed? [2]

6 a) Describe the principle of operation of an electrostatic precipitator used to remove ash and dust particles from the flue gases of a power station. [3] 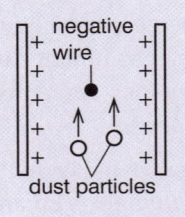
b) An electronic chip may be damaged if its metal pins become charged. With the aid of a diagram, explain how it is possible to charge an insulated metal pin simply by touching the pin in the presence of a nearby charged object. [2]

Electric circuits — Chapter 13

PREVIEW

At the end of this topic you will be able to:

- explain what is meant by potential difference
- describe series and parallel circuits in terms of current and voltage
- describe how to use an ammeter to measure current and a voltmeter to measure voltage
- recognise the circuit symbols for common electrical components and know their characteristics
- define resistance and carry out calculations involving current, voltage, resistance and power
- describe how mains electricity is supplied and costed
- identify dangers of mains electricity and explain safety features and devices to minimise dangers.

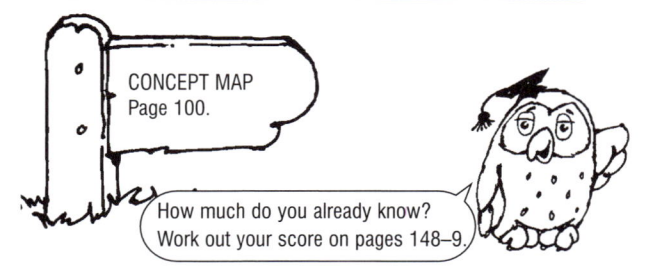

CONCEPT MAP Page 100.

How much do you already know? Work out your score on pages 148–9.

Test yourself

1. Two identical torch bulbs, a switch, an ammeter and a 1.5 V cell are connected in series with each other.
   a) Draw the circuit diagram. [2]
   b) The ammeter reading was 0.20 A when the switch was closed. How much energy was delivered to each torch bulb in one minute? [2]

2. A 1.5 V cell was connected in series with an ammeter, a switch and a torch bulb X. A second torch bulb Y was connected in parallel with X. The switch was then closed to light both torch bulbs.
   a) Draw the circuit diagram. [2]
   b) The ammeter reading was 0.30 A. Calculate the energy supplied by the cell in
   (i) one second (ii) one minute. [2]

3. In the circuit shown, ammeter A_1 reads 0.5 A and ammeter A_2 reads 0.3 A.

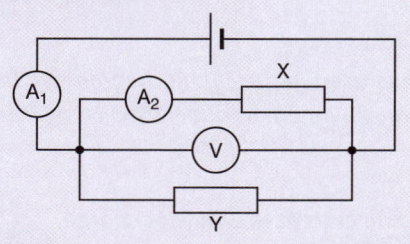

   a) Calculate the current through resistor Y. [1]
   b) The voltmeter in parallel with resistor Y reads 1.0 V when ammeter A_1 reads 0.5 A. Calculate the resistance of resistor Y. [2]

4. A current of 2.5 A is passed through a 6.0 Ω resistor. Calculate
   a) the p.d. across the resistor
   b) the power supplied to the resistor. [2]

5. a) Draw a circuit diagram to show a diode connected in series with a 1.5 V cell and a torch bulb lit up. [2]
   b) If the 1.5 V cell is connected in the circuit in the reverse direction, the torch bulb would not light. Why? [2]

6. Give the symbol and state the main characteristic of each of the following components:
   a) a light-dependent resistor
   b) a thermistor. [4]

7. An electric heater is rated at 240 V, 1000 W.
   a) Calculate the electrical energy delivered to the heater in 300 s.
   b) Calculate the current through the heater when it operates at its rated power. [3]

8. a) State the purpose of a fuse in an electric circuit.
   b) Explain how a fuse achieves its purpose. [3]

9. A set of Christmas tree lights contains 20 light bulbs rated at 6 W. The light bulbs are connected in series to be operated from 240 V mains. When in normal use, calculate
   a) the current through each bulb
   b) the voltage across each bulb. [4]

10. A microwave oven rated at 800 W is used for 15 minutes to heat some food. Calculate
    a) the number of units of electricity used
    b) the cost of the electricity used, if each unit of electricity is priced at 6.0p. [3]

Electric circuits

13.1 Current and potential difference

Note
The symbols used in the circuit diagrams in this chapter are explained on page 155.

Fact file

★ An **electric current** is a **flow of charge**. The unit of electric current is the **ampere** (A).

★ The **potential difference** (p.d.) between any two points in a circuit is the **work done per unit charge** when charge moves from one point to the other point. Voltage is an alternative word for potential difference.

★ The unit of charge is the **coulomb** (C). One coulomb is equal to the charge passing a point in a circuit in one second when the current is one ampere.

★ The unit of potential difference is the **volt** (V), equal to one joule per coulomb.

Four rules about current

1 The current entering a component is the same as the current leaving it. A component does not use up current; it uses the electrical energy supplied to it by the charge that passes through it.

2 At a junction, the total current leaving the junction is equal to the total current entering the junction.

3 Components in series pass the same current.

4 An ammeter is a meter designed to measure current. It is always connected in series with a component. An ideal ammeter has zero resistance.

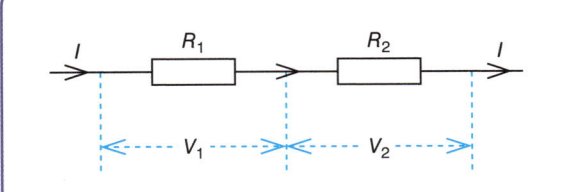

The combined resistance of two or more resistors in series = the sum of the individual resistances

Series resistors

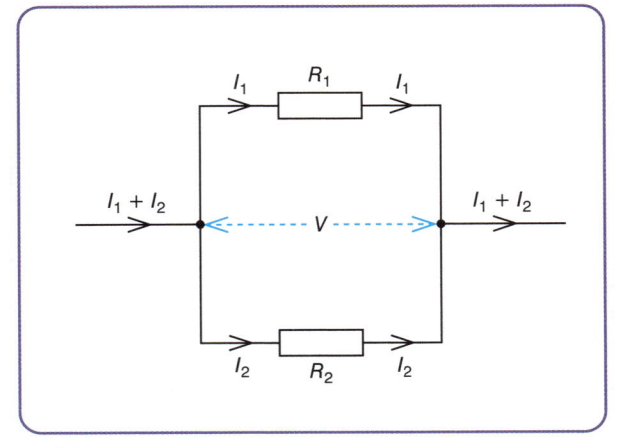

Parallel resistors

Four rules about voltage

1 The voltage across a component is the number of joules delivered to the component by each coulomb of charge that passes through it.

2 Components in parallel have the same voltage across them.

3 For two or more components in series, the total voltage is equal to the sum of the individual voltages.

4 A voltmeter is a meter designed to measure voltage (potential difference). It is always connected in parallel with a component. An ideal voltmeter has infinite resistance.

Four rules about power

Consider a component in a circuit which has voltage V across its terminals and which passes a steady current I.

1 In a time interval t, charge Q flows through the component where $Q = It$.

2 The electrical energy E delivered by charge Q is QV, since V is defined as the electrical energy delivered per unit charge.

3 Hence the electrical energy E delivered in time t is ItV.

4 The electrical power = $\dfrac{\text{electrical energy delivered}}{\text{time taken}} = IV$

Electric circuits

13.2 Resistance

Fact file

★ The **resistance** R of an electrical component is given by

$$R = \frac{\text{the voltage across the component}}{\text{the current through the component}}$$

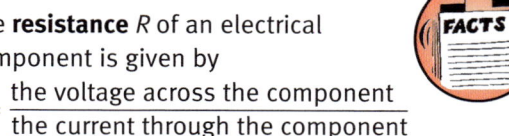

★ The unit of resistance is the **ohm** (Ω), defined as one volt per ampere.

★ **To calculate resistance**, use the equation

$$\text{resistance} = \frac{\text{voltage}}{\text{current}}$$

★ **Ohm's law** states that for a wire under constant physical conditions, the current is proportional to the voltage. This is equivalent to stating that its resistance is constant.

★ A **resistor** is a component designed to have a particular value of resistance. This resistance is caused by opposition to the motion of electrons round the circuit.

Note

The following prefixes are used for large or small values of current, voltage or resistance:

mega (M)	kilo (k)	milli (m)	micro (µ)
1 000 000	1000	0.001	0.000 001
10^6	10^3	10^{-3}	10^{-6}

What does current depend on?

Current depends on:
- the voltage of the cell, battery or power supply unit
- the resistance of the components in the circuit.

Resistors can be used to control the current in a circuit.

Measuring resistance

The diagram at the top of the next column shows how the resistance of a resistor may be determined using an ammeter and a voltmeter. Note that the voltmeter is in parallel with the resistor, and the ammeter is in series.

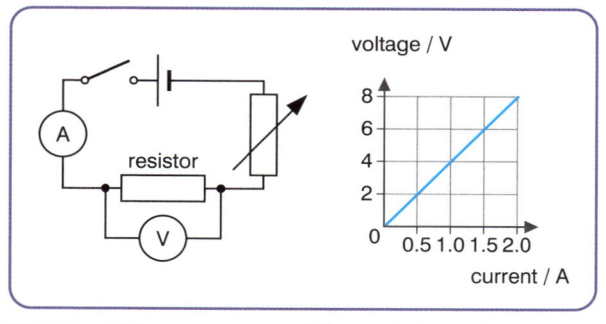

Measuring resistance   Voltage against current

1. With the switch closed, the variable resistor is adjusted to change the current in steps. At each step, the current and voltage are measured from the ammeter and the voltmeter, respectively.

2. The measurements are plotted as a graph of voltage (on the vertical axis) against current, as shown. The plotted points define a straight line passing through the origin.

3. The gradient of the line is measured. This is equal to the resistance of the resistor.

Questions

a) Determine the resistance of the resistor that gave the results plotted on the graph.

b) Calculate the current through this resistor when the voltage across it is **(i)** 5.0 V **(ii)** 0.1 V.

Resistance heating

All the electrical energy supplied to a resistor is transformed to thermal energy, heating the surroundings as a result.

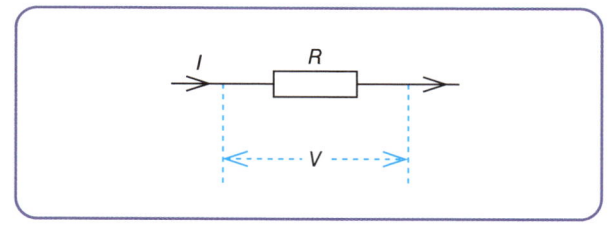

Heating effect

1. The voltage V across the resistor $= IR$, where I is the current through the component.

2. The power supplied to the resistor $P = IV = I^2R$. This is the rate of heat produced in the resistor.

Answers a) 4.0 Ω b) (i) 1.25 A (ii) 25 mA

Electric circuits

13.3 Components

The circuit shown on the previous page (top right) for measuring resistance may be used to investigate the variation of current with voltage for any device. The graphs below show the results of such investigations for different components, plotted with current on the *y*-axis and voltage on the *x*-axis.

★ For a wire-wound resistor at constant temperature, the graph is a straight line – the resistance is constant.

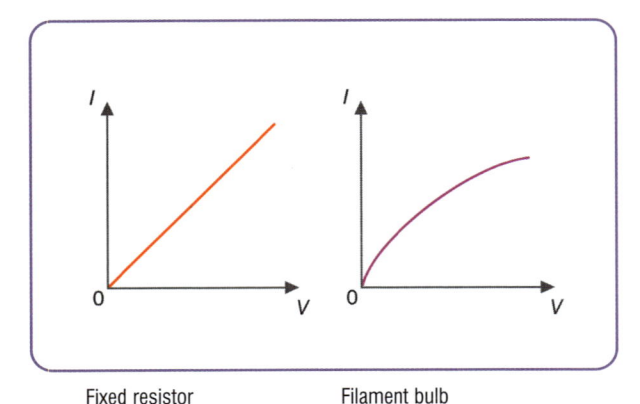

Fixed resistor   Filament bulb

★ For a filament bulb such as a torch bulb, the graph is a curve – the resistance increases as the filament becomes hotter.

★ For a diode in its forward direction, the graph shows that the resistance decreases as the current increases. In the reverse direction, the graph shows that the diode has an extremely high resistance.

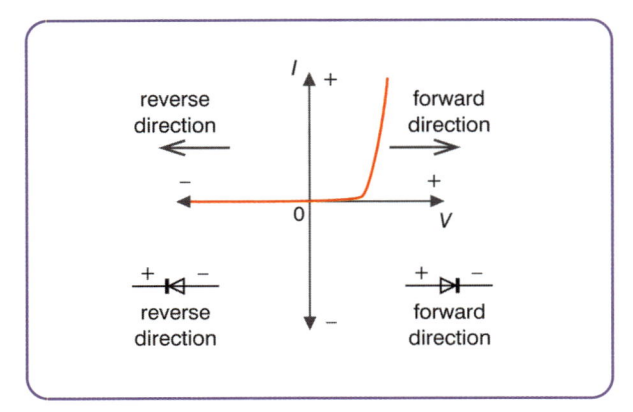

Diode

★ For a light-dependent resistor (LDR), its resistance depends on the intensity of light falling on it. Increasing the intensity makes the resistance lower; conversely, decreasing the intensity makes the resistance higher. More electrons are freed from the atoms if the light intensity is increased, causing the resistance to fall.

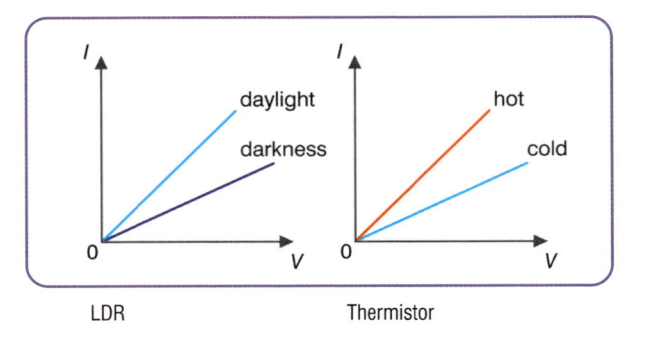

LDR   Thermistor

★ For a thermistor, the resistance decreases with increasing temperature and vice versa. More electrons are freed from the atoms if the temperature is increased, causing the resistance to fall.

Questions

A $1000\,\Omega$ resistor was connected in series with a thermistor, a milliammeter and a 2.0 V cell. The reading on the milliammeter was 1.0 mA. Calculate

a) the voltage across the $1000\,\Omega$ resistor when its current was 1.0 mA

b) the voltage across the thermistor when its current was 1.0 mA.

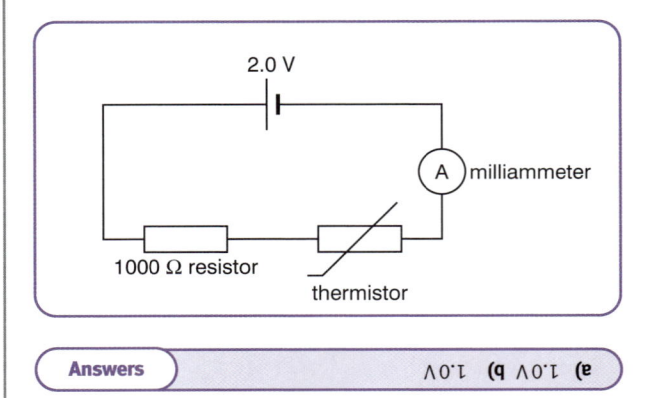

Answers: a) 1.0 V b) 1.0 V

Electric circuits

13.4 Mains electricity

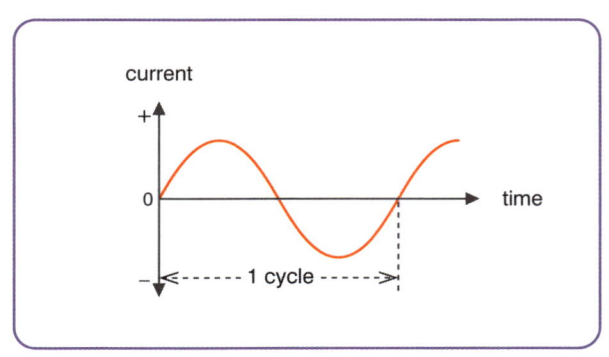

Alternating current

The three-pin plug

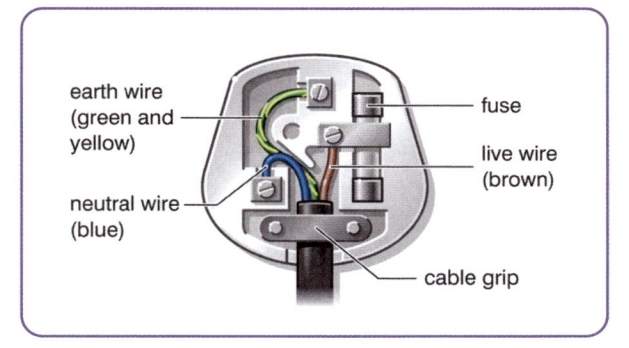

A mains plug

Alternating current

★ The electric current through a mains appliance alternates in direction. The current reverses direction, then reverses back each cycle.

★ The **frequency** of an alternating current is the number of cycles per second. In the UK, the mains frequency is 50 Hz.

Electricity costs

★ One kilowatt hour (kWh) is the electrical energy supplied to a one kilowatt appliance in exactly one hour.

★ The kilowatt hour is the unit of electricity for costing purposes.

★ A domestic electricity meter records the total number of units used.

Each circuit from the fuse board is protected with its own fuse. If the fuse 'blows', the live wire is therefore cut off from appliances supplied by that circuit.

The mains cable from the substation to a building is connected via the electricity meter to the circuits in the building at the distribution fuse board. The live wire from the substation is connected via a main fuse to the electricity meter.

The two wires used to supply an electric current to an appliance are referred to as the **live** and the **neutral** wires. The neutral wire is earthed at the nearest mains substation.

Mains wires need to have as low a resistance as possible, otherwise heat is produced in them by the current. This is why mains wires are made from copper. All mains wires and fittings are insulated.

The fuse in a lighting circuit is in the fuse box. Each light bulb is turned on or off by its own switch. When the switch is in the off position, the appliance is not connected to the live wire of the mains supply.

A **ring main** is used to supply electricity to appliances via wall sockets. A ring main circuit consists of a live wire, a neutral wire and the **earth wire** which is earthed at the fuse board. The wires of a ring main are thicker than the wires of a lighting circuit because appliances connected to a ring main require more current than light bulbs.

Each appliance is connected to the ring main by means of a three-pin plug which carries a fuse. An appliance with a metal chassis is earthed via the three-pin plug and the earth wire. This prevents the metal chassis from becoming live if a fault develops in the appliance. Appliances connected to the ring main can be switched on or off independently since they are in parallel with each other.

Mains circuits

Electric circuits

13.5 Electrical safety

Faults and fuses

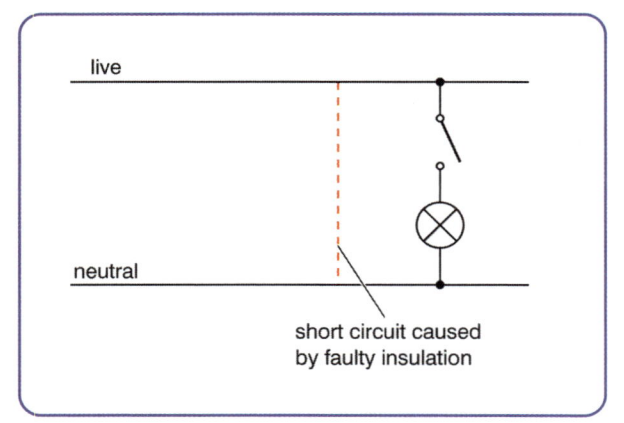

A short circuit

A **short circuit** occurs where a fault creates a low resistance path between two points at different voltages. The current through the short circuit is much greater than the current along the correct path between the two points; potentially enough to create a fire through overheating.

Fuses are intended to prevent excessive currents flowing. A fuse is a thin piece of resistance wire which overheats and melts if too much current passes through it. The fuse wire breaks when it melts, thus cutting the current off and protecting the appliance or the wires leading to it from overheating due to excessive current.

Faults in mains circuits can arise due to:
- **poor maintenance** e.g. frayed cables or damaged plugs or fittings such as sockets and switches
- **carelessness** e.g. coiling cables that are too long, which prevents heat escaping from them
- **overloading a circuit** e.g. too many appliances connected to the same circuit or connecting a powerful appliance to a low current circuit.

Earthing

Any appliance with a metal case must be earthed through the ring main to protect the user. If such an appliance is not earthed and a fault develops in which a live wire touches the case, anyone who subsequently touches the case will be electrocuted. The victim effectively provides a short circuit path to earth from the live case.

Circuit breakers

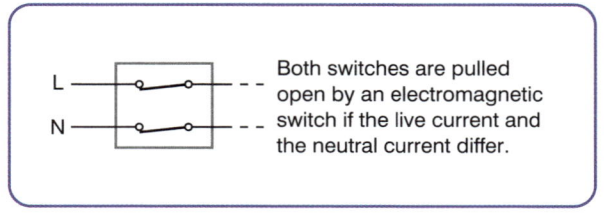

A residual current circuit breaker

A lethal electric shock is possible with currents as small as 50 mA passing through the body. The **residual current circuit breaker** is designed to cut an appliance off from the mains if the current in the live wire differs from the current in the neutral wire by more than 30 mA. This difference would arise if current leaks to earth from a poorly insulated live wire.

A **simple circuit breaker** is a switch operated by an electromagnet in series with the switch. When the switch is closed, if the current reaches a certain value, the electromagnet pulls the switch open and cuts the current off. The circuit breaker switch then needs to be reset once the fault causing the current rise has been remedied. A circuit breaker does not need to be replaced like a fuse each time it cuts the current off.

Double insulation

This is a safety feature of mains appliances like hand-held hair dryers and electric shavers which have insulated cases.

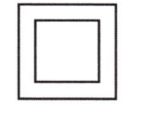

Double insulation symbol

Questions

State the purpose of a) a fuse b) a residual current circuit breaker.

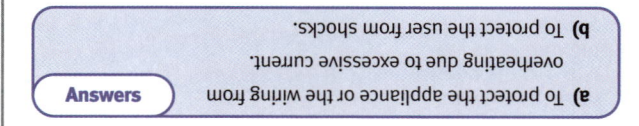

Answers
a) To protect the appliance or the wiring from overheating due to excessive current.
b) To protect the user from shocks.

Electric circuits

ROUND UP

How much have you improved? Work out your improvement index on page 149.

1 In this circuit, the ammeter reading was 0.25 A and the voltmeter reading was 3.0 V.

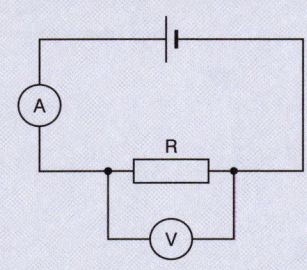

a) Calculate the resistance of resistor R. [1]
b) If a second resistor identical to R was connected in parallel with R how would the ammeter and voltmeter readings alter? [2]

2 a) A 1500 W, 240 V electric heater is connected to the ring main in a house and then switched on.
  (i) Calculate the current through the heater. [1]
  (ii) How many units of electricity would be used by this heater in 2 hours? [1]
b) (i) What is the function of the earth wire in a ring main circuit? [2]
  (ii) Given mains fuses rated at 3 A, 5 A and 13 A, which one would you choose for a microwave oven rated at 650 W, 240 V? [1]
  (iii) In **(ii)**, if the wrong fuse is chosen, what problems might occur? [2]

3 The circuit diagram shows two 5 Ω resistors P and Q in series with each other, an ammeter and a 3.0 V cell.

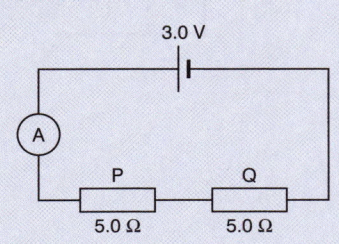

a) (i) What is the voltage across each resistor? [1]
  (ii) What is the current through each resistor? [1]
b) Hence calculate the power supplied to each resistor. [1]
c) A third 5 Ω resistor R is then connected in parallel with resistor P. How does this affect the current passing through each of the other two resistors? [2]

4 A 24 W heating element for a 12 V heater is to be made using a suitable length of resistance wire.
a) Calculate the expected current and the required resistance. [2]
b) The resistance wire has a resistance of 5 Ω per metre. Calculate the length of wire required to make this heating element. [2]
c) With the aid of a circuit diagram, describe how you could check the resistance per metre of a reel of this resistance wire. [5]

5 The following mains appliances were used in a household over a period of 24 hours:
  (i) two 100 W light bulbs, each for 6 hours
  (ii) a 5000 W electric oven for 2 hours
  (iii) a 3000 W electric kettle used four times for five minutes each time.
a) Calculate the number of units of electricity used in each case. [3]
b) Calculate the total cost of the electricity used if the unit price of electricity was 5p. [1]
c) How long would it take a 5000 W electric oven to use the same number of electricity units as a 100 W electric light bulb would use in 24 hours? [2]

6 a) Why is it dangerous to touch a mains appliance when you have wet hands? [3]
b) A mains electric mower should never be connected to the mains unless a residual current circuit breaker is used. Why? [3]
c) Why is it dangerous to use a mains electric mower with its mains cable coiled up? [2]

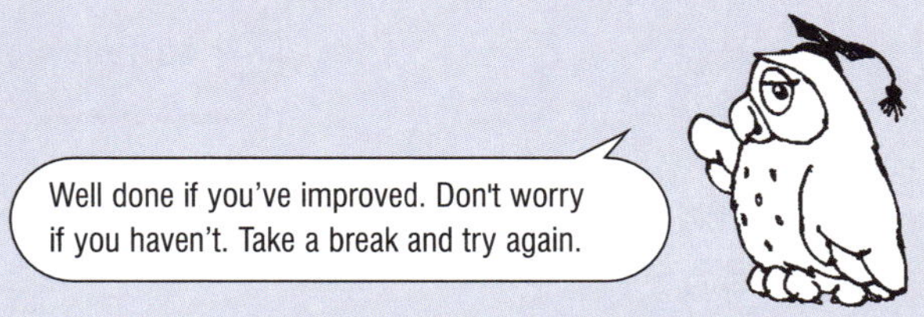

Well done if you've improved. Don't worry if you haven't. Take a break and try again.

Electric circuits

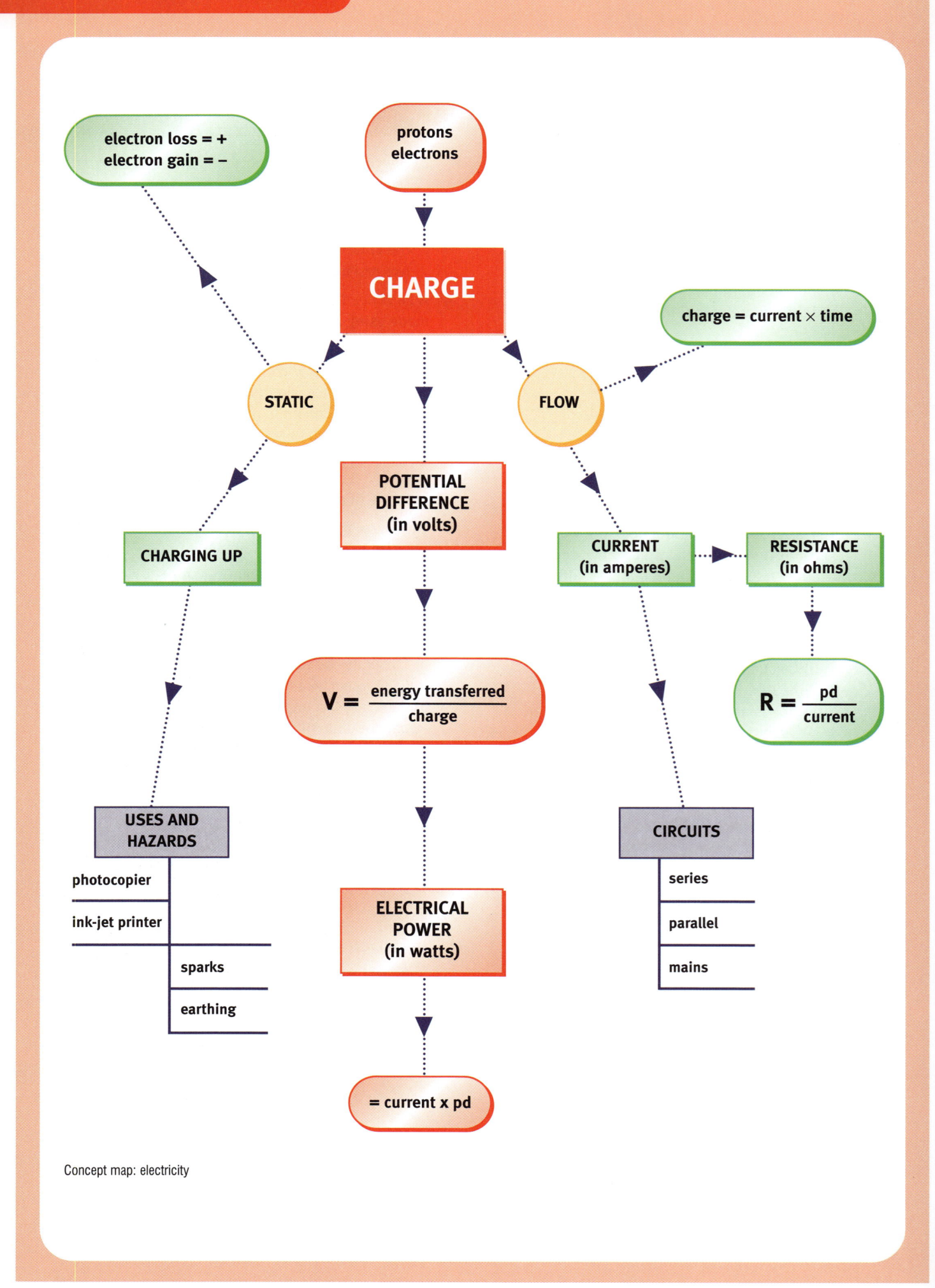

CHARGE

- protons / electrons
- electron loss = +
- electron gain = −
- charge = current × time

STATIC → CHARGING UP → USES AND HAZARDS
- photocopier
- ink-jet printer
- sparks
- earthing

FLOW → CURRENT (in amperes) → CIRCUITS
- series
- parallel
- mains

RESISTANCE (in ohms)

$$R = \frac{pd}{current}$$

POTENTIAL DIFFERENCE (in volts)

$$V = \frac{energy\ transferred}{charge}$$

ELECTRICAL POWER (in watts)

= current × pd

Concept map: electricity

Electromagnetism — Chapter 14

PREVIEW

At the end of this topic you will be able to:

- describe the operation of devices that contain an electromagnet
- explain the principle and operation of a moving-coil loudspeaker and an electric motor
- explain the principle and operation of an alternating current generator and a transformer
- explain how electric power is transmitted via the grid system.

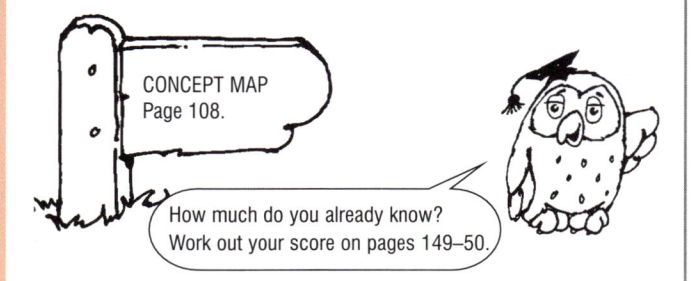

CONCEPT MAP Page 108.

How much do you already know? Work out your score on pages 149–50.

Test yourself

1. State a suitable material from which to make
   a) the core of an electromagnet
   b) a permanent magnet. [2]

2. a) One end of a bar magnet is held near a plotting compass, as shown. What is the polarity of this end of the bar magnet? [1]

   b) The north pole of a bar magnet repels pole P of another bar magnet. What is the polarity of P? [1]

3. Describe the lines of the magnetic field produced by
   a) a long, straight, vertical wire carrying a direct current [2]
   b) a solenoid carrying a direct current. [2]

4. State whether each of the following devices contains a permanent magnet or an electromagnet:
   a) a loudspeaker   b) a relay   c) an electric motor. [3]

5. a) The diagram shows a vertical wire between the poles of a U-shaped magnet, arranged so the magnetic field of the magnet is horizontal. When a current passes up the wire, the wire is forced outwards. If the magnetic field is reversed and the current is reversed, in which direction would the force on the wire then be? [1]

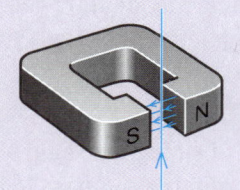

   b) Explain why a direct current electric motor cannot work on alternating current. [2]

6. a) State two ways in which the voltage from an alternating current generator would change if its rate of rotation was reduced. [2]

   b) Why is alternating current used to transmit electric power through the grid system? [3]

7. An aluminium plate placed between the poles of an electromagnet supplied with alternating current, as shown, becomes warm. Explain how this happens. [2]

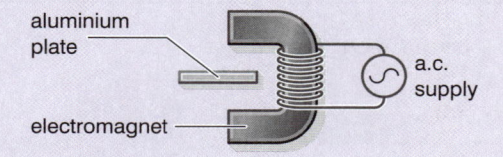

8. A transformer has 60 turns in its primary coil and 1200 turns in its secondary coil. A 240 V, 100 W lamp is connected to the terminals of its secondary coil. The primary coil is connected to an alternating voltage supply.

   a) Calculate the voltage of this supply if the lamp lights normally. [1]

   b) Calculate the maximum possible current through the primary coil when the 100 W lamp is on. [1]

Electromagnetism

14.1 Magnetism

Fact file

★ Two magnets act on each other at a distance.

★ The law of force for magnetic poles is that **like poles repel and unlike poles attract**.

★ Iron and steel can be magnetised and demagnetised.

★ Permanent magnets are made from steel because it is hard to demagnetise once magnetised.

★ Electromagnets are made from soft iron because it is easy to magnetise and demagnetise.

Magnetic field patterns

The lines of force of a magnetic field are defined by the direction of a plotting compass in the magnetic field. A bar magnet suspended on a thread aligns itself with the Earth's magnetic field. The end that points north is the north-seeking pole; the other end is the south-seeking pole.

Permanent magnets

A bar magnet produces lines of force which loop round from one end to the other end. The lines emerge from the north-seeking pole and end at the south-seeking pole. A U-shaped magnet has straight lines of force between its poles.

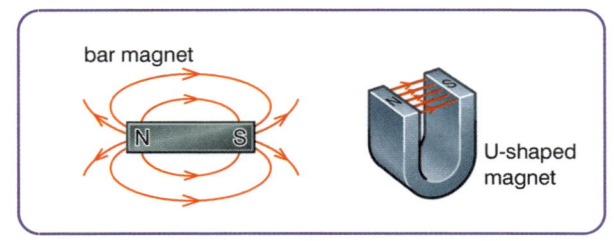

Magnetic fields

The magnetic effect of a steady electric current

Near a long straight wire, the magnetic field lines are concentric circles centred on the wire in a plane perpendicular to it.

Near a long solenoid, the magnetic field lines are concentrated at the ends, similar to the field of a bar magnet. The lines pass through the solenoid along its axis. In both examples, reversing the current reverses the field lines.

Electromagnets

An electromagnet consists of a solenoid with an iron core. When a current is passed through the coil of wire, the iron bar is magnetised. The magnetic field is much stronger than the field created by the empty coil. It can be switched off by switching the current off, and its strength can be altered by changing the current.

Using electromagnets

To lift scrap iron: a powerful electromagnet suspended from a crane cable is used to lift scrap iron in scrapyards. Switching the electromagnet off causes the scrap iron to fall off the electromagnet.

The relay: when current is passed through the coil of a relay, the electromagnet attracts a soft iron armature. The movement of this armature closes a switch which is part of a different circuit. When the current is switched off, the armature springs back to its normal position and the switch reverts to its original state.

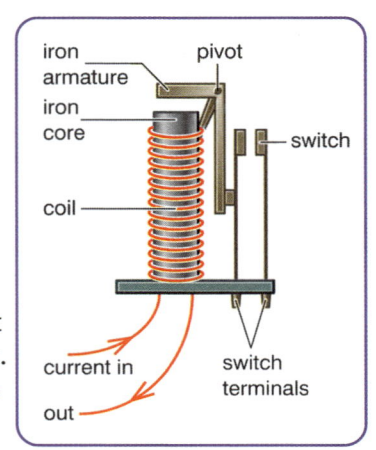

A normally open relay

The electric bell: the electromagnet coil is part of a 'make-and-break' switch. When current passes through the coil, the electromagnet attracts the soft iron armature which makes the hammer hit the bell. The movement of the armature opens the 'make-and-break' switch which switches the electromagnet off, allowing the armature to spring back to its initial position and close the switch. Current then passes through the electromagnet again, causing the sequence to be repeated.

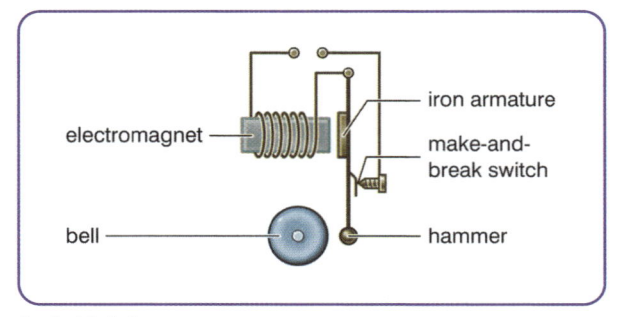

An electric bell

Electromagnetism

14.2 The electric motor

The motor effect

A force is exerted on a current-carrying wire placed at right angles to the lines of force of a magnetic field. The diagram shows a current-carrying wire between the poles of a U-shaped magnet. The force is perpendicular to the wire and to the lines of force of the magnet.

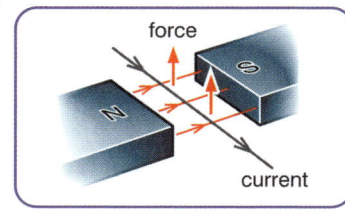

The force occurs because the magnetic field created by the wire interacts with the applied magnetic field (the magnetic field in which the wire is placed). The combined field is very weak on one side where the two fields are in opposite directions to each other. The force acts towards the side where the combined field is very weak.

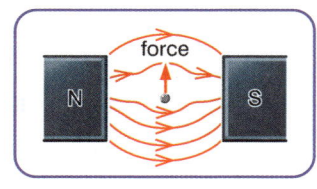

The motor effect

Combined fields

Fleming's left-hand rule is a convenient way to remember the force direction if you know the current direction and the direction of the applied magnetic field.

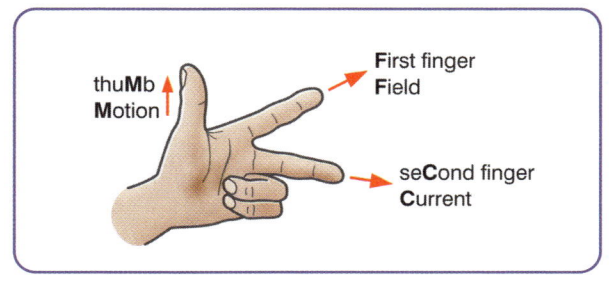

thuMb — Motion
First finger — Field
seCond finger — Current

Fleming's left-hand rule

The electric motor

A model electric motor is shown in the next diagram. The rectangular coil is on a spindle between the poles of a U-shaped magnet. Current enters and leaves the coil via a split-ring commutator.

Current passes along each side of the coil in opposite directions. Each side is therefore acted on by a force due to the magnetic field. The force on one side is in the opposite direction to the force on the other side.

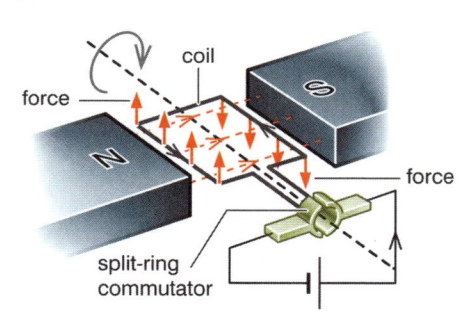

When the coil is parallel to the field, the forces on the sides rotate the coil. As the coil turns through the position at 90° to the field, the split-ring commutator reverses its connections to the battery, reversing the current direction round the coil. Therefore, the forces acting on each side continue to turn the coil in the same direction as before, so the coil rotates continuously in one direction.

The electric motor

Questions

For the electric motor above, what would be the effect of **a)** reversing the current direction **b)** reversing the current direction and reversing the direction of the magnetic field?

Practical electric motors

★ A mains electric motor works with alternating current because it has an electromagnet, not a permanent magnet. Each time the current reverses, the magnetic field does too, so the rotation direction is unchanged.

★ The armature may comprise 20 different coils, each at a fixed angle to the next. Each coil has its own pair of segments of a split-ring commutator. This produces a much steadier speed of rotation than a single coil.

★ The power supply is connected to the split-ring commutator using two spring-loaded graphite brushes which press on the commutator. Graphite conducts electricity and allows the commutator to turn with very little friction.

Answers: The rotation direction would **a)** reverse **b)** be unchanged

Electromagnetism

The loudspeaker

This contains a coil of insulated wire on a plastic tube in a magnetic field, as shown. The coil is at the centre of a diaphragm. When current is passed through the coil, it is forced to move by the magnetic field. With alternating current, the coil is forced to move to and fro. This vibrating motion makes the diaphragm vibrate, creating sound waves in the surrounding air with the same frequency as the alternating current.

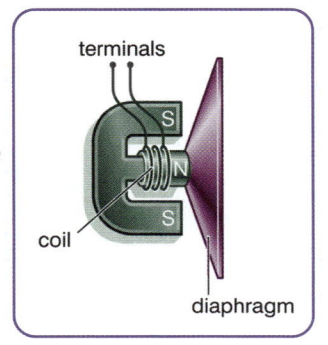

A loudspeaker

14.3 Electromagnetic induction

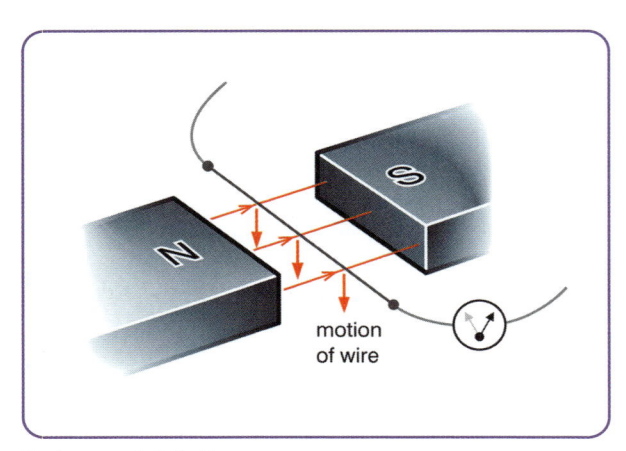

Electromagnetic induction

Fact file

★ When a wire cuts across the lines of force of a magnetic field, a voltage is induced in the wire.

★ If the wire is part of a complete circuit in which there is no other voltage source, the induced voltage drives a current round the circuit.

★ The faster the wire moves across the field lines, the greater the induced voltage.

★ The stronger the magnetic field, the greater the induced voltage.

Laws of electromagnetic induction

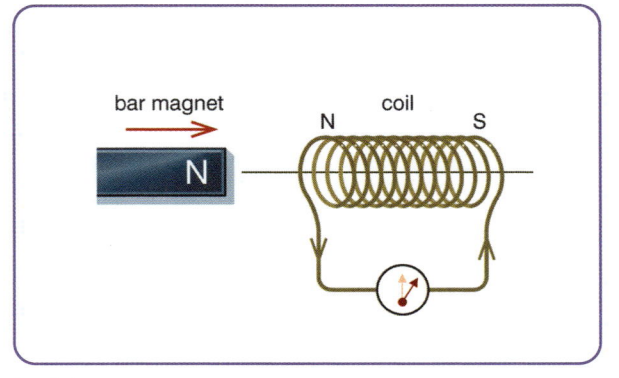

Lenz's law

Lenz's law: the induced current in a circuit is always in such a direction as to oppose the change which causes it. This can be tested by inserting a bar magnet into a coil connected to a centre-reading milliammeter. The direction of the induced current is given by the deflection of the pointer of the meter. Inserting the magnet generates a current which creates a magnetic pole to oppose the incoming pole.

Faraday's law of electromagnetic induction: the induced voltage is proportional to the speed at which the wire cuts the magnetic field lines. The induced current is small if the magnet is inserted slowly. If the magnet is inserted rapidly, the induced current is much larger.

The alternating current generator

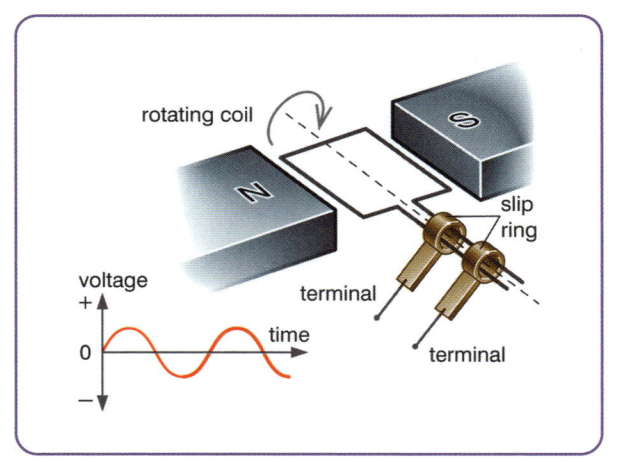

An a.c. generator

Electromagnetism

The a.c. generator consists of a rectangular coil of insulated wire which is made to rotate at steady speed in a uniform magnetic field. Work done to turn the coil is converted into electrical energy. The alternating voltage induced across the terminals of the coil can be displayed on an oscilloscope.

★ The frequency of the alternating voltage is equal to the frequency of rotation of the coil.

★ The peak voltage is proportional to the speed of rotation of the coil (Faraday's law). Rotating the coil faster would show more waves on an oscilloscope screen (because the frequency is greater) and make them higher (because the peak voltage is larger).

★ The peak voltage occurs when the sides of the coil cut across the field lines at 90°. The voltage is zero when the coil sides move parallel to the field lines.

★ A direct voltage can be generated if the two slip rings are replaced by a split-ring commutator, as shown. An oscilloscope display of this voltage would show each cycle as two positive half-cycles instead of a positive half-cycle followed by a negative half-cycle. Note that a battery connected to an oscilloscope would display a flat line above or below the zero level.

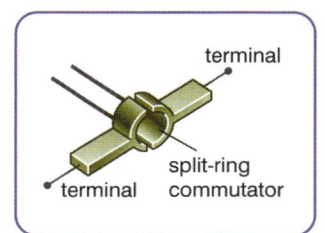

Producing direct current

The dynamo

In a dynamo, the magnet rotates and the coil remains stationary. The magnet and coil move relative to each other such that the coil windings cut across the magnetic field lines. Hence a voltage is induced.

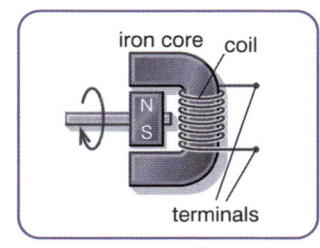

A dynamo

The microphone

Sound waves make the microphone diaphragm vibrate. A coil attached to the diaphragm moves in and out of the magnetic field of a permanent magnet, generating an alternating voltage across the coil terminals. The voltage from a microphone is usually referred to as an audio signal.

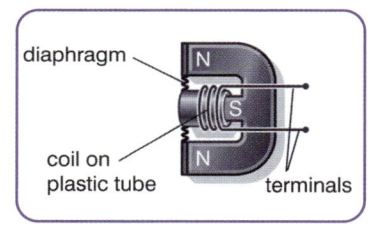

A microphone

Question

A bicycle is fitted with a dynamo lamp. Explain why the cyclist must pedal harder after switching the lamp on.

Magnetic recording

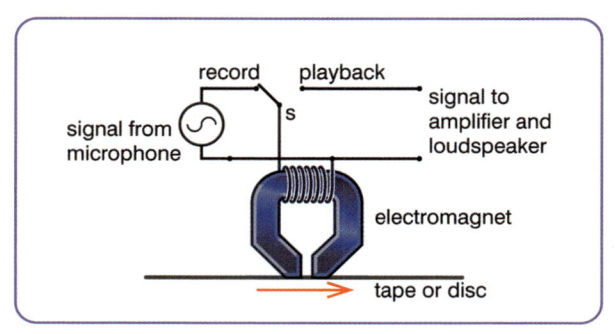

Magnetic recording

The tape or disc is coated on one side with a thin film of magnetic material.

Recording: the tape or disc is made to run at a steady speed past a recording head. This is a small electromagnet to which the audio signal is supplied. The changes of magnetism due to the audio signal are recorded by the magnetic film.

Playback: the tape or disc is made to run at a steady speed past the same recording head. This time, the recording head is connected to an amplifier and a loudspeaker. The changes in magnetism on the film induce an alternating voltage in the coil of the electromagnet. This is the audio signal recreated.

Answer

Electrical energy for the lamp is provided from work done by the cyclist. Hence the cyclist must do more work by exerting more force to keep the speed the same.

Electromagnetism

14.4 Transformers

How a transformer works

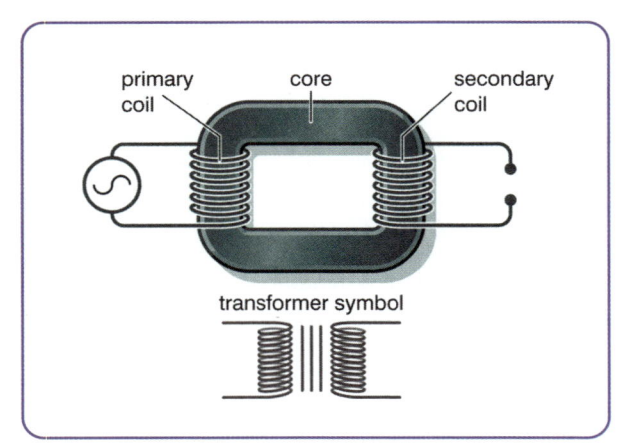

A model transformer

A transformer steps an alternating voltage up or down. It consists of two coils wound on an iron core.

1. The voltage to be transformed is applied to the **primary coil** of the transformer.
2. The alternating current through the windings of the primary coil creates an alternating magnetic field in the transformer's iron core.
3. The continuously changing magnetic field through the core induces an alternating voltage in the **secondary coil**.

The transformer rule

$$\frac{\text{voltage induced in the secondary coil } V_s}{\text{voltage applied to the primary coil } V_p} = \frac{\text{number of turns on the secondary coil } N_s}{\text{number of turns on the primary coil } N_p}$$

For a **step-up transformer**, the number of secondary turns is greater than the number of primary turns. Hence the secondary voltage is greater than the primary voltage.

For a **step-down transformer**, the number of secondary turns is less than the number of primary turns. Hence the secondary voltage is less than the primary voltage.

Transformer efficiency

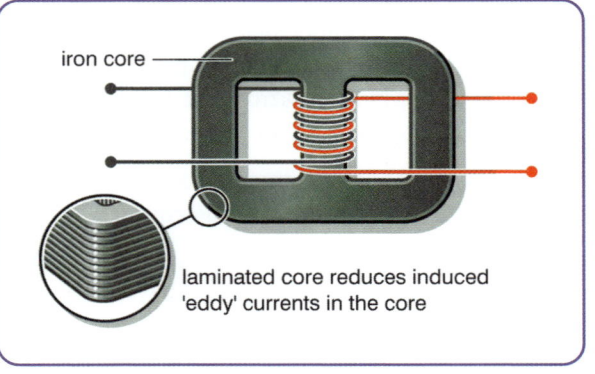

A practical transformer

The percentage efficiency of a transformer is defined as $\frac{\text{output power}}{\text{input power}} \times 100\%$.

For a transformer that is 100% efficient, the output power equals the input power. In other words, primary current × primary voltage = secondary current × secondary voltage. Thus if the voltage is stepped up, the current is stepped down and vice versa.

Questions

A transformer has a 100-turn primary coil and a 2000-turn secondary coil. A 240 V, 60 W lamp is connected to the secondary coil. Calculate **a)** the primary voltage needed to make the lamp light normally **b)** the primary current when the lamp lights normally, assuming the transformer is 100% efficient.

High-voltage transmission of electrical power

The grid system operates at high voltage because the higher the voltage, the less the current needed for the same power. Less power is therefore wasted due to resistance heating in the cables used to carry the current. Alternating voltages can easily be stepped up or down using transformers. Hence power is transmitted on the grid system using alternating voltage.

Answers: a) 12 V b) 5 A

Electromagnetism

ROUND UP

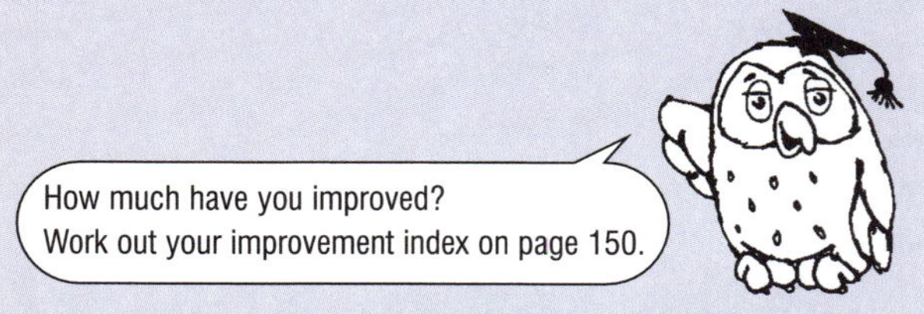

How much have you improved? Work out your improvement index on page 150.

1. **a)** With the aid of a diagram, explain the operation of a make-and-break switch in an electric bell or a buzzer. [8]
   b) The diagram shows the construction of a different type of electric bell. When the switch is closed, the iron bar is pulled into the electromagnet, causing the wooden striker X to hit the metal plate with a 'ding'. When the switch is released, the iron bar springs back and the other wooden striker Y hits the other plate with a 'dong'.

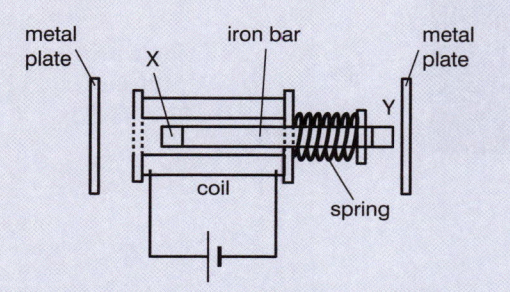

   (i) Why is it essential that the bar is made of iron? [1]
   (ii) When the switch is open, why is it necessary for the iron bar to be partly in and partly out of the solenoid? [1]
   (iii) Explain whether or not the device would work with an alternating current supply instead of a direct current supply. [2]

2. **a)** With the aid of a labelled diagram, explain the operation of a relay that is normally open. [6]
   b) A metal-detector consists of an electromagnet connected to a low voltage alternating current supply. When a piece of metal is held near the electromagnet, the current through the coil increases. Explain why this increase of current occurs. [2]

3. **a)** With the aid of a labelled diagram, explain the operation of an alternating current generator. [6]
   b) (i) Sketch the waveform produced by an alternating current generator. [2]
   (ii) Show on the waveform you have drawn a point where the coil is parallel to the magnetic field. [1]
   c) How does the voltage waveform of an alternating current generator change if the generator turns more quickly? [2]

4. **a)** The diagram shows the construction of a step-down transformer.

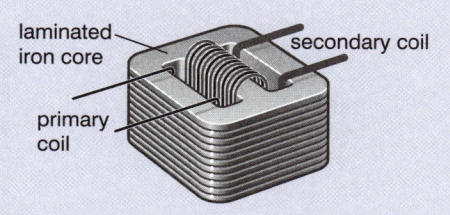

   (i) Explain the operation of this transformer. [2]
   (ii) Why are the windings of the secondary coil thicker than the windings of the primary coil? [1]
   (iii) Why is the core constructed from laminated iron plates? [2]
   b) A step-down transformer has a primary coil with 1200 turns and a secondary coil with 60 turns.
   (i) If the primary coil is connected to 240 V a.c. mains, what will the secondary voltage be? [1]
   (ii) The percentage efficiency of the transformer was measured and found to be 80%. If the primary current is not to exceed 0.1 A, what is the maximum current that can be delivered to a 12 V light bulb connected to the secondary coil? [2]

5. **a)** (i) Why is electrical power transmitted through the grid system at high voltage? [2]
   (ii) Domestic consumers in the UK are supplied with mains electricity at 240 V. In the USA, the mains voltage is 110 V. Which system is safer and why? [2]
   b) The cables used to distribute electricity through the grid system are often carried by pylons. Give one advantage and one disadvantage of using pylons rather than underground cables for this purpose. [2]

Well done if you've improved. Don't worry if you haven't. Take a break and try again.

Electromagnetism

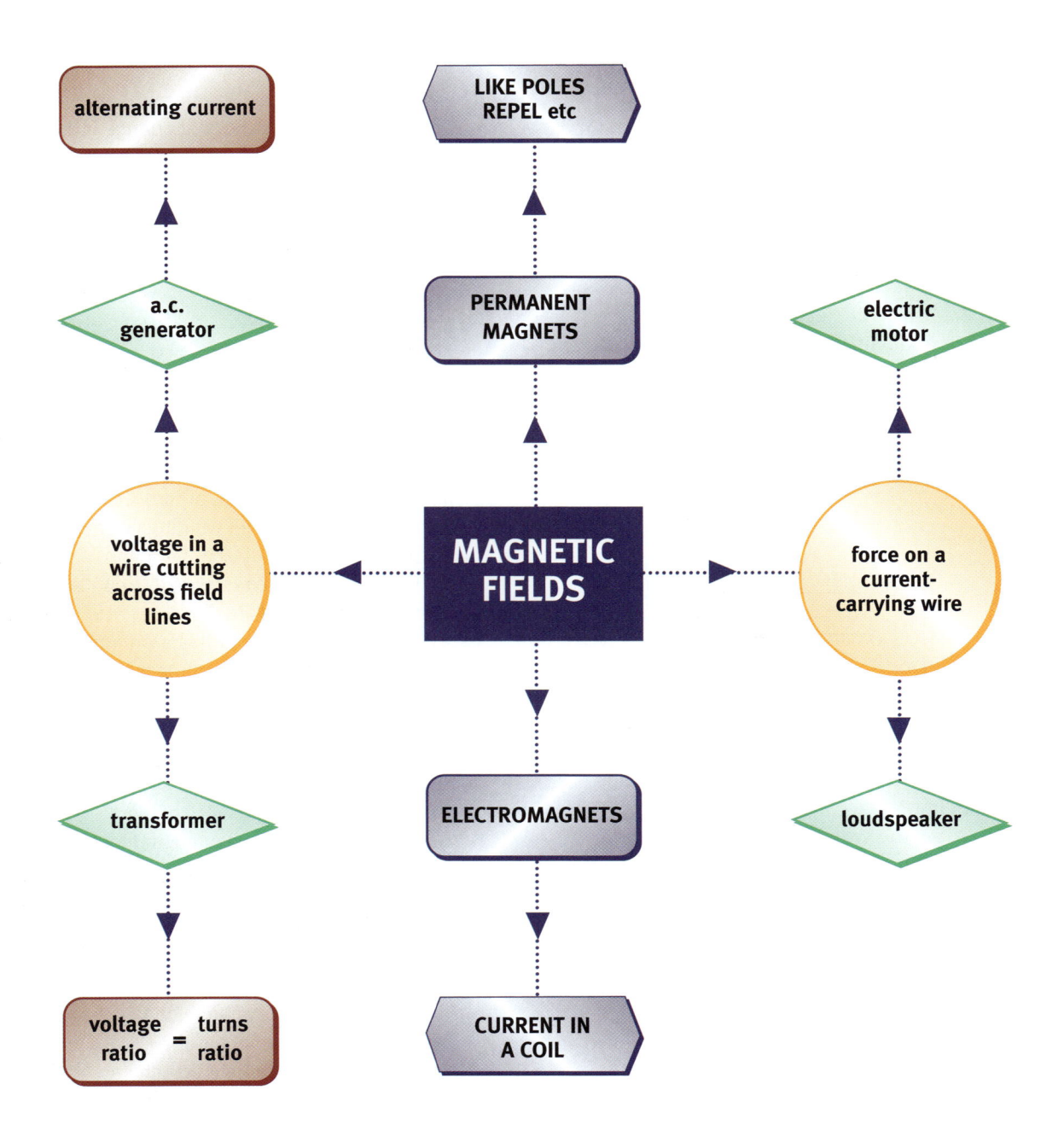

```
alternating current              LIKE POLES
        ▲                        REPEL etc
        ┊                            ▲
        ┊                            ┊
    a.c.                         PERMANENT          electric
  generator                       MAGNETS            motor
        ▲                            ▲                ▲
        ┊                            ┊                ┊
  voltage in a                                    force on a
  wire cutting  ◄┄┄┄┄  MAGNETIC  ┄┄┄┄►             current-
  across field          FIELDS                   carrying wire
     lines                                            ┊
        ┊                            ┊                ▼
        ▼                            ▼
   transformer                  ELECTROMAGNETS    loudspeaker
        ┊                            ┊
        ▼                            ▼
  voltage   turns              CURRENT IN
   ratio  = ratio                A COIL
```

Concept map: electromagnetism

Electronics and communications — Chapter 15

15.1 More about components and electric circuits

PREVIEW

At the end of this topic you will be able to:
- use the resistor colour code
- calculate the resistance of resistors in series or parallel
- calculate the voltages and currents in circuits containing no more than one source of voltage
- state the function of a capacitor and describe its use in control and smoothing circuits
- describe how a diode is used to protect other components and to rectify alternating current
- use an oscilloscope to display and measure waveforms
- describe the operation of a transistor as a switch
- use a multimeter to measure current, voltage and resistance.

CONCEPT MAP Page 120.

How much do you already know? Work out your score on pages 150–1.

Test yourself

1 a) Sketch a circuit showing a 10 Ω resistor in series with a 5 Ω resistor and a 1.5 V cell.
  b) **(i)** Calculate the total resistance of these two resistors in series.
  (ii) Calculate the current through each resistor in the circuit. [3]

2 The following diagram shows a 3 Ω resistor in parallel with a 6 Ω resistor. The two resistors are connected across the terminals of a 1.5 V cell.

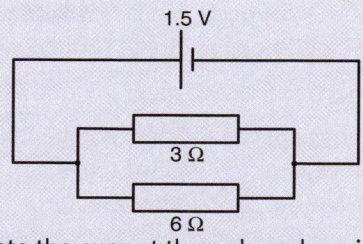

a) Calculate the current through each resistor and the current through the cell.
b) Calculate the total resistance of these two resistors in parallel. [4]

3 A thermistor is connected in series with a resistor, a milliammeter and a 1.5 V cell.
  a) Draw the circuit diagram for this arrangement.
  b) When the thermistor is at 20 °C, the milliammeter reading is constant. State and explain how the milliammeter reading would change if the temperature of the thermistor fell. [4]

4 The diagram shows a potential divider circuit consisting of a light-dependent resistor (LDR) in series with a 1000 Ω resistor R and a 5.0 V voltage supply unit. A voltmeter is connected across resistor R.

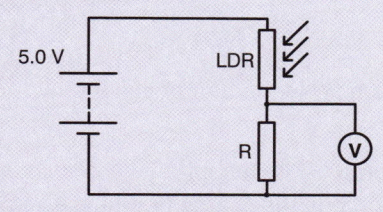

a) When the LDR is in darkness, the voltmeter reads 1.0 V.
  (i) What is the voltage across the LDR when the voltmeter reads 1.0 V?
  (ii) Calculate the resistance of the LDR when the voltmeter reads 1.0 V.
b) State and explain what change occurs in the voltmeter reading when the LDR is exposed to daylight. [6]

5 A capacitor, a switch, a light-emitting diode (LED) and a 1.5 V cell are connected in series with each other. When the switch is closed, the LED lights up briefly.
  a) Sketch the circuit diagram for this arrangement.
  b) Explain why the LED lights up briefly when the switch is closed. [3]

continues →

Electronics and communications

6 A diode is connected in series with a resistor and an alternating voltage supply unit.

a) Sketch the circuit diagram for this circuit.

b) An oscilloscope is then connected across the resistor to display the resistor voltage waveform. Sketch the waveform you would expect to observe on the oscilloscope screen. [2]

7 The circuit diagram shows a transistor being used to make a light-operated electric bell.

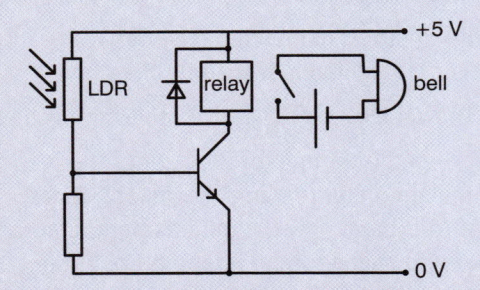

When the light-dependent resistor (LDR) is in darkness, the bell is off. When the LDR is illuminated, the bell rings. Explain why illuminating the LDR makes the bell ring. [4]

Recap

Units

★ The **ampere** (A) is the unit of electric current.

★ The **coulomb** (C) is the unit of electric charge. One coulomb is the charge that passes a point in a circuit in 1 s when the current is 1 A.

★ The **volt** (V) is the unit of potential difference (or voltage). One volt is one joule per coulomb.

The resistor colour code

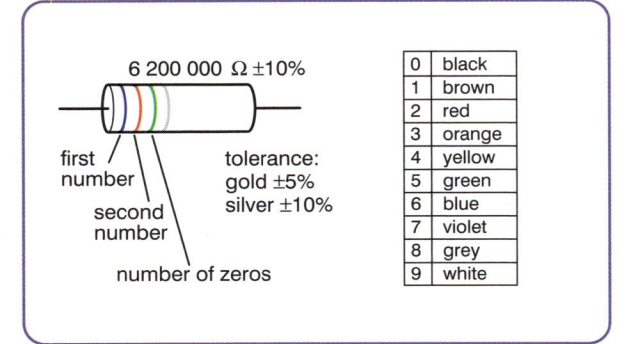

0	black
1	brown
2	red
3	orange
4	yellow
5	green
6	blue
7	violet
8	grey
9	white

tolerance: gold ±5%, silver ±10%

The resistor colour code

Resistance rules

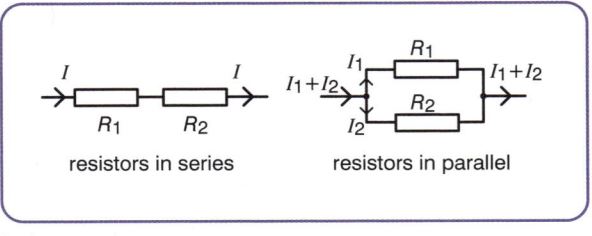

Resistance rules

For two or more resistors of resistance R_1, R_2, etc. in series,

total resistance $R = R_1 + R_2 +$ etc.

For two resistors of resistance R_1 and R_2 in parallel, the total resistance R is given by the equation

$$\frac{1}{R} = \frac{1}{R_1} + \frac{1}{R_2}$$

The potential divider

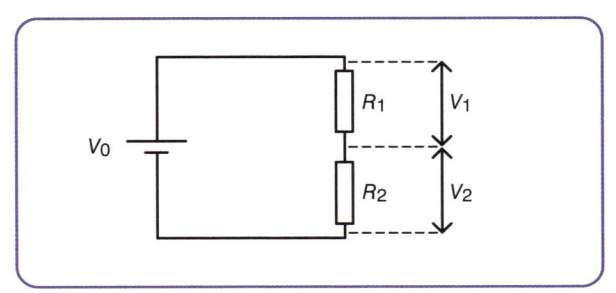

The potential divider

This consists of two resistors in series with a voltage V_0 across the combination, as shown in the diagram.

For two resistors R_1 and R_2, the voltage V_1 across R_1 and the voltage V_2 across R_2 are given by the equations

$$V_1 = \frac{R_1}{(R_1 + R_2)} V_0$$

$$V_2 = \frac{R_2}{(R_1 + R_2)} V_0$$

Electronics and communications

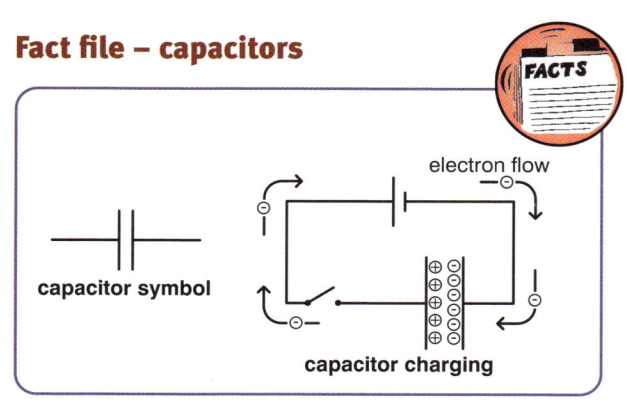

Fact file – capacitors

The capacitor (capacitor symbol; capacitor charging showing electron flow)

★ A **capacitor** is a device designed to store charge. Its symbol is shown above.

★ A simple capacitor consists of two parallel plates. When the switch is closed, electrons transfer from the negative terminal of the battery onto the plate the negative terminal is connected to. At the same time, electrons transfer from the other plate to the positive terminal of the battery. When the p.d. between the plates is equal to the p.d. of the power supply, the electron flow stops.

★ A practical capacitor consists of two strips of tin foil as plates, separated by insulating material.

★ Uses of a capacitor include:
- smoothing out voltage changes in a d.c. circuit, for example, to prevent sudden voltage changes in the voltage supply to a computer circuit which would seriously affect the operation of the circuit
- delaying the growth of voltage in a d.c. circuit when the circuit is switched on, for example, in a time delay circuit.

Fact file – diodes

★ A **diode** allows current to pass through in one direction only.

★ In a d.c. circuit, a diode can be used to prevent damage due to a battery being connected with incorrect polarity (the wrong way round).

★ A diode can be used to convert an alternating current into a direct current. The diagrams show how this can be achieved.

★ A light-emitting diode (LED) emits light when it conducts. See page 155 for the symbol.

1. **Half-wave rectification** is achieved using a single diode in series with a resistor and the alternating voltage supply unit.

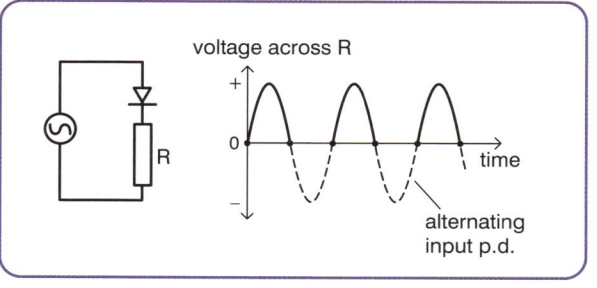

Half-wave rectification

2. **Full-wave rectification** is achieved using:
   a) two diodes and a transformer
   b) four diodes as a bridge rectifier.

In both circuits, a large capacitor connected across the output terminals produces a steady direct voltage by smoothing the full-wave voltage.

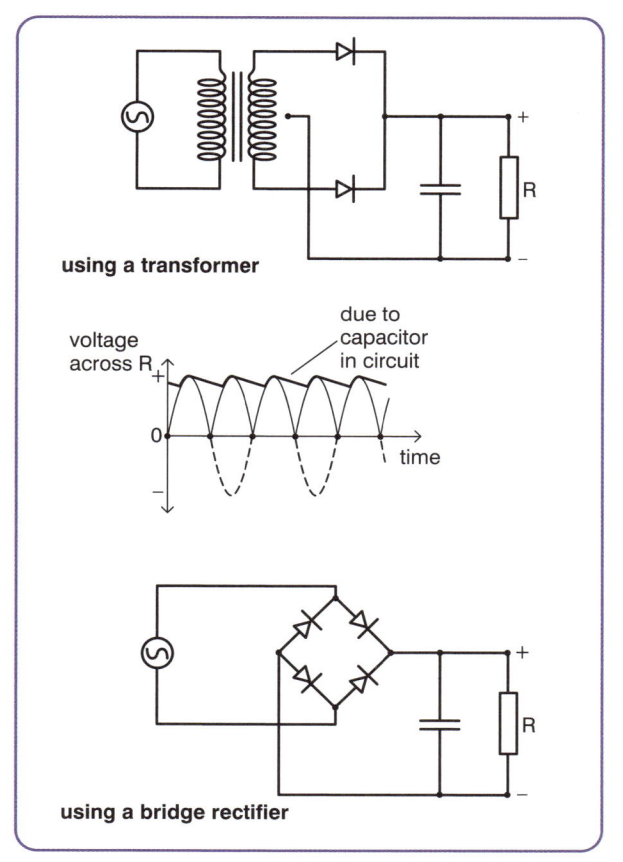

using a transformer

using a bridge rectifier

Full-wave rectification

Electronics and communications

Fact file – transistors

★ The current entering the **collector** and the **base** leaves via the **emitter** in normal use.

$$\text{emitter current } I_e = \text{collector current } I_c + \text{base current } I_b$$

★ The collector current is controlled by the base current and is proportional to it.

$$\text{current gain} = \frac{\text{collector current}}{\text{base current}}$$

★ The current gain varies from one transistor to another. Typically, the current gain of a transistor is about 200.

★ The base–emitter junction is a forward-biased diode. No current can enter the base unless the base–emitter voltage is about 0.7 V. The base–emitter voltage scarcely changes when current enters the base.

The diagram on the right shows how a transistor is used to switch a relay on or off. The switch S and resistor in series with the base of the transistor could be replaced by an LDR to make a light-operated relay, or by a thermistor to make a temperature-operated relay.

Fact file – use of a multimeter

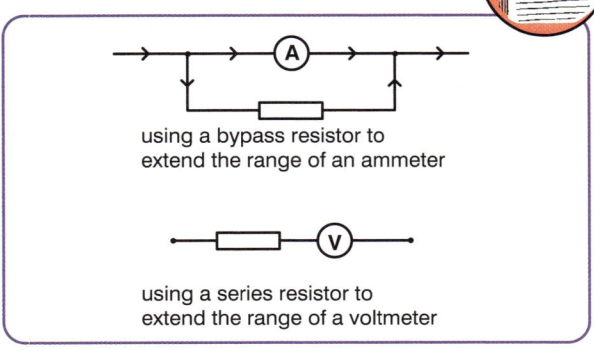

using a bypass resistor to extend the range of an ammeter

using a series resistor to extend the range of a voltmeter

Extending the range of a meter

★ The range of an **ammeter** can be extended by connecting a resistor in **parallel** with the meter. The extra current through the resistor does not pass through the meter. The meter reading is multiplied by a constant factor to give the total current.

the transistor

$$\text{current gain} = \frac{I_c}{I_b} = 200$$

typical current gain

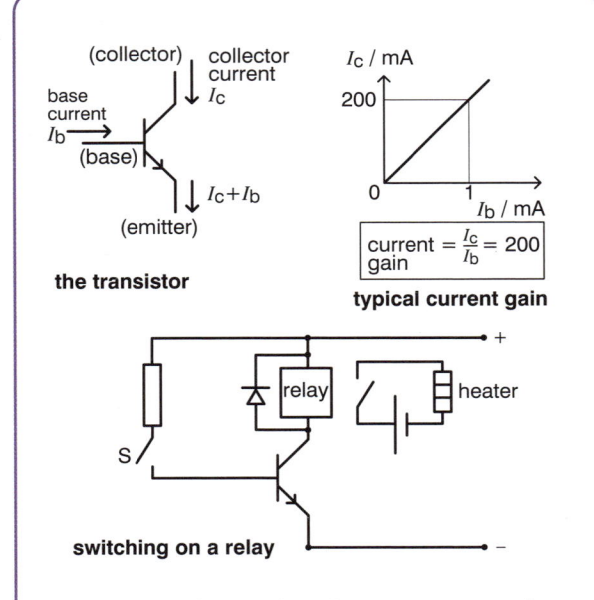

switching on a relay

1. When switch S is closed, current enters the base of the transistor.
2. As a result, current passes through the relay into the collector of the transistor.
3. The relay core is therefore magnetised and the relay switch is forced to close. This can be used to switch a high-current device on or off.
4. The diode in parallel with the relay coil is necessary to prevent the transistor from being damaged when it is switched off. Without the diode, switching the transistor off would cause a very large induced voltage in the relay coil. This high voltage would act across the transistor between its collector and emitter and destroy the transistor. The diode prevents this by short-circuiting the induced voltage.

Transistors in use

★ The range of a **voltmeter** can be extended by connecting a resistor in **series** with the meter. The extra voltage is dropped across the resistor, not across the meter. The meter reading is multiplied by a constant factor to give the total voltage.

★ A **multimeter** is used to measure voltage or current according to the position of one or more selector switches. These switches are used to connect the multimeter in series or in parallel with different resistors, chosen to extend the range by a desired factor.

Electronics and communications

ROUND UP

How much have you improved?
Work out your improvement index on pages 151–2.

1 The circuit diagram shows a variable resistor and two 6 V, 24 W bulbs connected to a 12 V voltage supply unit.

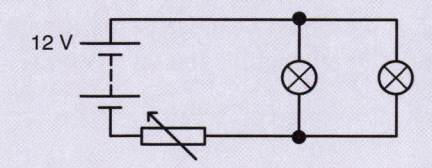

a) (i) Are the two bulbs in series or in parallel?

(ii) Is the current through the variable resistor more than, less than or the same as the current through the voltage supply unit?

b) The variable resistor is adjusted so that the bulbs light normally.

(i) Determine the voltage across and the current through each bulb when they light normally.

(ii) Calculate the voltage across and current through the variable resistor when the bulbs light normally. [6]

2 A set of Christmas tree lights consists of 20 12 V, 0.25 A torch bulbs in series with each other. They are designed to light normally when connected to the 240 V mains. Assume they operate normally.

a) How much current passes through the wires connecting the lights to the mains?

b) How much electrical energy is delivered to the whole set of lights each second? [3]

3 The circuit diagram shows a potential divider used to supply a variable voltage from a 9.0 V battery. The potential divider consists of a variable resistor R and a 1000 Ω resistor.

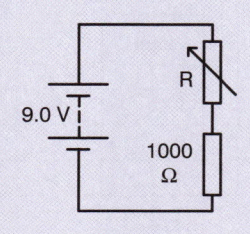

a) If the resistance of the variable resistor R is increased, what change occurs in

(i) the current from the battery
(ii) the voltage across the 1000 Ω resistor
(iii) the voltage across the variable resistor?

b) Calculate the voltage across the variable resistor when it is adjusted to 500 Ω. [5]

4 a) How many different resistances can be obtained using a 2 Ω, a 3 Ω and a 6 Ω resistor? Sketch each possible combination.

b) Calculate the maximum and the minimum total resistance in this set of combinations. [8]

5 a) A 3.0 V battery and two 10 Ω resistors are connected in series. Draw the circuit diagram and calculate the current and the voltage for each resistor.

b) A third 10 Ω resistor is connected in parallel with one of the resistors in the above circuit. Draw the new circuit diagram and calculate the current and the voltage for each resistor in this new circuit. [11]

6 a) With the aid of a labelled diagram, explain how a bridge rectifier converts alternating current to direct current. Sketch the output voltage waveform and the alternating voltage waveform on the same axes.

b) Add a capacitor to your diagram in **a)** to smooth the voltage output from the bridge rectifier. Indicate on your waveform diagram how the capacitor affects the output voltage of the bridge rectifier. [8]

7 The diagram below shows a temperature-controlled heater. When the temperature of the thermistor falls, the heater is switched on.

a) Explain in terms of the current in each part of the circuit why the heater is switched on when the temperature of the thermistor falls.

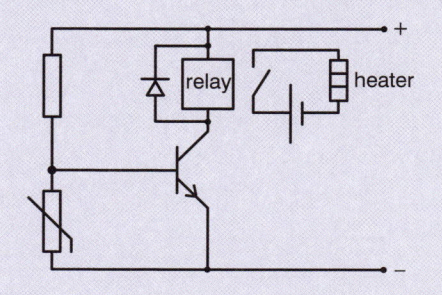

b) Explain the function of the diode. [6]

113

Electronics and communications

15.2 Electronic control

PREVIEW

At the end of this topic you will be able to:

- explain what is meant by a digital circuit and how an LED is used as a logic indicator
- give the symbol and truth table for NOT, AND, OR, NAND and NOR gates
- work out the truth table for a combination of logic gates
- explain the operation of sensor-controlled logic circuits used to switch devices on or off
- explain the operation of time-delay logic circuits and latches.

How much do you already know? Work out your score on page 152.

Test yourself

1. **a)** Identify the logic gate shown.
   b) Write the truth table for this logic gate. [5]

2. The diagram shows an LED and a resistor used as a logic indicator connected to the output of a NOT gate. 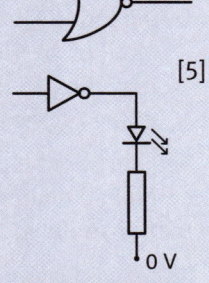 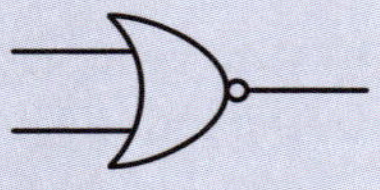
   a) State and explain what the logic state of the NOT input should be for the LED to light up.
   b) Why is it essential to connect a resistor in series with the LED? [4]

3. Write the truth table for the logic circuit shown. [4]

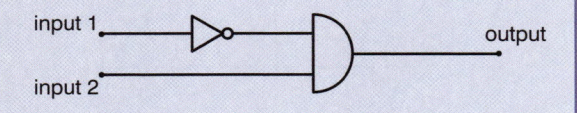

   input 1 ──▷○──┐
                 ├──D── output
   input 2 ──────┘

4. **a)** The circuit diagram shows a time delay circuit used to operate an alarm. Explain how this circuit works.

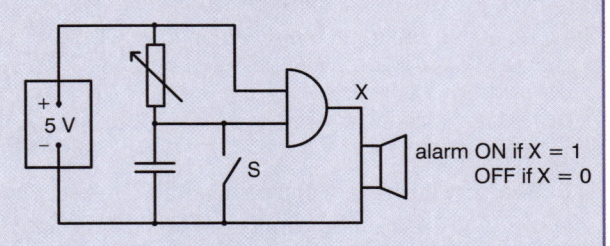

   alarm ON if X = 1
   OFF if X = 0

   b) The time delay can be changed by altering the variable resistor. State and explain what change should be made to the variable resistor to lengthen the time delay. [7]

Logic gates and states

A **logic gate** is an example of a **digital circuit**. This is a circuit in which the voltage is either high (1) or low (0). No other voltage level occurs. There can only be two states (1 or 0) for the voltage at any point.

The output state of a logic gate is determined by the input states. A **truth table** is a table showing the output state for all possible input states.

The **NOT gate** is sometimes called an **inverter**. Its output state is *NOT* the same as its input state.

The logic state at a point in a logic circuit can be displayed using a **logic indicator**. This consists of a light emitting diode (LED) in series with a resistor. The diagram below shows a logic indicator connected to the output of a NOT gate. When the NOT input is 0, the LED is lit up, indicating the NOT output is 1.

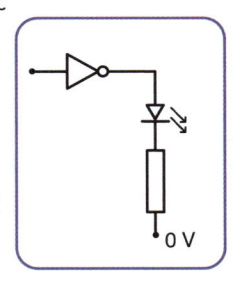

A logic indicator

Input		Symbol and output			
		AND	NAND	OR	NOR
A	B				
0	0	0	1	0	1
0	1	0	1	1	0
1	0	0	1	1	0
1	1	1	0	1	0

Truth tables and symbols for different types of logic gate

Electronics and communications

Logic gates in sensor circuits

Sensors may be used to supply the input voltages to a logic circuit. The diagram shows a light sensor and a pressure sensor connected to an AND gate. The output voltage is high only when the switch is closed and the light sensor is in darkness.

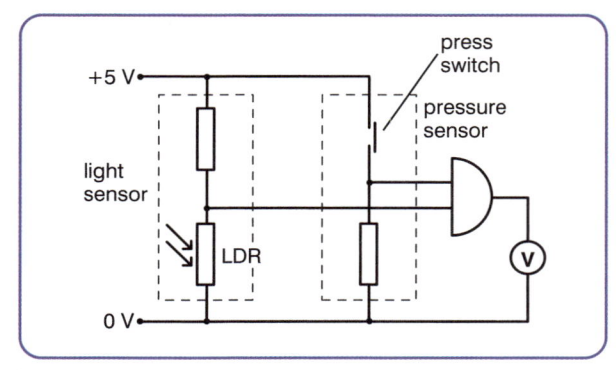

Using sensors

Relay control

The diagram below shows a transistor connected to the output of a logic gate. The transistor is used to operate a relay. When the logic gate output is high, current enters the base of the transistor (the transistor is on) and so current passes through the relay, causing the relay switch to close. Some relays can be operated directly from the output of a logic gate.

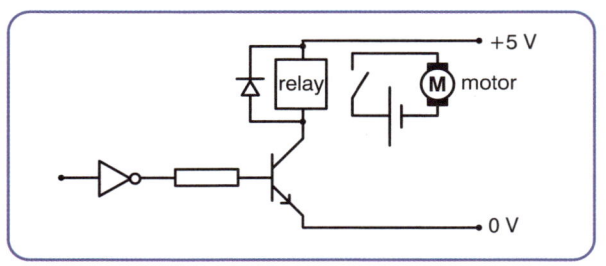

Relay control

Time-delay circuits

Closing the switch in the circuit at the top of the next column causes the capacitor to charge up through the resistor. When the voltage across the capacitor reaches the required voltage, the LED indicator at the output of the OR gate is switched on. The time delay can be increased by using a larger capacitor or using a larger resistance.

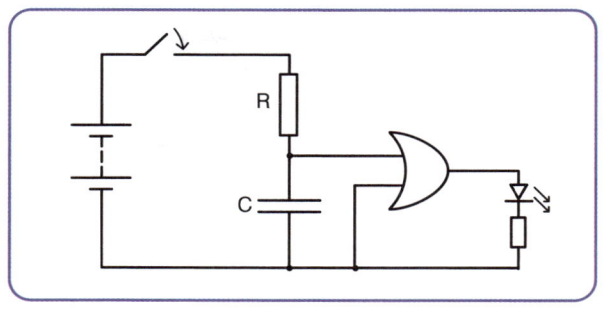

Time-delay circuit

Memory circuits

A **latch** is a logic circuit in which the output voltage stays in a certain logic state (0 or 1) after the input condition that caused that state has changed. The diagram shows how an OR gate is used as a simple latch. When a 1 is applied to input A, the output state changes to 1 and this is fed back to the other input B, which therefore holds the output at 1. Even if the logic state of input A changes to 0, the output remains at 1.

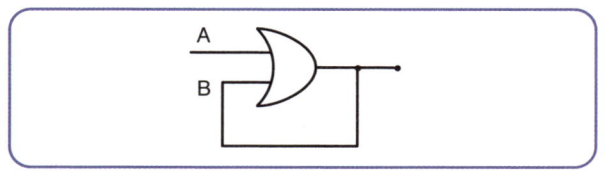

An OR latch

Here is a more complicated latch, which includes a **reset** switch to reset the output to 0 when the input is 0. This type of circuit is called a **bistable circuit** because its output can be latched to 0 or 1 according to the logic state of input S.

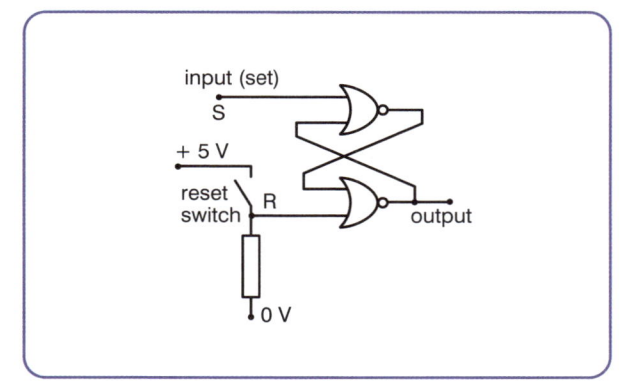

Using NOR gates in a bistable circuit

115

Electronics and communications

ROUND UP

How much have you improved? Work out your improvement index on page 152.

1. Copy and complete the truth table below for each combination of logic gates.

input A	input B	output
0	0	
0	1	
1	0	
1	1	

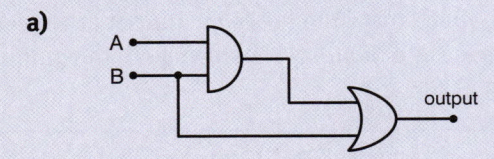

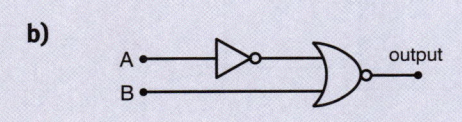

a)

b)

[8]

2. The diagram below shows an alarm system consisting of a window sensor, a key-operated sensor, a logic circuit and an alarm. The window sensor gives logic 0 if the window is open and logic 1 if the window is closed. The key sensor gives logic 1 or 0 according to the position of a switch in the sensor. The system is designed to switch the alarm on (logic state 1) only if the switch is closed (logic state 1) and the window is open (logic state 0).

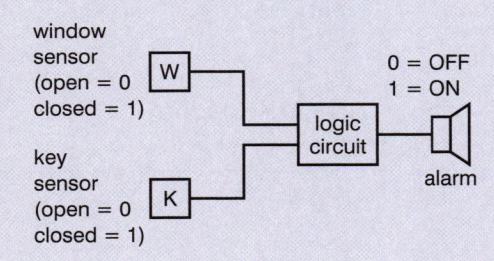

a) Complete the truth table for this system.

window sensor	key sensor	alarm
0	0	
0	1	
1	0	
1	1	

b) Design a logic circuit for this system using an AND gate and a NOT gate. [6]

3. The diagram shows a time-delay circuit consisting of a resistor, a capacitor, a two-pole switch S, an OR gate and a voltmeter.

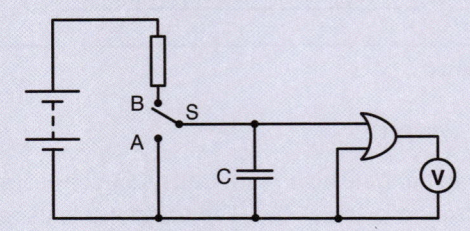

a) When the two-pole switch is at A, what is the reading on the voltmeter?

b) State and explain what happens to the voltmeter reading when this switch is moved from A to B. [5]

4. An OR gate is connected to the output of a bistable latch, as shown, to operate a siren when switch X is closed.

a) Explain what is meant by the term 'latch' in electronics.

b) Which switch would you press to turn the siren off?

c) Which switch would you press to test the siren? [3]

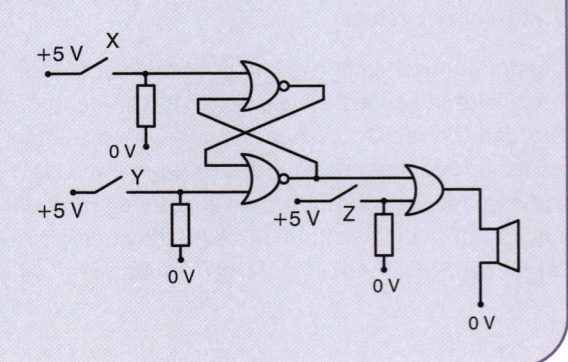

Electronics and communications

15.3 Communication systems

PREVIEW

At the end of this topic you will be able to:

- describe the difference between analogue and digital signals
- explain the differences between AM, FM and digital transmission
- recall the building blocks in a communications system and describe the function of each
- describe different methods of storing and retrieving information
- explain the benefits of digital systems for transmitting and storing information.

How much do you already know? Work out your score on page 153.

Test yourself

1. State whether each of the following systems transmits information in digital or analogue form.
   a) fax transmission
   b) FM radio
   c) a satellite microwave link
   d) CD music system [4]

2. Here are some building blocks of different communications systems, listed alphabetically:

   decoder   encoder   modulator   receiver   regenerator   transmitter

   a) Which of these building blocks are not needed in an AM broadcasting system?
   b) Which are essential in an optical fibre link carrying telephone calls? [4]

3. Information in digital form can be stored on a magnetic disc or on a compact disc (CD).
   a) State one advantage a magnetic disc has over a CD.
   b) State one advantage a CD has over a magnetic disc. [3]

4. To receive a satellite TV programme, a dish receiver and a decoder are necessary.
   a) Why is it essential to fit the dish outdoors, pointing in a certain direction?
   b) What type of electromagnetic waves is the dish designed to receive?
   c) Why is it necessary to fit a decoder between the dish aerial and the TV set? [3]

5. a) What is the advantage of broadcasting radio programmes using FM instead of AM transmission?
   b) Why is it not possible to broadcast TV programmes in the same waveband as FM radio programmes?
   c) A single cable can carry many telephone calls at the same time. How is this possible? [4]

Recap on electromagnetic waves

Look back at **optical fibre and radio communications**.

COMMUNICATIONS Page 60.

Analogue transmission

The building blocks of an analogue transmission system for radio or TV broadcasts or telephone calls are shown at the top of the next page.

★ The **oscillator** generates electrical waves at the carrier wave frequency.

★ The **transducer** (e.g. a microphone for audio signals) converts the analogue signal that is to be carried into an electrical waveform.

★ The **modulator** imposes the waveform of the analogue signal onto the carrier wave. The modulation could be AM or FM.

★ The **transmitter** converts the electrical waves into electromagnetic waves, if these are to be used to carry the signal to the receiver.

★ The **receiver** detects the carrier waves, reconverts them back to electrical waves if necessary, and passes them into a **rectifier circuit**. This circuit passes the positive part of the waves through to the **demodulator circuit** which lets the analogue signal through, but stops the carrier waves.

★ An **amplifier** makes the analogue signal larger. The signal can be recorded or supplied to a speaker if it is an audio signal, or to a TV monitor if it is a TV signal.

117

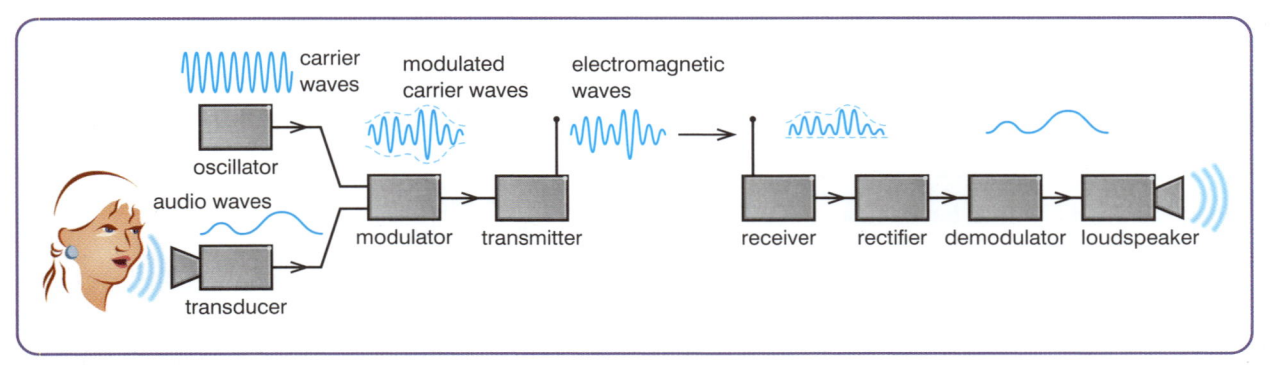

Electronics and communications

Analogue transmission using amplitude modulation

Digital transmission

To transmit information in digital form, a code is needed. Examples of codes used to convert information to digital form include the Morse code, Braille, bar codes and the ASCII code used in computer circuits. An **encoder** and a **decoder** are necessary building blocks of any digital transmission system.

Computers and fax machines are digital systems in which information is stored, processed and transmitted as **bytes** of data, each byte consisting of a sequence of **bits** (binary digits, 1s and 0s). The **ASCII code** is based on eight-bit bytes.

Analogue signals can be converted into digital signals before being transmitted. The amplitude of the analogue signal is **sampled** or measured at frequent intervals, and each sample is converted to a data byte which is then used to modulate the carrier wave. This process is called **pulse code modulation** (PCM).

The higher the carrier frequency, the greater the amount of information that can be carried. Optical fibres can carry many more simultaneous telephone calls than a microwave beam, which can carry many more calls than a pair of copper wires.

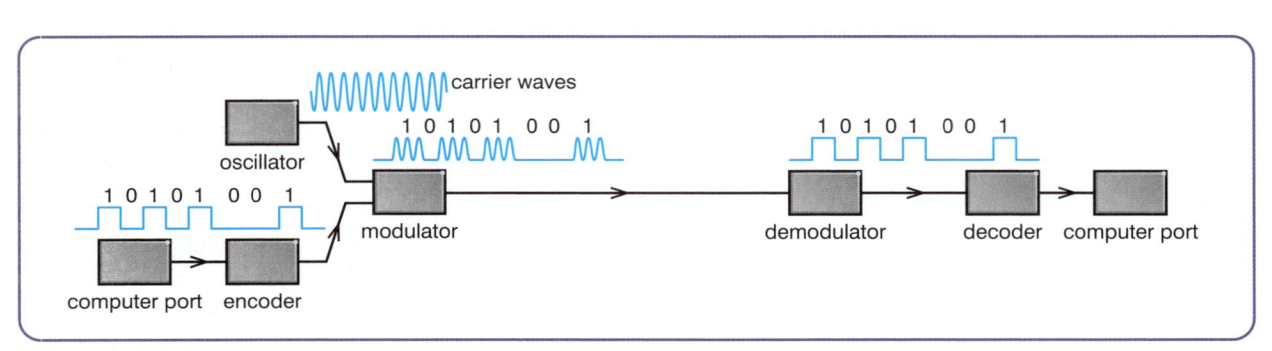

Digital transmission

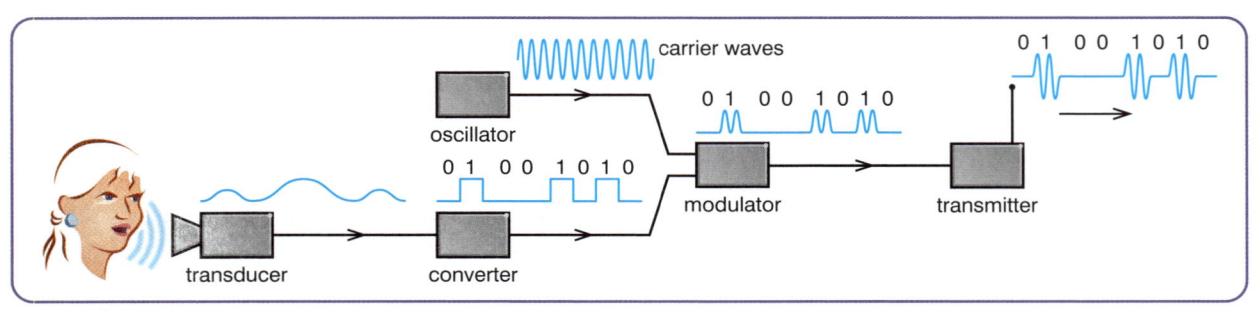

Pulse code modulation

Electronics and communications

Information storage

Magnetic tape is used to store audio and video signals.

TAPE RECORDER Page 105.

Computer discs are used to store and retrieve information in digital form. A computer disc has a thin magnetic film on its surface. A motor-controlled head magnetises the part of the surface next to it when it is supplied with a voltage pulse. In this way, data bytes are stored on the disc as it turns under the head. When reading data from the disc, the same head is used to detect changes of magnetisation on the disc. As the disc moves past the head, these changes of magnetisation induce a stream of voltage pulses in the head. Data on a disc can be changed.

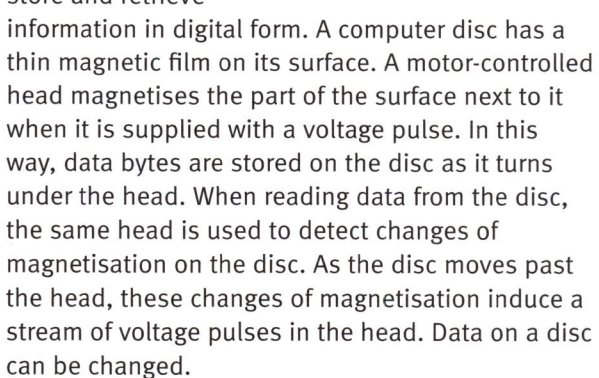

Compact discs (CDs) store data permanently in digital form. The surface of the disc is etched with tiny pits, the absence or presence of a pit representing a binary 0 or 1. Light from a laser diode is reflected off the disc onto a detector. The presence of a pit prevents light being reflected off the disc. As the disc turns, the detector receives a stream of light pulses which it converts into electrical pulses. In this way, bytes of data are read off the disc. In a CD music system, the data bytes are used to recreate the audio signal. Because electrical noise is eliminated in digital systems, CD music systems are of much higher quality than taped music systems.

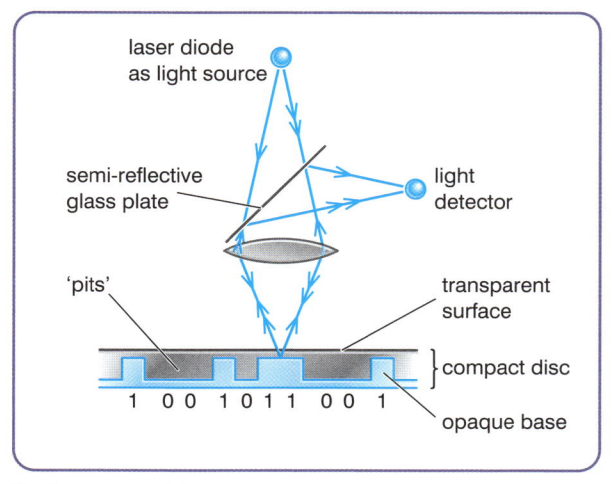

Reading a compact disc

ROUND UP

How much have you improved? Work out your improvement index on page 153.

1. State one advantage of using
   a) digital transmission instead of analogue transmission for telephone calls
   b) optical fibres instead of copper wires for transmitting a signal. [2]

2. Why are an encoder and a decoder necessary for digital transmission but not for analogue transmission? [3]

3. Storage of a single TV picture in digital form takes about 0.5 million bits. The picture on a TV screen is renewed 25 times per second.
   a) How much data can be stored on a three-hour video tape?
   b) A CD-ROM can store about 10 000 million bits. What would be the maximum duration of a TV programme stored on a CD-ROM? [2]

4. State and explain the type of communication system most suitable for
   a) linking together a network of computers in a room
   b) video conferencing between two continents
   c) maintaining contact with a ship at sea. [3]

5. Vinyl records were once a very popular means of replaying recorded music. The record player consisted of a turntable, and an arm with a needle attached to a small pressure transducer at the end. The audio signal was recreated as a result of the needle following a spiral track of variable depth on the record disc. These have now largely been replaced by CD music systems and magnetic tape cassette systems.
   a) State if (i) a CD music system (ii) a vinyl record player is digital or analogue.
   b) State two advantages a CD music system has over a vinyl record player. [4]

Well done if you've improved. Don't worry if you haven't. Take a break and try again.

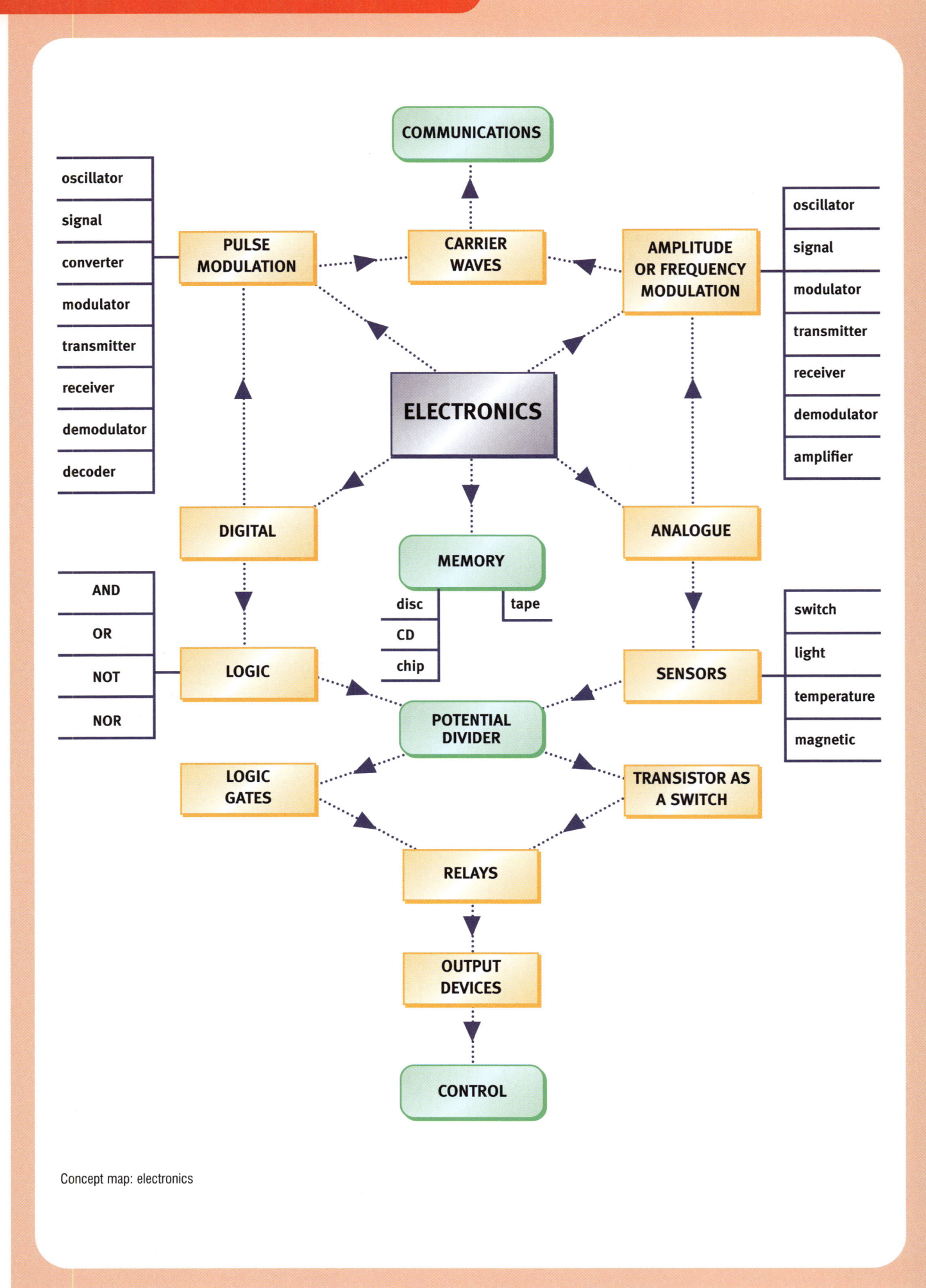

Electronics and communications

Concept map: electronics

- **COMMUNICATIONS**

- **PULSE MODULATION**
  - oscillator
  - signal
  - converter
  - modulator
  - transmitter
  - receiver
  - demodulator
  - decoder

- **CARRIER WAVES**

- **AMPLITUDE OR FREQUENCY MODULATION**
  - oscillator
  - signal
  - modulator
  - transmitter
  - receiver
  - demodulator
  - amplifier

- **ELECTRONICS**

- **DIGITAL**

- **MEMORY**
  - disc
  - CD
  - chip
  - tape

- **ANALOGUE**

- **LOGIC**
  - AND
  - OR
  - NOT
  - NOR

- **SENSORS**
  - switch
  - light
  - temperature
  - magnetic

- **LOGIC GATES**

- **POTENTIAL DIVIDER**

- **TRANSISTOR AS A SWITCH**

- **RELAYS**

- **OUTPUT DEVICES**

- **CONTROL**

Radioactivity   Chapter 16

PREVIEW

At the end of this topic you will be able to:

- explain the structure of the atomic nucleus and the term isotope
- explain radioactivity in simple terms
- describe the characteristics of the three main types of emission from radioactive substances
- explain what is meant by background radioactivity
- explain the term half-life and interpret half-life graphs and related data
- understand that emissions from radioactive substances have harmful effects
- describe uses of radioactivity.

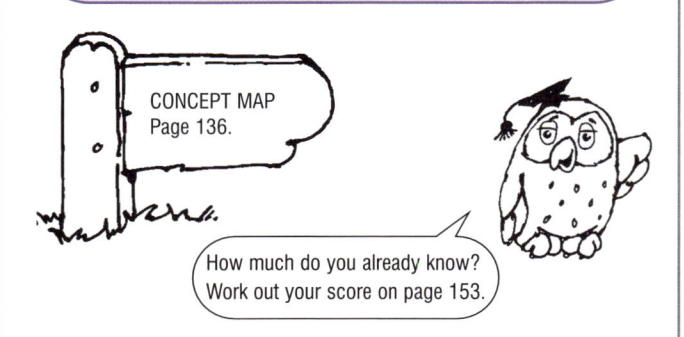

CONCEPT MAP Page 136.

How much do you already know? Work out your score on page 153.

Test yourself

1. State whether each of the following particles carries positive charge, negative charge or is uncharged.
   a) the electron b) the proton c) the neutron
   d) the alpha particle e) the beta minus particle [5]
2. State how many protons and how many neutrons are present in each nucleus of the following isotopes.
   a) $^{4}_{2}He$ b) $^{235}_{92}U$ [4]
3. What type of charge does the nucleus of the atom carry? [1]
4. State the three types of emissions from naturally occurring radioactive substances, and state which type of radioactive emission is most easily absorbed. [4]
5. What is background radioactivity? [1]
6. Name a scientific instrument used to measure radioactivity. [1]
7. The *half-life* of the *isotope* of carbon $^{14}_{6}C$ is 5500 years. Explain what is meant by the terms in italics. [2]
8. What is meant by nuclear fission? [2]
9. Why is it important to store radioactive waste from a nuclear reactor for thousands of years? [2]
10. State two uses of radioactive isotopes. [2]

16.1 Inside the atom

A scientific puzzle

Radioactivity was discovered in 1896 by **Henri Becquerel**. When he developed an unused photographic plate, he found an image of a key on it. He realised this was caused by radiation from a packet containing uranium salts, which had been on top of a key with the photographic plate underneath. The puzzle of explaining the radiation was passed by Becquerel to a young research worker, **Marie Curie**. She painstakingly analysed the uranium salts and discovered the radiations were emitted from the uranium atoms, which formed other types of atoms in the process. She and her husband Pierre discovered and named two new radioactive elements, polonium and radium. It was shown that the emissions contained two types of radiation: alpha radiation which is positively charged and easily absorbed, and beta radiation which is negatively charged and much less easily absorbed. Later gamma radiation was discovered which is uncharged and much more penetrating.

Symbol for radioactive sources

Radioactivity

The structure of the atom

Ernest Rutherford used alpha radiation to probe the atom. He knew that alpha radiation consisted of positively charged particles. He found that when a beam of alpha particles was directed at a thin metal foil, some of the particles bounced back off the foil. He deduced that:

- the atom contains a tiny positively charged nucleus, where most of its mass is located
- the rest of the atom consists of empty space through which negatively charged electrons move as they orbit the nucleus.

Further investigations showed that the nucleus contains two types of particles, **protons** and **neutrons**.

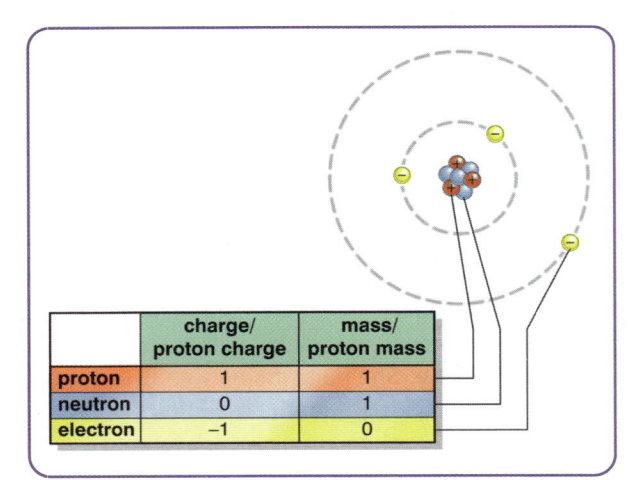

	charge/proton charge	mass/proton mass
proton	1	1
neutron	0	1
electron	−1	0

A lithium atom

Atoms and molecules

★ An **element** is a substance which cannot be split into simpler substances. A **compound** is a substance containing two or more elements combined in fixed proportions.

★ An **atom** is the smallest particle of an element which is characteristic of that element.

★ A **molecule** is formed when two or more atoms join together.

★ The lightest atom is hydrogen. The heaviest naturally occurring atom is uranium.

★ The **periodic table of the elements** places the elements in order of increasing **atomic number** (symbol Z). The atomic number of an element is the number of protons in its nucleus.

Isotopes

★ The number of protons in the atomic nucleus of an element (the **atomic number Z** of the element) is constant for that element.

★ The number of neutrons in the atomic nuclei of a given element can vary from one atom to another.

★ The term **isotope** describes a particular type of atom of a given element. For example, chlorine has two isotopes, one with 17 protons and 18 neutrons, and the other with 17 protons and 20 neutrons.

★ Since protons and neutrons each have a mass of one atomic mass unit, the total number of protons and neutrons in a nucleus gives the mass of the nucleus in atomic mass units. This is called the **mass number A** of the nucleus. Because electrons have very little mass in comparison, the mass of an atom in atomic mass units is equal to A.

★ An isotope is defined by the symbol

$$^{A}_{Z}X$$

where X is the chemical symbol of the element, Z is the number of protons in the nucleus (the atomic number) and A is the number of protons and neutrons in the nucleus (the mass number).

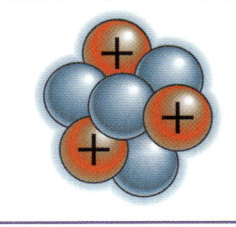

Why doesn't the nucleus fly apart due to repulsion of the positive protons? The nucleus is held together by the **strong nuclear force**.

Questions

Work out the number of protons and neutrons in each of the following isotopes. **a)** $^{238}_{92}U$ **b)** $^{14}_{6}C$ **c)** $^{22}_{10}Ne$

Answers: a) 92p + 146n b) 6p + 8n c) 10p + 12n

Radioactivity

16.2 Radioactive isotopes

Stable and unstable nuclei

A nucleus is **stable** if the strong nuclear force between its neutrons and protons is much greater than the electrostatic force of repulsion between the protons. Some nuclei are **unstable** because the electrostatic forces of repulsion are larger than the strong attractive forces.

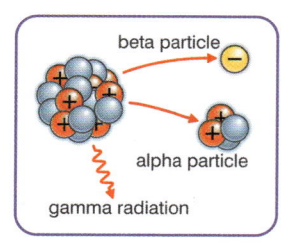

An unstable nucleus

★ A large nucleus with **too many protons and neutrons** is unstable. It becomes stable by emitting an **alpha particle**. This is a particle consisting of two protons and two neutrons.

★ A smaller nucleus with **too many neutrons** is unstable. It becomes stable by emitting a **beta particle**. This is an electron created in the nucleus and instantly emitted.

★ A nucleus may still possess **excess energy** after an alpha or beta particle has been emitted. It may then release the excess energy as **gamma radiation**. This is electromagnetic radiation of very short wavelength.

★ The daughter nucleus might itself be radioactive, and may emit a further alpha or beta particle.

★ An unstable nucleus is said to **disintegrate** when it emits an alpha particle or beta particle. When it emits gamma radiation, it is said to **de-excite**.

★ The **activity** of a radioactive source is the number of nuclei per second that disintegrate.

The Geiger counter

This consists of a Geiger tube connected to an electronic counter. Each particle from a radioactive source that enters the tube is registered on the electronic counter as one count. If the Geiger tube is pointed at a radioactive source, the activity of the source can be monitored by counting the number of particles entering the tube in a measured time interval and calculating the **count rate** (the number of counts per second), which is proportional to the activity.

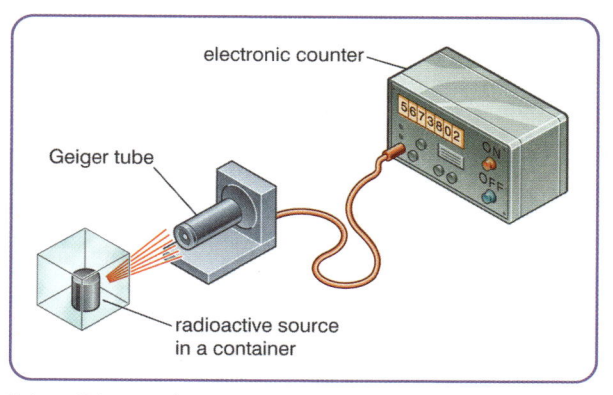

Using a Geiger counter

Background radioactivity

A Geiger counter will detect a low level of radioactivity even with no source present. This is called **background radioactivity** and is due to cosmic radiation and naturally occurring radioactive isotopes in rocks such as granite.

Questions

A Geiger counter records 1980 counts in 300 seconds when it is held at a fixed distance from a radioactive source. Without the source present, it records 120 counts in 300 seconds.

a) Why does the Geiger tube count when no source is present?

b) Calculate the count rate due to the source.

c) Give two reasons why the count rate is less than the activity of the source.

$E = mc^2$

This famous equation was first derived by **Albert Einstein**. He showed that if energy E is given to (or taken away from) an object, the mass of the object increases (or decreases) by a mass m in accordance with the equation $E = mc^2$, where c is the speed of light. The energy given out when a nucleus disintegrates can be calculated from the difference in mass of the parent nucleus and its products.

Answers

a) Background radioactivity
b) 6.2 counts per second
c) The radiation spreads out from the source in all directions so most of it misses the tube; absorption by the air between the tube and the source.

Radioactivity

16.3 Radioactive emissions

Ionisation

Ions are atoms that have become charged, either by removing electrons or by adding them.

When the particles produced from radioactive substances pass through a gas, they cause the gas molecules to ionise. In a **cloud chamber**, tiny droplets form along the path of an alpha particle due to the trail of ions created by the particle. The path of each alpha particle is visible in the cloud chamber.

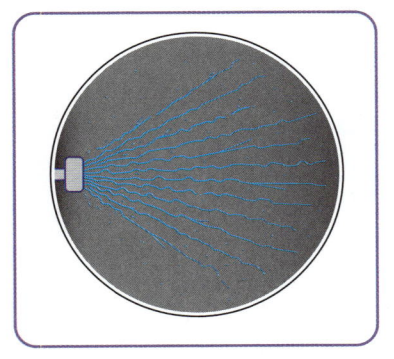

Alpha-particle tracks in a cloud chamber

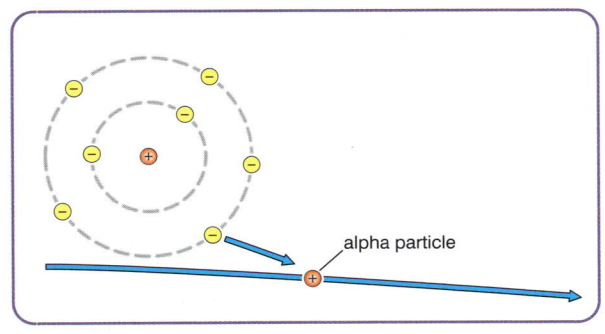

Ionisation

The properties of alpha, beta and gamma radiation

	alpha	beta	gamma
charge	+2	−1	0
absorption	thin paper	few mm of aluminium	several cm of lead
range in air	fixed*, up to 10 cm	variable*, up to 1 m	spreads without limit
ionising effect	strong	weak	very weak

(* = for a given source)

Equations for radioactive change

★ **Alpha emission**

An alpha particle (symbol $^4_2\alpha$) consists of two protons and two neutrons. An unstable nucleus that emits an alpha particle therefore loses two units of charge and four units of mass. (Remember each proton has a mass of 1 atomic mass unit and a charge of +1 and a neutron has the same mass as a proton and is not charged.)

An unstable nucleus $^A_Z X$ has Z protons and $(A-Z)$ neutrons in its nucleus. If it emits an alpha particle, it becomes a nucleus with two fewer protons and two fewer neutrons.

$$^A_Z X \longrightarrow {}^{A-4}_{Z-2} Y + {}^4_2 \alpha$$

★ **Beta minus emission**

A beta particle (symbol β) is an electron created in an unstable nucleus, then instantly emitted. A neutron in the nucleus suddenly becomes a proton, creating the beta particle at the same time. The total number of neutrons and protons in the nucleus is therefore unchanged, but there is one more proton.

$$^A_Z X \longrightarrow {}^A_{Z+1} Y + {}^0_{-1} \beta$$

The mass number of the beta particle is 0 because it is an electron. Its charge is opposite to that of a proton, so its proton number is written as −1.

Note
In both equations, the numbers balance along the top and along the bottom.

Questions

a) Write down the equation representing
   (i) alpha emission from the unstable nucleus $^{238}_{92} U$ to form a nucleus of thorium (Th)
   (ii) beta emission from the unstable nucleus $^{27}_{12} Mg$ to form a nucleus of aluminium (Al).

b) State how many protons and how many neutrons are present in each nucleus in your equations.

Answers

a) (i) $^{238}_{92} U \longrightarrow {}^{234}_{90} Th + {}^4_2 \alpha$
   (ii) $^{27}_{12} Mg \longrightarrow {}^{27}_{13} Al + {}^0_{-1} \beta$
b) U-238 = 92 p + 146 n; Th-234 = 90 p + 144 n; Mg-27 = 12 p + 15 n; Al-27 = 13 p + 14 n

Radioactivity

16.4 Half-life

The **half-life** of a radioactive isotope is the time taken for half its atoms to disintegrate. This time is a characteristic of the isotope. Long-lived radioactive isotopes have nuclei that are less unstable than short-lived isotopes. For example, uranium-238 has a half-life of more than 4500 million years.

The **number of atoms** of a radioactive isotope decreases with time. Radioactive disintegration is a **random** process, and the number of atoms that disintegrate per second is proportional to the number of radioactive atoms present at that time. For example, suppose 10% of the atoms of a certain radioactive isotope X disintegrate every 10 seconds. The table below shows how the number of atoms of X changes, starting with 10 000.

A graph showing how the number of atoms of X decreases with time is shown below. This type of curve is called a **decay curve**.

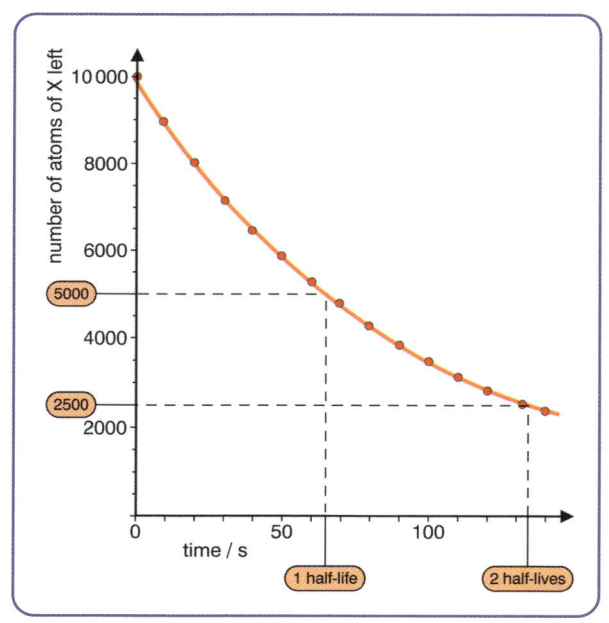

A decay curve

> **Questions**
>
> a) Use the graph to estimate the half-life of X.
> b) Estimate the time taken for the number of atoms to fall to 25% of 10 000.

The **activity** of a radioactive isotope decreases with time. This is because the activity is proportional to the number of atoms of the isotope left. The shape of the activity–time curve is the same as the decay curve, provided the 'daughter' isotope is stable.

Radioactive dating

␡ocks formed millions of years ago can be dated using radioactivity. Ancient materials can also be dated using radioactivity.

★ Some igneous rocks contain the uranium isotope U-238, formed by volcanic activity long ago. These can be dated by measuring the proportion of an isotope of lead, Pb-206, relative to U-238. The uranium isotope has a half-life of 4500 million years, emitting alpha particles and forming the stable isotope Pb-206 via a series of relatively short-lived radioactive isotopes. A decay curve like the one on the left may be used to work out the age of a rock from the proportion of U-238 remaining.

★ Rocks containing trapped argon gas can be dated by measuring the proportion of the gas to the radioactive potassium isotope, K-40, which produces the gas as a result of radioactive change. K-40 is an unstable isotope with a half-life of 1250 million years, producing the argon isotope Ar-40. This gas is trapped when the molten rock solidifies. Hence the age of the rock can be determined by measuring the relative proportions of the two isotopes and then using a decay curve.

> **Answers**
> a) 67 s b) 134 s

Time/s	0	10	20	30	40	50	60	70
Number of atoms left	10 000	9000	8100	7290	6561	5905	5314	4783
Decrease in number of atoms of X	1000	900	810	729	656	591	531	478

Radioactivity

16.5 Using radioactivity

In each of the uses of radioactivity described below, think about the choice of the radioactive isotope in terms of:
- the half-life of the isotope
- absorption of radioactive emissions
- whether or not the daughter isotope is stable.

Medical uses

Tracers for diagnosis: the cause of certain illnesses can be pinpointed using **radioactive tracers**. For example, an underactive thyroid gland can be detected by giving the patient food containing the radioactive isotope iodine-131. This is a beta emitter with a half-life of 8 days.

A correctly functioning thyroid gland will absorb iodine and store it. A Geiger tube pointed at the neck will therefore show an increased reading if the patient's thyroid gland is functioning correctly. The amount of radioactivity is too small to harm the gland, and the isotope decays after a few weeks.

> **Questions**
>
> 1 a) Why is a beta emitter chosen?
>
>   b) Why is an isotope with a half-life of a few minutes not chosen?

Gamma therapy: gamma radiation from the radioactive isotope cobalt-60 is used to destroy cancerous tissues. The gamma radiation penetrates the body and passes into the diseased tissue. A lead collimator (filter) is used to direct the gamma radiation onto the cancer cells. The half-life of cobalt-60 is 5 years.

> **Questions**
>
> 2 a) Why is a gamma emitter chosen?
>
>   b) Why is an isotope with a half-life of a few years chosen?

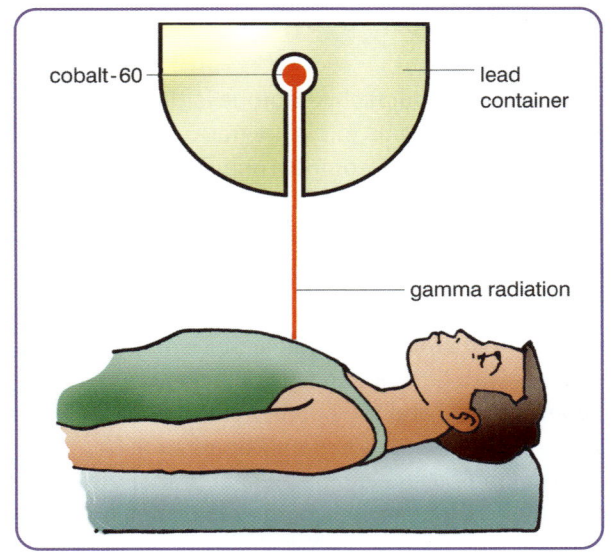

Treating cancer

Industrial uses

Thickness of metal foil: a detector measures the amount of beta radiation passing through the metal foil feeding out of a production line. If the foil becomes too thick, the detector reading falls and feeds a signal back to increase the pressure on the foil and make it thinner.

Pipeline cracks: the crack in a leaking underground pipe can be located by putting a radioactive tracer into the flow. A Geiger counter is then moved on the ground along the pipeline. Its reading is higher where the fluid in the pipe leaks into the ground. A beta-emitting isotope with a half-life of a few hours is suitable for this purpose.

Some other uses

Irradiation of food: gamma radiation is used to kill the bacteria responsible for food poisoning in certain foods. This makes the food safer to eat, and prolongs its shelf-life.

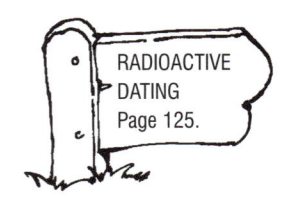

RADIOACTIVE DATING Page 125.

> **Answers**
>
> 1 a) Beta radiation from the thyroid can be detected outside the body.
>
>   b) There would be no radioactivity left in the iodine by the time it reached the thyroid.
>
> 2 a) Gamma radiation easily penetrates the body.
>
>   b) The source only needs to be replaced every few years.

Radioactivity

16.6 Nuclear reactors

Releasing energy from the nucleus

★ The uranium-235 nucleus is unstable and splits into two approximately equal 'daughter' nuclei, and two or three neutrons. This splitting process is called **fission**.

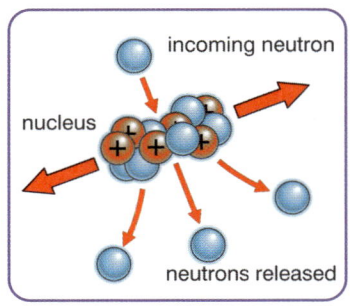

Fission

★ Energy is released when a U-235 nucleus splits, which is carried away as kinetic energy by the daughter nuclei and neutrons.

★ Fission can be induced by bombarding U-235 nuclei with neutrons.

★ A controlled **chain reaction** is created if there are sufficient U-235 nuclei. One neutron from each fission event goes on to cause the fission of another nucleus.

Radioactive waste

Radioactive waste from a nuclear reactor is classified as:
- **low level waste** such as clothing worn by personnel – the clothing fibres may contain radioactive dust particles
- **intermediate level waste** such as metal cladding from spent fuel rods – the cladding becomes radioactive inside the reactor
- **high level waste** such as fission products, unused uranium and plutonium.

Treatment and storage of radioactive waste

★ Low level radioactive waste from Britain's nuclear reactors is stored in sealed containers in a shallow trench at Sellafield.

★ Intermediate level waste is stored in sealed drums at several sites in Britain. An underground storage site at Sellafield is being developed to store all Britain's intermediate level and low level waste.

★ High level waste includes spent fuel rods, which are highly radioactive because the nuclei produced by fission of uranium-235 are unstable. The spent fuel rods therefore generate heat due to radioactive decay. The rods are placed initially in cooling ponds until they are cool enough to be transported safely to Sellafield. There they are reprocessed to recover unused uranium and plutonium. The rest of the high level waste is stored in sealed containers at Sellafield.

Why radioactivity is harmful

Radiation from radioactive substances produces ions. Ionising radiation damages living cells in two ways:
1 by penetrating the cell membranes which causes the cell to die
2 by breaking the strands of DNA molecules in the cell nucleus, which may cause cell mutation.

★ **Alpha radiation** is easily absorbed, highly ionising and therefore very harmful.

★ **Beta radiation** is less easily absorbed and less ionising. However, it can penetrate deep into the body from outside so it too is very harmful.

★ **Gamma radiation** easily penetrates soft tissue and is absorbed by bones, where its ionising effect can produce immense damage.

There is no lower limit below which ionising radiation is harmless. Therefore, extreme care is essential when radioactive substances are used and legal regulations for using radioactive substances must be observed. In a school laboratory, students under the age of 16 are not allowed to carry out experiments with radioactive materials.

Questions

a) Why is a storage box for radioactive substances made of lead?

b) Why is it essential for tongs used for handling radioactive substances to have long handles?

Answers
a) Lead is the best absorber of radioactivity.
b) The tongs keep the source as far away from the user as possible.

Radioactivity

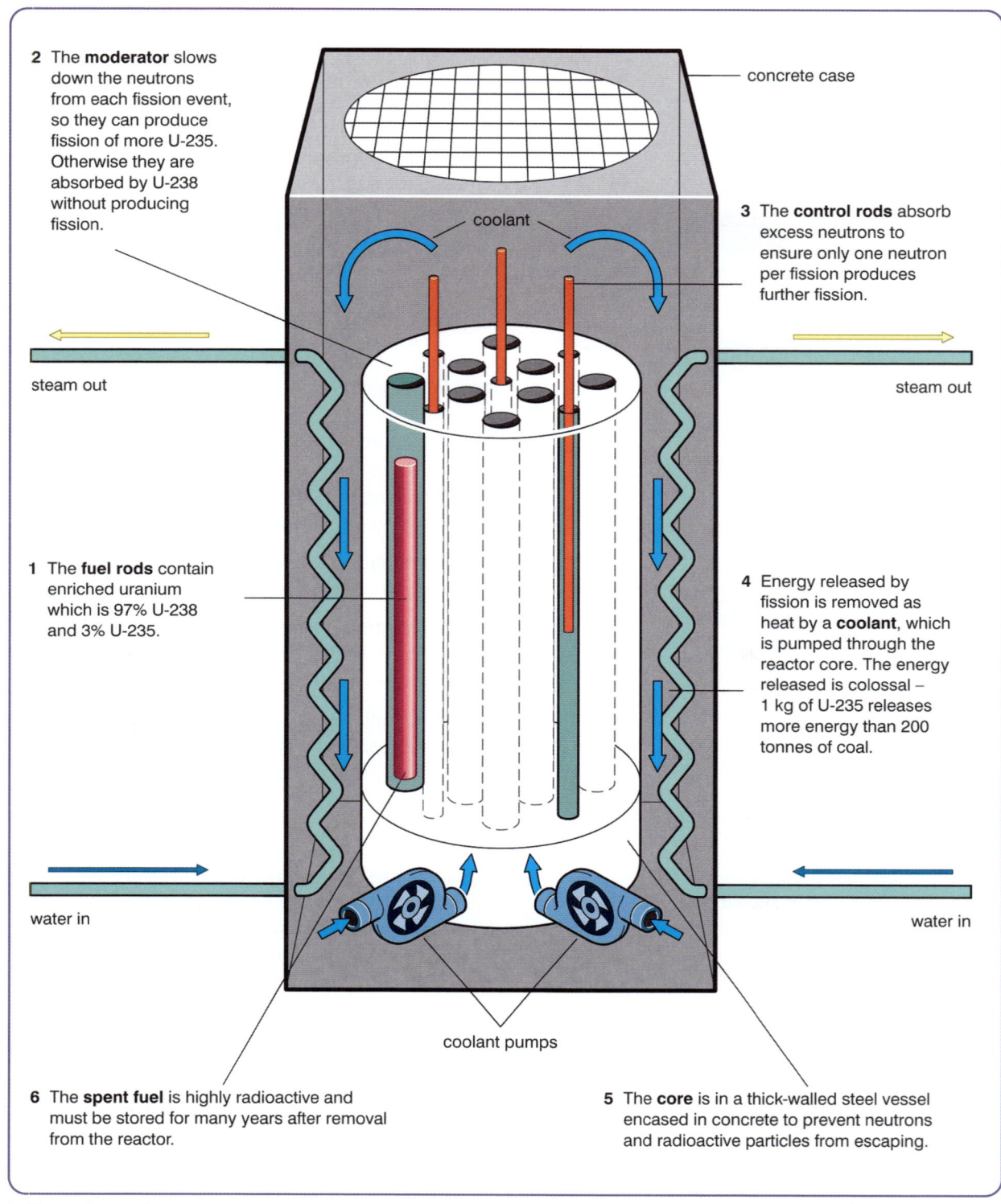

2 The **moderator** slows down the neutrons from each fission event, so they can produce fission of more U-235. Otherwise they are absorbed by U-238 without producing fission.

concrete case

coolant

3 The **control rods** absorb excess neutrons to ensure only one neutron per fission produces further fission.

steam out

steam out

1 The **fuel rods** contain enriched uranium which is 97% U-238 and 3% U-235.

4 Energy released by fission is removed as heat by a **coolant**, which is pumped through the reactor core. The energy released is colossal – 1 kg of U-235 releases more energy than 200 tonnes of coal.

water in

water in

coolant pumps

6 The **spent fuel** is highly radioactive and must be stored for many years after removal from the reactor.

5 The **core** is in a thick-walled steel vessel encased in concrete to prevent neutrons and radioactive particles from escaping.

Inside a nuclear reactor

Radioactivity

ROUND UP

How much have you improved?
Work out your improvement index on pages 153–4.

1. Natural uranium consists of about 99% $^{238}_{92}$U and about 1% $^{235}_{92}$U.
   a) How many protons and how many neutrons are present in each type of atom? [4]
   b) What is the name for different types of atoms of the same element? [1]
   c) $^{238}_{92}$U has a half-life of about 4500 million years. Explain what is meant by *half-life*. [1]

2. One type of smoke detector uses an alpha particle source, as shown.

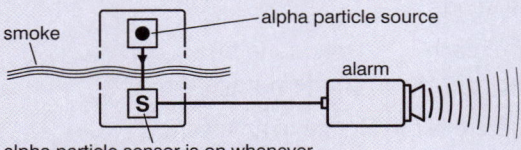

   a) Why is an alpha source used rather than a beta or a gamma source? [2]
   b) Why is it important for the alpha source to have a half-life of more than 5 years? [1]

3. a) $^{220}_{82}$Rn emits alpha particles to form an isotope of the element polonium (Po). Write down the equation for this process. [2]
   b) Radon-220 has a half-life of 52 s. A pure sample of this isotope had an initial activity of 400 disintegrations per second. What was its activity after (i) 104 s (ii) 208 s? [2]

4. The thickness of hot rolled steel plate produced in a factory was monitored using a gamma source and detector, as shown below.

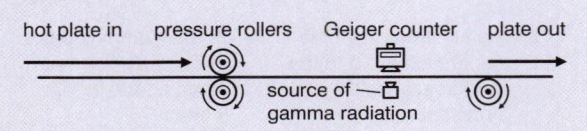

   a) Why was gamma radiation used instead of alpha or beta radiation? [3]
   b) The counter reading increased every second as shown in the table below.

Time / s	0	1	2	3	4	5	6	7	8	9	10
Counter reading	0	204	395	602	792	1004	1180	1340	1505	1660	1825

   (i) What was the average count rate over the first 5 seconds? [1]
   (ii) What was the average count rate over the last 2 seconds? [1]
   (iii) What happened to the thickness of the plate? [1]

5. a) Background radioactivity accounts for 87% of the exposure to ionising radiations of the average person in Britain. Explain what is meant by
   (i) background radioactivity [1]
   (ii) ionising radiation. [1]
   b) State two further sources of ionising radiation. [2]
   c) Explain how you would use a Geiger counter and a stopwatch to measure background radioactivity. [2]

6. In a test to identify the type of radioactivity produced by a radioactive source, the following results were obtained with different sheets of materials placed between the source and the Geiger tube.

material	count rate / counts per second
none	450
tin foil	235
1 mm aluminium	230
10 mm aluminium	228
10 mm lead	160

Use these results to decide what types of radiation are emitted by the source. Explain your answer. [4]

7. a) Why is it essential to use long-handled tongs to move a radioactive source? [1]
   b) Cobalt-60 is a radioactive isotope that emits gamma radiation. It is used in hospitals to treat cancer.
   (i) What is gamma radiation and why is it necessary to use gamma radiation for this purpose? [2]
   (ii) With the aid of a diagram, explain how the gamma radiation is concentrated on the tumour. [3]

Chapter 17 More about the atom

17.1 Electrons

PREVIEW

At the end of this topic you will be able to:
- describe how a beam of electrons is produced and how it can be deflected
- explain how an X-ray tube works
- describe the appearance of a line spectrum and a continuous spectrum of light
- explain in simple terms how a line spectrum is produced.

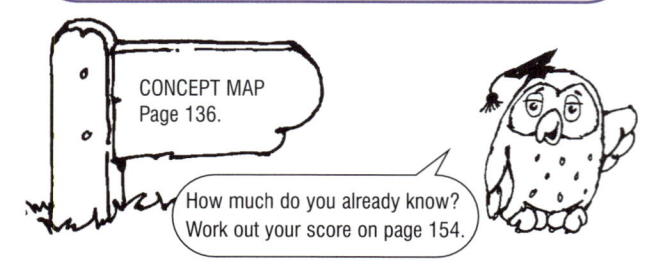

CONCEPT MAP Page 136.

How much do you already know? Work out your score on page 154.

Test yourself

1. **a)** What type of charge is carried by an electron?
   b) In an electron tube, electrons are emitted from a wire filament and attracted towards the anode.
      (i) What is done to the filament to make it emit electrons?
      (ii) What is done to the anode to make it attract electrons? [3]

2. The diagram shows a beam of electrons passing through the space between two parallel metal plates P and Q.

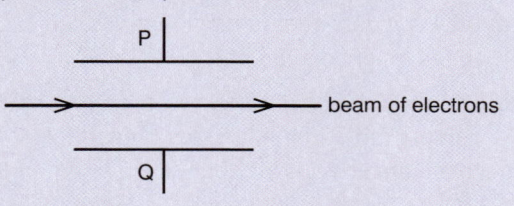

   a) Sketch the path of the beam if plate P is made positive and plate Q is made negative. Label the path **a**.
   b) Sketch the path of the beam if the speed of the electrons is increased by increasing the anode voltage, keeping the voltage between P and Q the same as in **a**. Label the path **b**. [2]

3. In an X-ray tube, electrons from a filament wire are attracted onto a metal anode which is positive relative to the filament wire.
   a) Whereabouts in the tube are the X-rays produced?
   b) How is the X-ray beam affected by increasing the anode voltage? [4]

4. Describe the appearance of a continuous spectrum of light. [2]

Electron beams – the electron gun

The electron gun is used to produce a beam of electrons in a vacuum tube. The kinetic energy gained by each electron is equal to the work done on the electron when it moves from the filament to the anode.

KE of each electron = work done by anode voltage V = eV

where e is the charge of an electron.

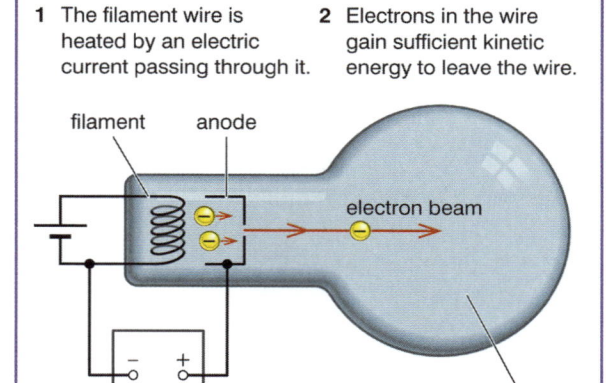

1. The filament wire is heated by an electric current passing through it.
2. Electrons in the wire gain sufficient kinetic energy to leave the wire.
3. The electrons from the wire are attracted to the anode because the anode is positive relative to the wire.
4. Some electrons pass through a small hole in the anode to form a beam.

The electron gun

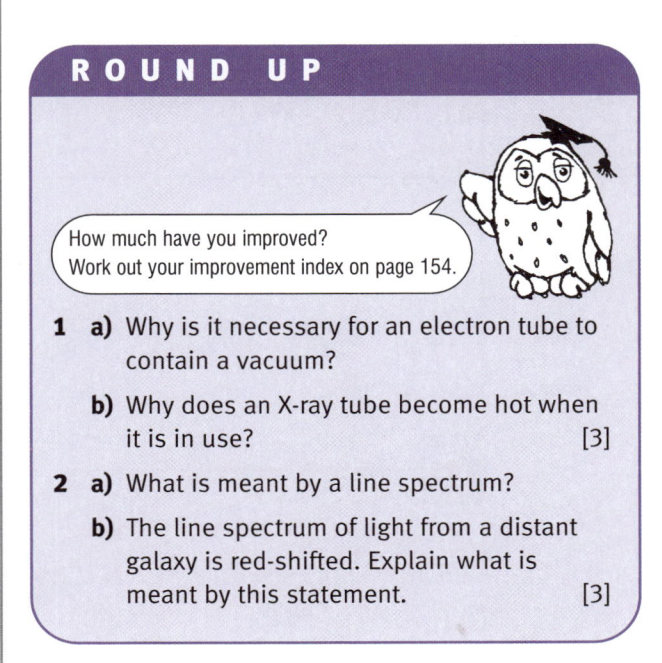

More about the atom

Deflection of electron beams

Using a pair of deflecting plates: the beam of electrons is directed between two oppositely charged parallel metal plates (Y_1 and Y_2 in the diagram). The beam is attracted towards the positive plate. Its path is an arc. If the beam speed is increased by increasing the anode voltage, the beam deflects less. This system is used in an oscilloscope.

Using deflecting coils: the beam of electrons is directed between two current-carrying coils. The beam is deflected by the magnetic field of the coils. This system is used to deflect an electron beam in a television tube.

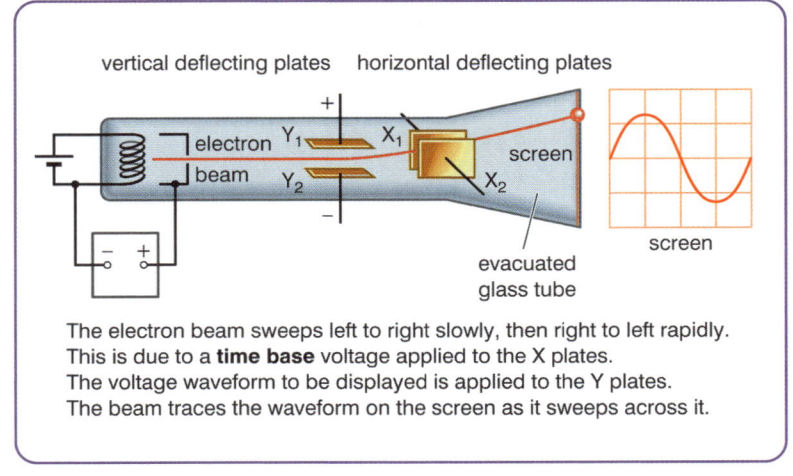

The electron beam sweeps left to right slowly, then right to left rapidly. This is due to a **time base** voltage applied to the X plates. The voltage waveform to be displayed is applied to the Y plates. The beam traces the waveform on the screen as it sweeps across it.

An oscilloscope tube

The X-ray tube

In an X-ray tube, electrons in a beam are attracted through a high voltage onto a metal anode. On impact, the kinetic energy of the electrons is converted into X-radiation and heat.

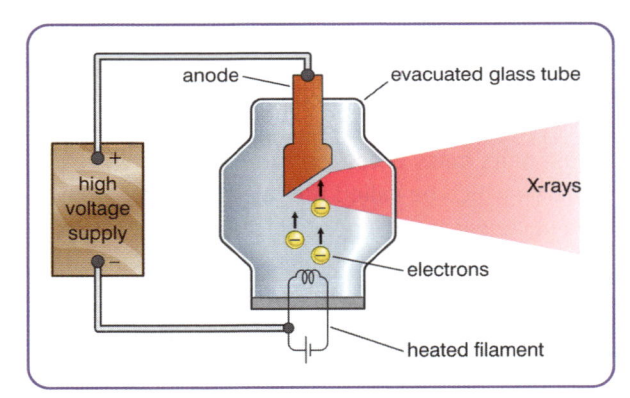

The X-ray tube

Optical spectra

Electrons in an atom are arranged in **shells**, each at a fixed energy level and able to hold a certain number of electrons. When an electron transfers to an inner shell from an outer shell, it releases energy as a **photon** of electromagnetic radiation.

The wavelength of a photon depends on its energy. Since the colour of light depends on its wavelength, the spectrum of light from an atom contains certain colours only. This is called a **line spectrum**. In comparison, the spectrum of light from a hot wire filament is **continuous**. This is because some electrons in a metal are not trapped in shells and can move about freely inside the metal.

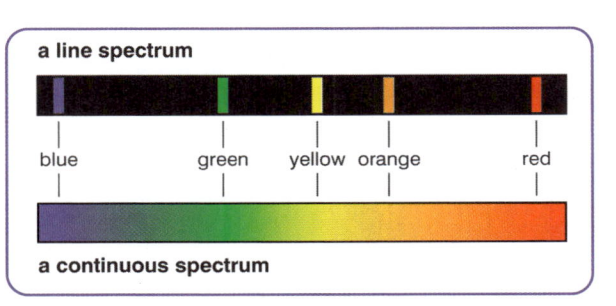

Optical spectra

ROUND UP

How much have you improved? Work out your improvement index on page 154.

1. a) Why is it necessary for an electron tube to contain a vacuum?

   b) Why does an X-ray tube become hot when it is in use? [3]

2. a) What is meant by a line spectrum?

   b) The line spectrum of light from a distant galaxy is red-shifted. Explain what is meant by this statement. [3]

More about the atom

17.2 More about the nucleus

PREVIEW

At the end of this topic you will be able to:
- describe the evidence for the nuclear model of the atom
- calculate the number of protons and neutrons in a nucleus, given the mass number and the atomic number of the nucleus
- describe how unstable nuclei become stable
- describe the quark model of the neutron and the proton.

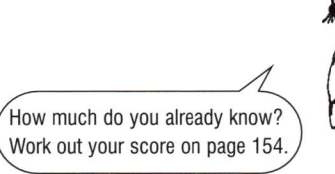

How much do you already know? Work out your score on page 154.

Test yourself

1. a) Calculate the atomic mass and the atomic number of an atom with 6 protons and 8 neutrons.
   b) Calculate the number of protons and the number of neutrons present in an atom of the isotope $^{224}_{88}$Ra. [4]

2. a) Why do most alpha particles directed at a thin metal foil pass straight through the foil?
   b) Why are alpha particles travelling straight towards a nucleus repelled by the nucleus? [3]

3. a) The isotope $^{16}_{8}$O is stable. The isotope $^{17}_{8}$O is unstable. How does this isotope become stable?
   b) The neutron-to-proton ratio for light nuclei is 1. What is this ratio for very heavy nuclei? [3]

4. a) The isotope in **1b** can be fissioned by a neutron. What is fission?
   b) Why are the fuel rods of a nuclear reactor much more radioactive after removal from a nuclear reactor than before being placed in the reactor? [7]

5. a) How many quarks are present in a neutron or a proton?
   b) State the quark content of a proton. [2]

Probing the nucleus

Lord Rutherford showed that most of the atom is empty space. He proved that:
- most of its mass is concentrated in a tiny volume which he called the nucleus of the atom
- the nucleus carries a positive charge equal to Ze, where Z is the atomic number of the element and e is the magnitude of the charge of the electron.

He arrived at these conclusions by measuring the scattering of alpha particles by thin metal foils, as shown in the diagram below.

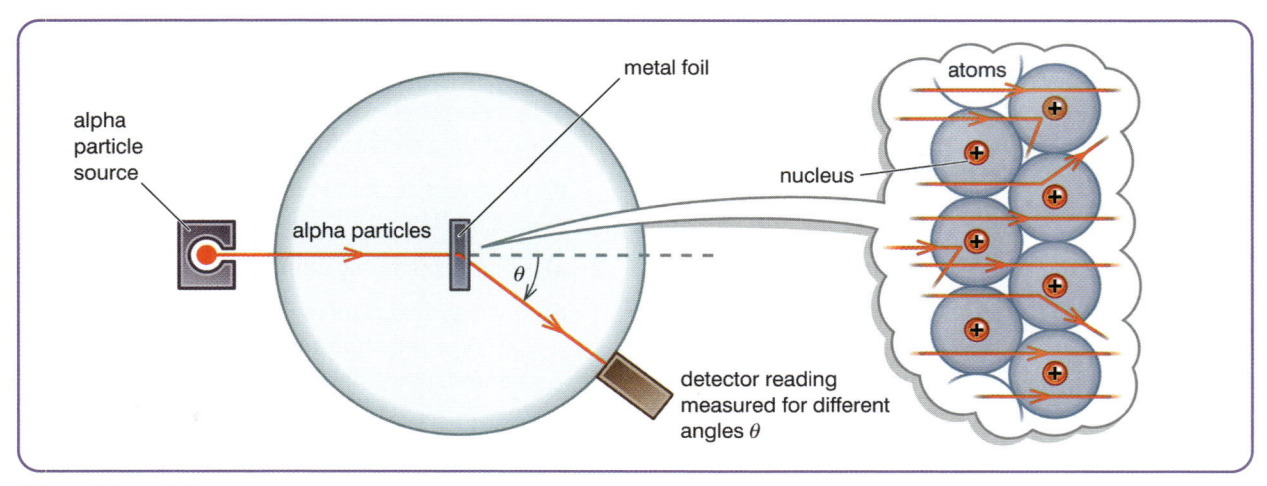

Alpha particle scattering

More about the atom

The measurements showed that:
- most of the alpha particles were undeflected
- the proportion of alpha particles scattered decreased as the angle θ was increased
- about one in 10 000 of the incident alpha particles was deflected by more than 90°
- some of the alpha particles bounced off the foil back towards the source.

Rutherford realised from these results that the atom must be mostly empty space with most of its mass concentrated in a tiny volume he referred to as the nucleus. He assumed the nucleus to be positively charged, repelling alpha particles because they carry positive charge too. Based on this model, he then worked out the expected proportion of alpha particles deflected at each position. His experimental results agreed exactly with his predictions, demonstrating his nuclear model of the atom conclusively.

Stable and unstable nuclei

There must be a very strong attractive force between the neutrons and protons in a stable nucleus, otherwise they would fly apart because of the electrostatic repulsion of the protons. The force holding the protons and neutrons together in a nucleus is called the **strong nuclear force**. Unstable nuclei disintegrate, because this force is not strong enough to prevent the particles in the nucleus flying apart.

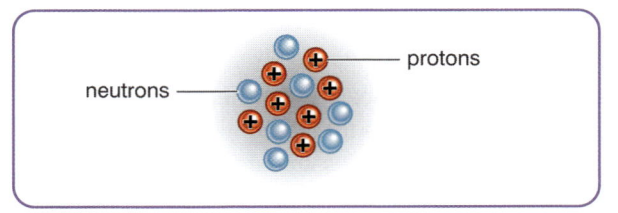

The strong nuclear force

Every known type of nucleus can be plotted on a graph of neutron number N on the y-axis against proton number Z on the x-axis, as shown. All the isotopes of an element appear on this graph at the same horizontal position (same Z) and at different vertical positions, corresponding to different neutron numbers.

The N–Z plot

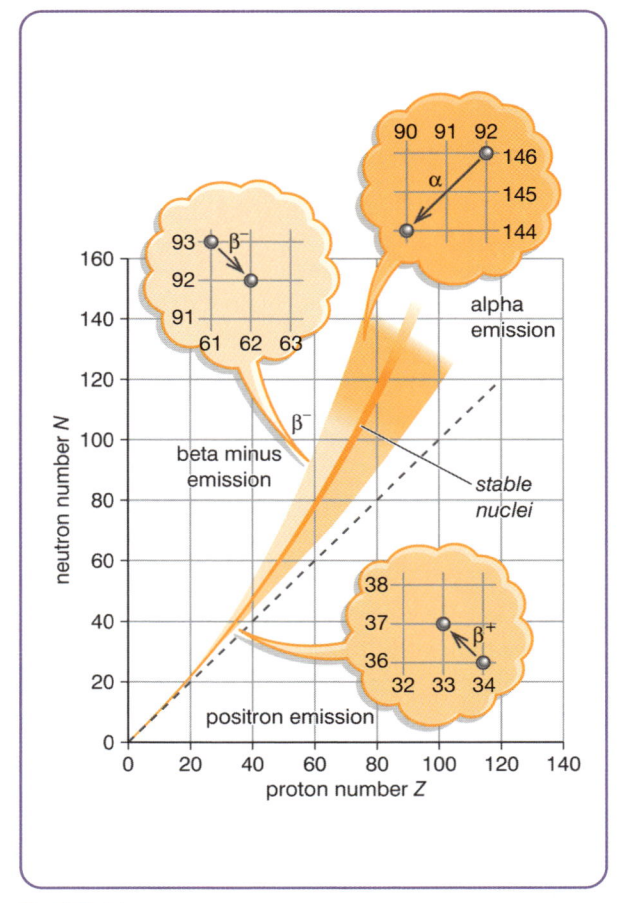

The N–Z plot

Stable nuclei form a well defined line on the N–Z plot. This line is straight from $Z = 0$ to about $Z = 20$, and then it curves up towards increasing N. This means that:
- stable nuclei up to about $Z = 20$ have equal numbers of neutrons and protons in their nuclei
- stable nuclei beyond $Z = 20$ have more neutrons than protons. For the largest stable nuclei, the number of neutrons N is approximately equal to $1.5 Z$.

More about the atom

When an **alpha particle** is emitted, the nucleus formed has two fewer protons and two fewer neutrons than the original nucleus. This change is shown on the N–Z plot and is represented by the equation below.

$$^A_Z X \rightarrow {}^4_2 \alpha + {}^{A-4}_{Z-2} Y$$

A **β⁻ particle** is emitted by a nucleus that has too many neutrons to be stable. Such a nucleus becomes stable by changing one of its neutrons into a proton. A β⁻ particle is created in the nucleus and emitted at the instant of change.

The change is shown on the N–Z plot and is represented by the equation below.

$$^A_Z X \rightarrow {}^0_{-1} \beta + {}^A_{Z+1} Y$$

Neutron-rich nuclei are above the stability line on the N–Z plot, so β⁻ emission moves such a nucleus down towards the stability belt from above.

A **β⁺ particle**, also called a **positron**, is the antiparticle of the electron. Proton-rich nuclei have too many protons to be stable. Such a nucleus becomes stable by changing one of its protons into a neutron. A β⁺ particle is created in the nucleus and emitted at the instant of change. This change is shown on the N–Z plot and is represented by the equation below.

$$^A_Z X \rightarrow {}^0_{+1} \beta + {}^A_{Z-1} Y$$

Since proton-rich nuclei are below the stability line on the N–Z plot, positron emission moves such a nucleus up towards the stability belt from below.

Antiparticles

There is an **antiparticle** for every particle. A particle and its antiparticle **annihilate** each other and turn into radiation when they meet. The positron was discovered in 1932 as a result of observing cosmic ray tracks in a cloud chamber. Now we know that positrons are produced by unstable nuclei that have too many protons.

The PET scanner

Antimatter in the form of positrons is used in medicine to scan the brain. Before the scan is carried out, the patient is given a drink of water containing a tiny amount of a positron-emitting isotope. Each positron travels no more than about a millimetre before it is annihilated by an electron, causing the emission of two bursts of gamma radiation travelling in opposite directions. A ring of detectors connected to a computer registers a positron emission when opposite detectors respond at the same time. The computer is programmed to map out the location of the positron-emitting isotope in the body to give a three-dimensional image of the brain.

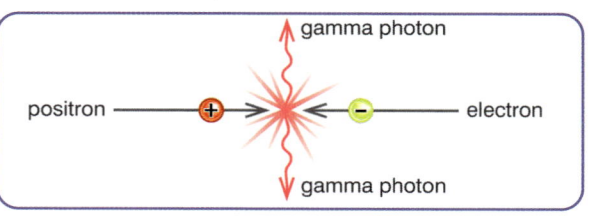

Annihilation

Quarks

The **Stanford Linear Accelerator** (SLAC) was built to accelerate electrons through 20 000 million volts almost to the speed of light, and make them collide with nuclei in a solid target. The resulting measurements proved that there are three tiny 'hard' particles inside each proton or neutron. These particles inside a neutron or proton are called **quarks**.

The measurements showed that there are two types of quark, referred to as the **up** quark and the **down** quark. An up quark carries a charge of $+\frac{2}{3}e$ and a down quark carries a charge of $-\frac{1}{3}e$, where e is the magnitude of the charge carried by an electron.

★ A proton consists of two up quarks and a down quark (uud).

★ A neutron consists of one up quark and two down quarks (udd).

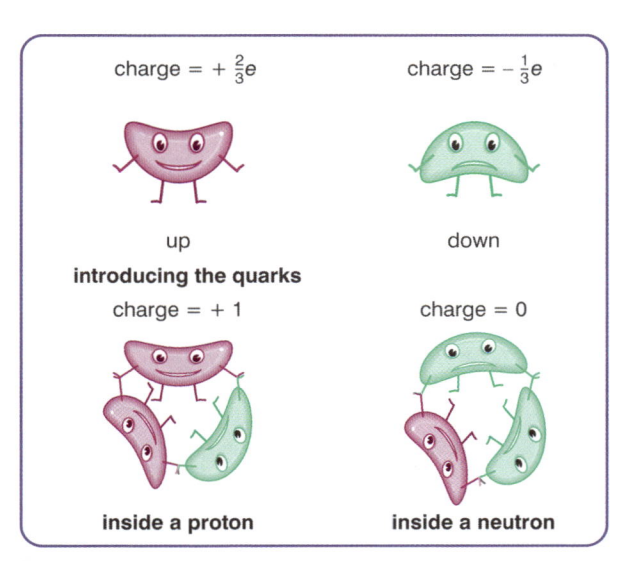

More about the atom

charge = $+\frac{2}{3}e$ charge = $-\frac{1}{3}e$

up   down

introducing the quarks

charge = $+1$ charge = 0

inside a proton   inside a neutron

The quarks

Back to beta decay

As you saw on page 134, a neutron-rich nucleus becomes stable when one of its neutrons changes into a proton. This happens because a down quark in a neutron suddenly changes into an up quark. A β^- particle is created in this change to conserve the total charge. The β^- particle is instantly emitted from the nucleus.

β^- emission β^+ emission

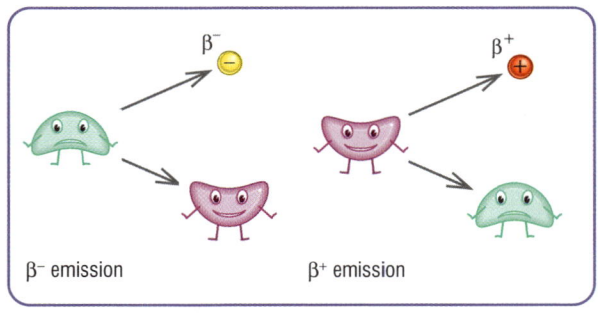

β decay

A proton-rich nucleus becomes stable when one of its protons changes into a neutron. This happens because an up quark in a proton suddenly changes into a down quark. A β^+ particle is created in this change to conserve the total charge. The β^+ particle is instantly emitted from the nucleus.

ROUND UP

How much have you improved? Work out your improvement index on page 154.

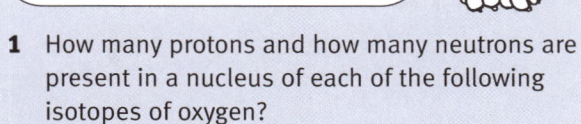

1. How many protons and how many neutrons are present in a nucleus of each of the following isotopes of oxygen?

   a) $^{14}_{8}O$ b) $^{16}_{8}O$ c) $^{19}_{8}O$ [3]

2. a) Which one of the isotopes in question **1** is stable?

   b) The other two isotopes are unstable. What type of radiation would you expect from each of these unstable isotopes?   [3]

3. How many up quarks and how many down quarks are present in

   a) the nucleus of a hydrogen atom?

   b) an alpha particle?   [3]

4. The cobalt isotope $^{60}_{27}Co$ emits β^- radiation.

   a) How many protons and how many neutrons are in the nucleus of an atom of this isotope?

   b) How many protons and how many neutrons are present in the nucleus after a β^- particle has been emitted?

   c) Use the quark model to describe this change.   [6]

Well done if you've improved. Don't worry if you haven't. Take a break and try again.

More about the atom

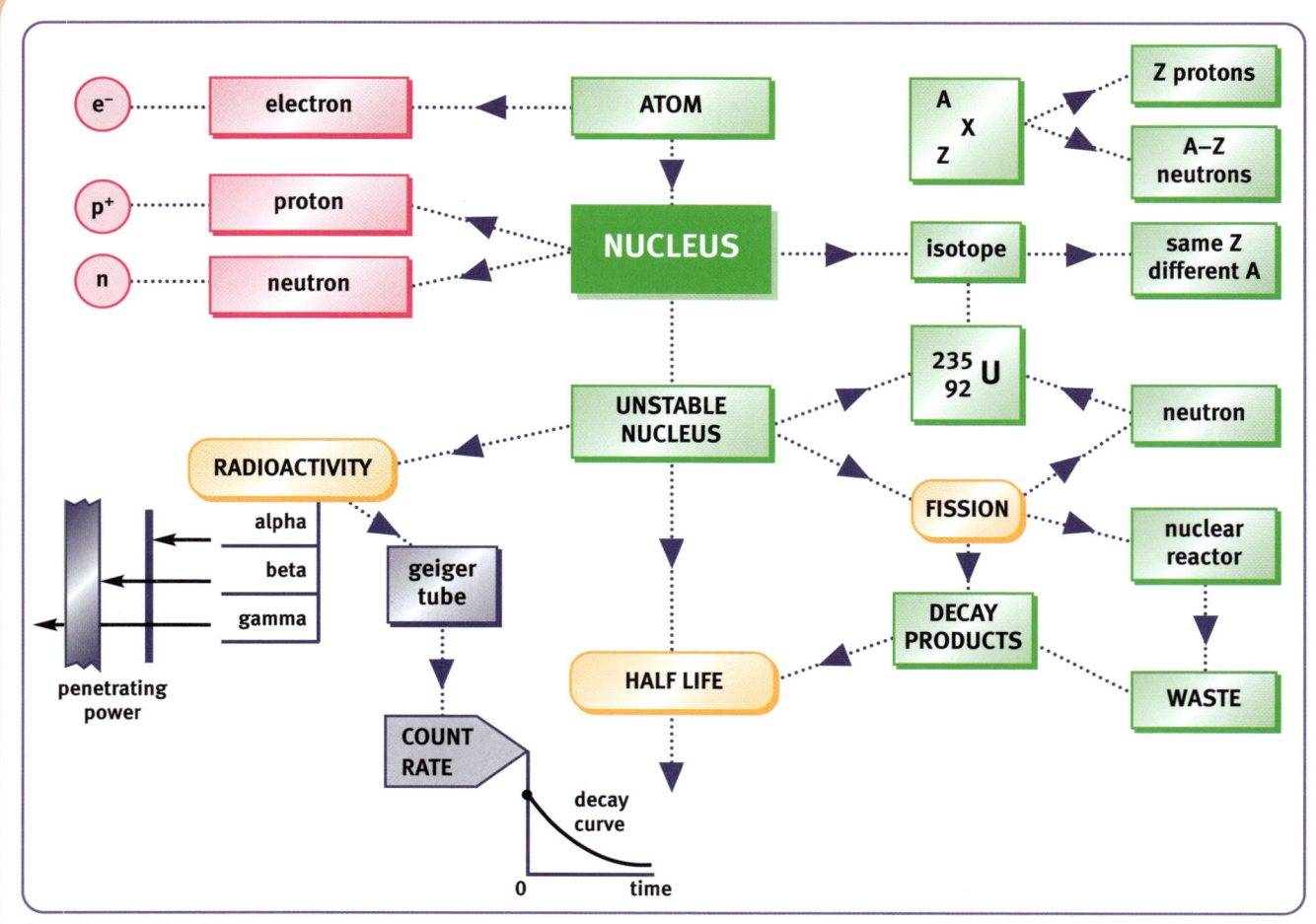

Concept map: radioactivity

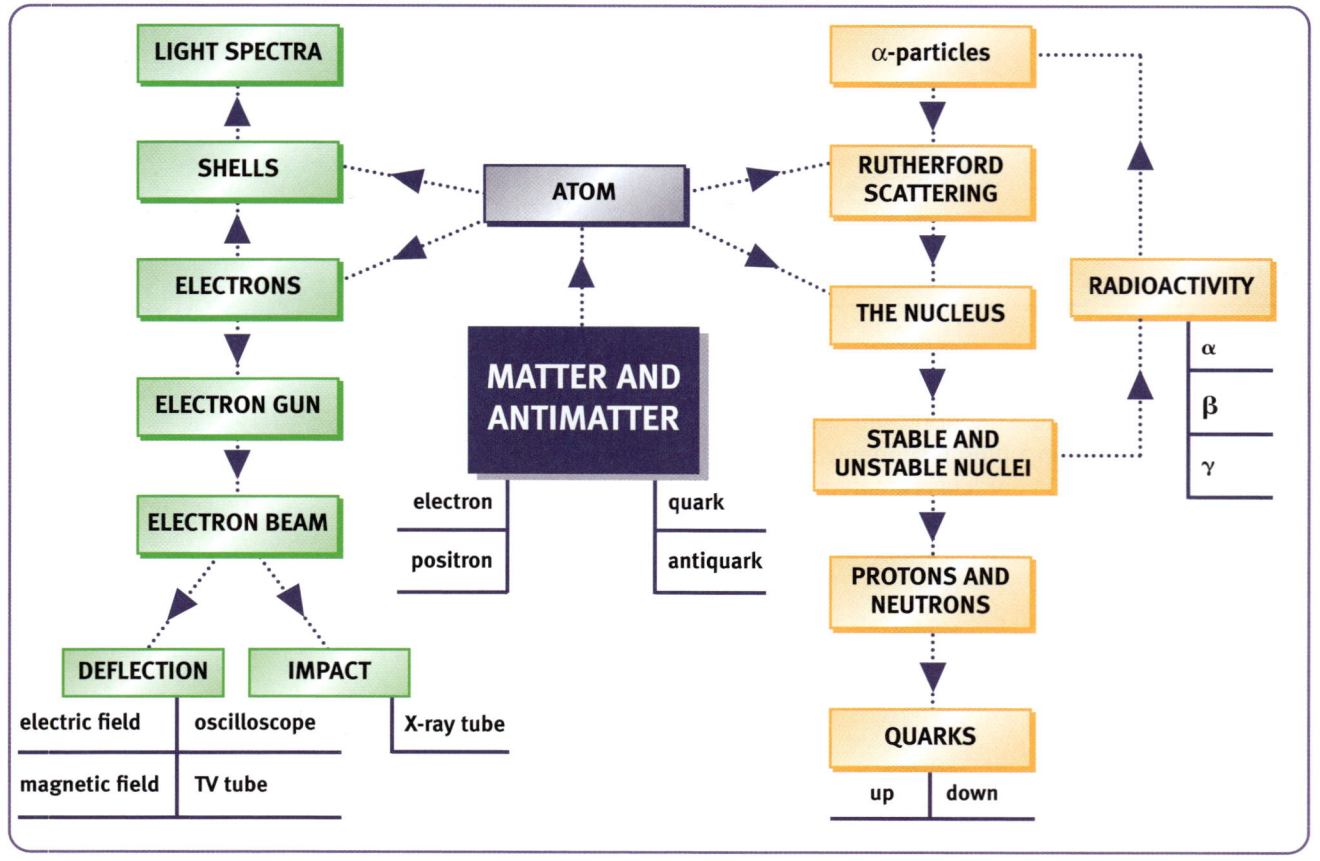

Concept map: more about the atom

Answers

1 Test yourself (page 2)
Beyond the Earth

1. VMJUN (✓ for each correct answer)
2. The mass of the planet (✓). The distance from the Sun to the planet (✓).
3. As it orbits the Sun, its distance from Earth changes (✓) and the amount of its sunlit surface we see changes (✓).
4. The stars we see each night are in the opposite direction to the Sun (✓). As the Earth moves round the Sun, the stars we see at night change during the year (✓).
5. a) Mars (✓) b) Jupiter (✓)
6. a) speeding up (✓) b) moving towards the Sun (✓)
7. nuclear fusion (✓)
8. A massive star exploding at the end of its life (✓) releasing an enormous amount of energy in a short time (✓).
9. The light spectrum from the star is shifted towards the red end of the spectrum (✓) due to the star receding (✓).
10. Distant galaxies are moving away from us (✓) at speeds in proportion to their distances away (✓).

Your score: ☐ out of 22

1 Round up (page 9)
Beyond the Earth

1. a) The force of gravity on each planet due to the Sun acts towards the Sun (✓). This force stops each planet leaving the Solar System (✓).
   b) In both cases, a body with relatively small mass orbits a body with much more mass (✓)
2. The Earth spins eastwards (✓), so the constellations appear to move across the sky westwards (✓).
3. a) planets reflect sunlight (✓)
   b) Sketch A is when Venus is in position 2, nearer Earth (✓). Its disc appears larger and crescent shaped (✓).
4. Moon (✓), Sun (✓), Pole star (✓), Andromeda galaxy (✓)
5. a) Jupiter shown in the opposite direction to the Sun (Sun Earth Jupiter) (✓).
   b) (i) Mars is smaller, further from the Sun, has two moons and has no oxygen in its atmosphere (✓✓✓✓).
      (ii) Jupiter is larger, not solid, further from the Sun than Earth, and spins faster (✓✓✓✓).
      (iii) Saturn is larger, not solid, further from the Sun than Earth, and has a ring system (✓✓✓✓).
6. a) It is close to the Sun (✓) and can therefore only be seen just before sunrise (✓) or just after sunset (✓).
   b) Neptune's orbit is circular (✓) whereas Pluto's orbit is elliptical and partly inside Neptune's orbit (✓).
   c) Neptune (✓)
   d) They become cold and dark when they move away from the Sun (✓), so cannot be seen (✓) until the Sun's gravity pulls them round back near the Sun (✓).
7. a) It is red (✓) and much larger than the Sun (✓).
   b) The Sun will become a red giant (✓) and then collapse to become a white dwarf (✓) before radiating all its energy (✓) and becoming invisible (✓).
   c) A massive star which explodes after the white dwarf stage (✓) because its internal pressure is too great (✓).
8. a) They must acquire sufficient speed to overcome gravity (✓) to gain orbital height (✓) then go into orbit (✓).
   b) Its mass (✓) and density are smaller (✓).
9. See page 8 (✓✓✓✓).
10. a) The Universe originated in a massive explosion (✓) and has been expanding ever since (✓).
    b) The Universe will continue to expand (✓) at a rate which might decrease or increase (✓).
    c) Four points from: Earth-like planets probably orbit other stars (✓); life might exist or have existed in primitive form (e.g. microbes) on other planets (✓); a meteorite thought to be from Mars contains evidence of microbes on Mars long ago (✓); radio telescopes have not detected communications signals from other planets or stars (✓); intelligent life on a planet may be short-lived in terms of the age of the planet (✓).

Your score: ☐ out of 60

Your improvement index: $\dfrac{\Box/60}{\Box/22} \times 100\% = \Box\,\%$

2 Test yourself (page 11)
Energy resources and energy transfer

1. B (✓)
2. weight – the newton (✓), power – the watt (✓)
3. 1200 J (✓)
4. a) KE = 6 J (✓), PE = 2 J (✓)
   b) KE = 8 J (✓), PE = 0 (✓)
5. 10 (✓) (= 4 + 6 (✓))
6. PE loss = 2000 J (✓), KE gain = 250 J (✓), therefore required ratio = 8 (✓)

Answers

7 Metals contain electrons which move about freely inside the metal (✓). When the metal is heated, the electrons at the point of heating gain kinetic energy (✓) which they transfer to other parts of the metal (✓).

8 **a** and **b** (✓✓)

9 **c** only (✓)

10 **b)** heat due to friction (✓)   **c)** electrical energy (✓)
   d) sound (✓)   **e)** light (✓)   **f)** heat due to electrical resistance (✓)

Your score: ☐ out of 24

2 Round up (page 18)
Energy resources and energy transfer

1 **a)** chemical energy in the battery → electrical energy → sound energy (✓)
  b) gravitational potential energy → kinetic energy (✓) + work done against air resistance (✓)

2 **a) (i)** 800 J (✓)   **(ii)** 40 J/s (✓)   **b)** 0.2 (= 20%) (✓)

3 **a)** 2750 J (✓)   **b)** 5.0 m (✓)

4 **a)** 80 MJ (✓)   **b)** 1.6 MW (✓)

5 **a)** 6.75 kWh (✓)   **b)** 40.5p (✓)

6 **a)** 22.5 kJ (✓)   **b) (i)** 16.8 kJ (✓)   **(ii)** 26 W (✓)

7 **a)** China is a better thermal insulator but shiny metal radiates less (✓). The china teapot is likely to be better unless it has very thin walls (✓).
  b) There is a larger open surface in the wide-brimmed cup so there is more evaporation (✓) and thermal radiation (✓) from the wide-brimmed cup. Hence the tea in it loses thermal energy faster and it cools more quickly (✓).
  c) A double-glazed unit traps a layer of still air between its two panes (✓). This is a good thermal insulator (✓).
  d) (i) Condensation occurs where moist air meets a cold surface (✓). A classroom full of people will be full of moist air and in winter, the windows will be cold enough to cause condensation (✓).
  (ii) The inner glass pane is warmer than the outer pane (✓) so the moist air does not come into contact with a cold surface (✓).

Your score: ☐ out of 26

Your improvement index: $\dfrac{\boxed{}/26}{\boxed{}/24} \times 100\% = \boxed{}\%$

3.1 Test yourself (page 20)
Density

1

Mass	1000 g	30.6 kg (✓)	60 g	55 kg	5.4 kg (✓)
Volume	120 cm³	25.5 m³	54.5 cm³ (✓)	0.022 m³ (✓)	0.0020 m³
Density	8.3 g/cm³ (✓)	1.2 kg/m³	1.1 g/cm³	2500 kg/m³	2700 kg/m³

2 **a) (i)** 83 g (✓)   **(ii)** 0.083 kg (✓)
  b) (i) 8.3×10^{-5} m³ (✓)   **(ii)** 83 cm³ (✓)

3 **a)** 1.5×10^{-3} m³ (✓)   **b)** 2.86 kg (✓)   **c)** 1910 kg/m³ (✓)

4 **a)** 35 m³ (✓)   **b)** 42 kg (✓)

Your score: ☐ out of 14

3.1 Round up (page 21)
Density

1 **a) (i)** 5.4×10^6 mm³ (✓)   **(ii)** 5400 cm³ (✓)   **(iii)** 5.4×10^{-3} m³ (✓)
  b) 13.5 kg (✓)

2 **a)** volume = $\pi(0.55 \times 10^{-3})^2 \times 1.5/4 = 3.6 \times 10^{-7}$ m³ (✓)
  b) (i) 2.8×10^{-3} kg (✓)   **(ii)** 2.8 g (✓)
  c) 0.53 m (✓)

3 **a)** volume of patch = volume of droplet = 0.1 mm³ (✓) = $\pi(350/2)^2\, t$ (where t = thickness) (✓), therefore $t = 0.1/(\pi(350/2)^2) = 1.0 \times 10^{-6}$ mm (✓)
  b) $t = 1.0 \times 10^{-9}$ m (✓)

4 **a)** Assume you are a uniform cylinder of length equal to your height and of radius equal to your waistline divided by 2π (✓) (e.g. height = 1.6 m, waistline = 0.60 m; volume = $\pi(0.60/2\pi)^2 \times 1.6 = 0.046$ m³ (✓))
  b) Estimate your density using density = mass/volume (✓); result not too different from water (✓). Claim is reasonable.

Your score: ☐ out of 16

Your improvement index: $\dfrac{\boxed{}/16}{\boxed{}/14} \times 100\% = \boxed{}\%$

3.2 Test yourself (page 22)
Specific heat capacity and specific latent heat

1 **a)** 7.4×10^5 J (✓)   **b)** 2.3×10^4 J (✓)   **c)** 9000 J (✓)
  d) 21 000 J (✓)

2 The mass of water is much greater than the mass of concrete (✓). Therefore, supplying a certain amount of energy to the concrete would raise its temperature far more (✓) than supplying the same amount of energy to the water (✓).

Answers

3. **a)** 11 kJ for the aluminium (✓); 403 kJ for the water (✓); 414 kJ in total (✓)
   b) 170 kJ for the copper (✓); 12770 kJ for the water (✓); 12940 kJ in total (✓)
4. **a)** 60 kJ for the steel (✓); 270 kJ for the water (✓); 330 kJ in total (✓) **b)** 330 000 J/2500 W (✓) = 130 s (✓)
5. energy needed = 340 × 100 = 34 000 J (✓); time taken = 34 000/40 = 850 s (✓)
6. energy needed = 2.3 × 0.5 = 1.15 MJ (✓); time taken = $1.15 \times 10^6/3000$ = 380 s (✓)

Your score: ☐ out of 22

3.2 Round up (page 24)
Specific heat capacity and latent heat

1. **a)** Water in wet clothing turns to vapour (✓). Latent heat is needed for this process. This energy is supplied by the body (✓).
   b) The liquid gains energy from the skin (✓) which it uses to become vapour (✓). The skin loses energy and becomes cooler (✓).
2. energy to melt the ice = 2.5 × 340 000 = 850 kJ (✓); energy to heat water = 2.5 × 4200 × 20 = 210 kJ (✓); total energy needed = 1060 kJ (✓)
3. **a)** 1.2 kg (✓) **b)** $2.3 \times 10^6 \times 1.2$ = 2.76 MJ (✓)
   c) $2.76 \times 10^6/3000$ (✓) = 920 s (✓)
4. **a)** 20 × 300 = 6000 g (✓)
   b) 6 × 4200 × (42 − 15) = 680 kJ (✓)
   c) 680 000/300 (✓) = 2270 W (✓)
5. **a)** energy needed to heat the water to boiling point = 1 × 4200 × (100 − 20) = 336 000 J = 0.34 MJ (✓); energy needed to vaporise the water = 2.3 × 1 = 2.3 MJ (✓); total energy needed = 2.3 + 0.3(4) = 2.6 MJ (✓)
   b) 1000/2.6 (✓) = 380 kg/s (✓)

Your score: ☐ out of 21

Your improvement index: $\frac{\square/21}{\square/22} \times 100\% = \square\%$

3.3 Test yourself (page 25)
The gas laws

1. **a)** 373 K (✓) **b)** −196 °C (✓)
2. **a)** See page 25 (✓✓).
   b) $p_2 = \frac{p_1 V_1 T_2}{V_2 T_1}$ (✓) = $\frac{120 \times 5 \times 250}{4 \times 300}$ (✓) = 125 kPa (✓)

3.
mass / g	10	10	10	10	10
volume / m³	0.01	0.02	0.02	0.03 (✓)	0.02
pressure / kPa	100	50 (✓)	100	50	60
temperature / K	300	300	600 (✓)	450	360 (✓)

4. **a)** 290 K (✓)
   b) $V_2 = \frac{p_1 V_1 T_2}{p_2 T_1}$ (✓) = $\frac{110 \times 60 \times 273}{100 \times 290}$ (✓) = 62 cm³ (✓)
5. The gas molecules move faster at a higher temperature (✓) so they hit the sides of the container harder (✓) and more often (✓) (which causes a greater pressure).

Your score: ☐ out of 18

3.3 Round up (page 27)
The gas laws

1. **a)** $V_2 = \frac{p_1 V_1 T_2}{p_2 T_1}$ (✓) = $\frac{105 \times 1.20 \times 10^{-4} \times 273}{101 \times 294}$ (✓)
   = 1.16×10^{-4} m³ (✓)
   b) $p_2 = \frac{p_1 V_1 T_2}{V_2 T_1}$ (✓) = $\frac{105 \times 1.20 \times 10^{-4} \times 373}{1.20 \times 10^{-4} \times 294}$ (✓)
   = 133 kPa (✓)
2. **a)** $V_2 = \frac{p_1 V_1 T_2}{p_2 T_1}$ (✓) = $\frac{150 \times 1.50 \times 10^{-4} \times 273}{100 \times 315}$ (✓)
   = 1.95×10^{-4} m³ (✓)
   b) Mass = volume × density (✓) = 2.44×10^{-4} kg (✓)
3. **a) (i)** use pV/T = constant correctly (✓); p_2 = 164 kPa (✓)
   (ii) use pV/T = constant correctly (✓); p_2 = 205 kPa (✓)
   b) The high pressure of the air in the can could cause an explosion (✓).
4. **a)** The gas molecules hit the sides of the container more often because the volume is smaller (✓), so the rate of impacts on the sides is greater (✓) (which makes the pressure greater).
   b) Volume is increased to 0.005 m³ (✓), therefore
   $p_2 = \frac{p_1 V_1 T_2}{V_2 T_1}$ (✓) = $\frac{110 \times 0.004 \times 293}{0.005 \times 283}$ (✓) = 91 kPa (✓).

Your score: ☐ out of 22

Your improvement index: $\frac{\square/22}{\square/18} \times 100\% = \square\%$

Answers

4 Test yourself (page 29)

Waves

1. Any four from: sound waves, water waves, waves on a string, seismic waves, electromagnetic waves (radio, microwaves, infrared, visible, ultraviolet, X-rays, gamma rays) (✓✓✓✓).

2. a) Longitudinal waves vibrate along the direction in which the wave travels (✓); transverse waves vibrate at 90° to the direction in which they travel (✓).
   b) longitudinal (✓)

3. Any electromagnetic wave can pass through a vacuum (✓); any other type of wave needs a medium (✓).

4. wavelength = 40 mm (✓); amplitude = 15 mm (✓)

5. a) Frequency = $\frac{speed}{wavelength} = \frac{20\,mm/s}{40\,mm} = 0.50$ Hz (✓)
   b) 30 (✓)

6. a) −15 mm below middle (✓) b) +15 mm above middle (✓)

7. There is no hard surface to reflect them (✓). The amplitude becomes less and less as they run up the shore (✓).

8. Refraction is the change of direction (✓) due to a change of speed when waves pass across a boundary (✓).

9. a) increased (✓) b) decreased (✓)

10. a) 850 Hz (✓) b) 1.0 mm (✓)

Your score: ☐ out of 23

4 Round up (page 33)

Waves

1. a) (i) sound waves (✓)
      (ii) radio waves (✓), waves on a rope (✓)
   b) (1) Light is transverse; sound is longitudinal (✓).
      (2) Light can travel through a vacuum; sound cannot (or sound requires a medium; light does not) (✓).
      (3) Light travels faster than sound (✓).

2. (✓✓) (✓✓)

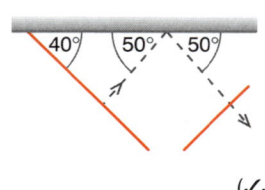

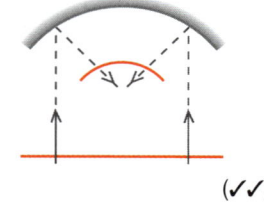

3. a) diffraction (✓) b) (i) increase (✓) (ii) decrease (✓)
   (iii) increase (✓)

4. a) Its wavelength becomes smaller (✓). Its frequency stays the same (✓).
   b) (✓✓)

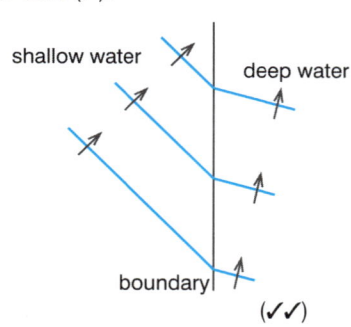

5. a) 0.50 m (✓) b) (i) 0.40 m/s (✓) (ii) 2.0 Hz (✓)

6. a) diffraction (✓)
   b) The spreading becomes less (✓).

7. a) 3.0 m (✓)
   b) The radio waves from the station are polarised (✓). As the aerial is turned, it moves more and more out of line with the plane of polarisation (✓) until it can no longer detect the signal (✓).
   c) The wire mesh reflects radio waves onto the aerial (✓).

8. a) The bow waves would form a sharper 'V' at the bow (✓).
   b) The bow waves would form a less sharp 'V' (✓).

Your score: ☐ out of 30

Your improvement index: $\frac{\Box/30}{\Box/23} \times 100\% = \Box\%$

Answers

5 Test yourself (page 34)
Sound waves and seismic waves

1. a) longitudinal (✓)
   b) Primary waves are longitudinal (✓); secondary waves are transverse (✓).
2. It produces a note at a precise frequency (✓).
3. a) (i) increases (✓) (ii) decreases (✓)
   b) The thicker string (✓) because it would produce sound at a lower pitch if it was at the same tension, and the pitch increases if the tension is increased (✓).
4. A reflected sound wave from a hard smooth surface (✓).
5. a) The amplitude increases (✓); the wavelength is unchanged (✓).
   b) The amplitude decreases (✓); the wavelength is shorter (✓).
6. diffraction (✓)
7. a) C (✓) b) B (✓)
   c) They sound deeper (✓) (because the higher frequencies are cut out).
8. a) Ultrasonic pulses are directed towards the sea bed (✓). On hitting the sea bed the pulses are reflected back to the surface (✓). Each pulse is timed from when it is emitted to when it is detected after reflection (✓). The time taken t for each pulse to reach the sea bed = $0.5 \times$ the time from when it is emitted to when it is detected (✓). The depth of the sea bed = speed of ultrasound in water $\times$ time t (✓).
   b) Two of: medical imaging; crack detection; cleaning (✓✓).
9. a) 0.17 mm (✓) b) (i) no change (✓) (ii) increases (✓)
10. a) The plates of the Earth's crust press against each other at certain parts (✓). An earthquake occurs when one of the plates gives way (✓).
    b) S waves are transverse (✓); transverse waves cannot pass through a liquid (✓); the outer core is liquid (✓).

Your score: ☐ out of 32

5 Round up (page 40)
Sound waves and seismic waves

1. a) 850 m (✓)
   b) Sound the siren briefly every 10 seconds and measure the time between each pulse being emitted and its return (✓). The timing becomes shorter if the ship is approaching the cliffs (✓).
2. a) The surface pushes and pulls the air near it back and forth (✓). The air near the speaker pushes and pulls on the air further away (✓).
   b) A small loudspeaker is lighter (✓) and so can vibrate faster (✓).
3. a) amplitude less (✓), horizontal spacing the same (✓)
   b) The waves are stretched out horizontally (✓).
4. a) 3400 Hz (✓) b) 68 mm (✓)

5. The glass panes reflect most of the sound (✓). Some sound penetrates the room because the glass panes vibrate when they reflect the sound waves (✓).
6. a) 37.5 mm (✓)
   b) (i) Without the paste, the ultrasound pulses from the probe would be almost completely reflected at the air–body boundary (✓). With the paste, the pulses from the probe travel directly into the body from the paste without passing into the air (✓).
      (ii) Reflection at each internal boundary is partial (✓); the pulses spread out as they move away from the probe (✓).
7. a) (i) B = outer core (✓), C = mantle (✓); D = crust (✓)
      (ii) B = molten (✓); A, C, D = solid (✓✓✓)
   b) They are more common where the plates of the Earth's crust meet (✓).
8. a) longitudinal (✓)
   b) (i) See page 37 (✓✓✓).
      (ii) The outer core is liquid (✓); S waves are transverse waves and therefore cannot travel through liquid (✓).
      (iii) The speed of a seismic wave increases with depth (✓). The seismic waves not moving directly towards the centre are therefore refracted away from the centre (✓).
      (iv) See page 37. S waves cannot reach the other side of the Earth from the epicentre (✓). Also, P waves cannot reach part of this zone because they refract back to the surface (✓). L waves therefore arrive without being preceded by P or S waves (✓).

Your score: ☐ out of 38

Your improvement index: $\dfrac{☐/38}{☐/32} \times 100\% = ☐\%$

6 Test yourself (page 42)
Light

1. a) The angle between the reflected ray and the normal = the angle between the incident ray and the normal (✓).
   b) 1.20 m (✓)
2. a) towards (✓) b) less than 30° (✓)
   c) The light ray is totally internally reflected (✓).
3. (i) reflection (✓) (ii) refraction (✓) (iii) reflection (✓)
4. Non-vertical light rays from any point at the bottom of the pool are refracted at the surface (✓) away from the normal (✓) and therefore appear to come from an image of the bottom of the pool nearer the surface than the bottom (✓).
5. a) decrease (✓) b) decrease (✓)
6. red, orange, yellow, green, blue, indigo, violet (✓)
7. a) red (✓)
   b) The surface absorbs all colours except blue (✓) which it reflects (✓). Therefore in red light, no light is reflected so it appears black (✓).
8. a) Reflection of a light ray incident in a transparent substance at a boundary with a less refractive substance or air (✓).

b) fibre optics used in the endoscope or in communications (✓)
c) Total internal reflection only happens if the angle of incidence is greater than the critical angle (✓) whereas reflection at a flat mirror happens at any angle of incidence (✓).

9 communications, to carry light pulses (✓); medicine, to see inside the body (✓)

10 a) more (✓)
b) The wavelength of blue light is less than that of any other colour (✓); blue light is diffracted less than any other colour when it enters the microscope (✓), therefore separate images seen in blue light can be closer together than seen in any other colour (✓).

Your score: ☐ out of 28

6 Round up (page 48)
Light

1

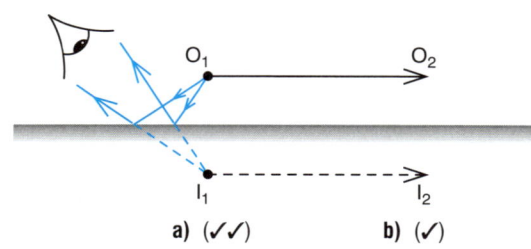

a) (✓✓)   **b)** (✓)

c) Image I_1 is directly opposite O_1 and image I_2 is directly opposite O_2 (✓). Hence distance I_1I_2 is the same as distance O_1O_2 (✓).

2 a) 2.0 m (✓)
b) The top of the mirror needs to be just above eye level (✓) to be able to see the head (✓). The bottom of the mirror needs to be opposite the midpoint between the floor and eye level (✓) to be able to see the feet (✓).
c) Two of: in a periscope; to make a corner cube reflector; to read a scale (✓✓).

3 a) See page 45 (✓✓).
b)

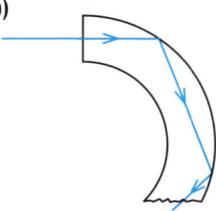

(✓✓)

c) The angle of incidence at the point of incidence becomes less than the critical angle, and so light is refracted out, not internally reflected (✓).
d) communications, to carry light pulses (✓); medicine, to see inside the body (✓)

4 (i) towards (✓)   **(ii)** away (✓)   **(iii)** away (✓)
5 (i) diffraction (✓)   **(ii)** reflection (✓)
   (iii) total internal reflection (✓)   **(iv)** refraction (✓)
6 See p 46. (✓✓) for correct refraction at each boundary (✓) for correct order of colours
7 a) less (✓)
b) diffraction causes image details to merge (✓)
less diffraction with blue light than any other colour (✓) because its wavelength is less (✓)
8 The wider the lens, the less the diffraction of light (✓), giving more detail in the image (✓).

Your score: ☐ out of 35

Your improvement index: $\dfrac{\Box/35}{\Box/28} \times 100\% = \Box\%$

7.1 Test yourself (page 50)
Waves and rays

1 a) interference (✓)   **b)** The pattern disappears (✓).
2 a) longer (✓)   **b) (i)** decrease (✓)   **(ii)** decrease (✓)
3 a) refraction (✓)   **b)** dispersion (✓)
4 a) (i) real (✓)   **(ii)** inverted (✓)   **b)** away from (✓)
c) larger (✓)

Your score: ☐ out of 11

Answers

7.1 Round up (page 52)
Waves and rays

1. a) Light from a point on the bottom of the pool refracts away from the normal on entering the air from the water (✓) as in the diagram (✓) showing the observer seeing the image nearer the surface (✓).

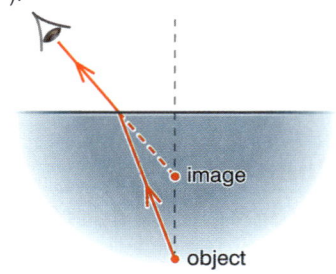

   b) White light is split into the colours of the spectrum by the camera lens (✓). The image of a white object becomes tinged with colour (✓).

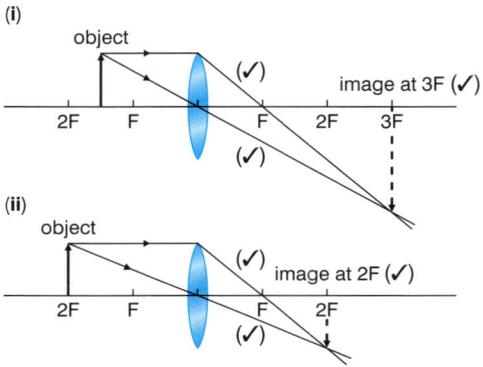

2. a) (i) object, image at 3F (✓), 2F, F, F, 2F, 3F (✓)(✓)

   (ii) object, image at 2F (✓), 2F, F, F, 2F (✓)(✓)

   b) (i) real (✓) (ii) real (✓)

3. a) (i) 2.26×10^8 m/s (✓) (ii) 2.0×10^8 m/s (✓)

   b) The diagram should show the light ray in glass nearer the normal than in water (✓).

Your score: ☐ out of 16

Your improvement index: $\dfrac{\Box/16}{\Box/11} \times 100\% = \Box\,\%$

7.2 Test yourself (page 53)
The eye

1. a) protects the front of the eye (✓), refracts light (✓)
   b) controls the amount of light entering the eye (✓)
   c) receives the image (✓)

2. a) The nearest point to the eye at which an object can be seen in focus (✓).
   b) thickest (✓)
   c) (i) There are muscle fibres around the rim of the eye lens (✓). When the fibres contract, they make the eye lens thicker (✓).
   (ii) thickest (✓)

3. a) The eye muscles relax (✓) so the eye lens becomes thinner (✓) enabling distant objects to be seen in focus (✓)
   b) The eye pupil becomes smaller (✓) because the iris becomes larger (✓).

4. a) The ability to see clearly near objects but not distant objects (✓).
   b) a concave lens (✓)

Your score: ☐ out of 16

7.2 Round up (page 54)
The eye

1. a) It would be fainter (✓).
   b) The retina is nearer the front of the eye than it ought to be (✓), so the image is out of focus (✓).

2. Only the rays passing through the centre of the eye lens reach the retina (✓). The other rays would not reach the same point, so the image would be blurred (✓), but the pinhole cuts out these other rays so the image is clear (✓).

3. a) The ability to see clearly near objects (✓) but not distant objects (✓).
   b) A concave lens is needed (✓) to enable the eye lens to focus light on the retina.

4. a) a convex lens (✓)
   b) a concave lens (✓)

Your score: ☐ out of 11

Your improvement index: $\dfrac{\Box/11}{\Box/16} \times 100\% = \Box\,\%$

Answers

7.3 Test yourself (page 55)
Optical instruments

1. a) To allow light into the camera briefly (✓).
   b) To control the amount of light entering the camera (✓).

2. The camera needs to be refocused (✓) by moving the lens towards the film (✓).

3. a) real (✓)   b) away (✓)   c) larger (✓)

4. a) virtual (✓)   b) upright (✓)   c) magnified (✓)

5. See page 52 (✓✓).

Your score: ☐ out of 12

7.3 Round up (page 56)
Optical instruments

1. Move the screen towards the lens (✓); move the slide away from the lens until the image is in focus (✓); repeat if the image is still too large (✓).

2. It becomes smaller (✓) and further away (✓).

Your score: ☐ out of 5

Your improvement index: $\dfrac{\boxed{}/5}{\boxed{}/12} \times 100\% = \boxed{}\%$

8 Test yourself (page 57)
Electromagnetic spectrum

1. radio (✓), microwaves (✓), infrared (✓), visible (✓), ultraviolet (✓), X-rays and gamma rays (✓)

2. See page 58 (✓✓✓✓✓✓).

3. visible light (✓) and radio (✓)

4. a) X-rays and gamma radiation (✓✓)
   b) infrared radiation (✓)
   c) ultraviolet light (✓)

5. X-rays or gamma radiation can (✓); radio waves, microwaves, visible light cannot (✓).

6. a) X-rays (✓)
   b) ultraviolet light (✓)

7. a) microwave radiation (✓)
   b) (i) To focus microwave radiation from the satellite onto the dish aerial (✓).
      (ii) Metal reflects microwaves (✓).

8. The pigment in the ink does not absorb visible light (✓). It absorbs ultraviolet light and emits visible light (✓). Under a UV lamp, the ink is therefore visible (✓).

9. a) (i) infrared radiation (✓)
      (ii) X-rays and gamma radiation (✓)
   b) radio waves and microwaves (✓)

10. a) infrared radiation (✓)
    b) visible light and infrared radiation (✓)

Your score: ☐ out of 33

8 Round up (page 62)
Electromagnetic spectrum

1. a) X-rays and gamma rays (✓), ultraviolet (✓), visible (✓), infrared (✓), microwave (✓), radio (✓)
   b) (i) Any two of: travel at the same speed in a vacuum; transverse waves; do not need a substance/pass through a vacuum; can be reflected or refracted or diffracted; make charged particles vibrate (✓✓).
      (ii) visible (✓), ultraviolet (✓), X-rays and gamma rays (✓)
      (iii) radio (✓), microwaves (✓), infrared (✓), visible (✓)

2. a) cooker 0.12 m (✓), satellite 0.03 m (✓)
   b) faster, uses less energy, cooks the food throughout (✓)

3. a) Long wave radio waves follow the Earth's curvature (✓), medium wave radio waves reflect from the ionosphere (✓).
   b) (i) The frequency of the electromagnetic waves that carry the audio or TV signals (✓).
      (ii) If they broadcast at the same frequency, the broadcasts would interfere with each other where they overlap (✓).
   c) The satellite signals are much weaker (✓); a dish is used to focus them onto an aerial (✓).

4. a) Ultraviolet light in bright sunlight would be absorbed by the powder molecules in the clothing (✓). The molecules would emit visible light, making the clothes seem brighter (✓).
   b) (i) It damages the retinal cells of the eye (✓); it causes sunburn (✓).
      (ii) To absorb ultraviolet light from sunlight (✓), to prevent sunburn (✓).

5. a) Their bodies emit infrared light which can be detected by an infrared camera (✓).
   b) (i) infrared light (✓)
      (ii) A conventional heating element consists of resistance wire surrounded by an electrical insulator in a metal tubing (✓); conduction of heat from the resistance wire to the metal tubing is very slow and so the hob takes much longer to heat up than a ceramic hob (✓).

Answers

6. a) (i) To attract electrons from the heated filament (✓).
   (ii) The X-rays need to originate from a small spot on the anode (✓) otherwise the image they produce will be blurred (✓).
   b) (i) X-rays pass through soft tissues and are absorbed by bone (✓). X-rays blacken photographic film (✓).
   (ii) The stomach consists of soft tissues only (✓). The barium meal in the stomach enables the lining of the stomach to be seen because barium absorbs X-rays (✓).

7. a) X, There are more cycles per second of the waveform at the higher frequency (✓). Each pulse needs the same number of cycles per second (✓), so more pulses per second are possible at higher frequencies (✓).
   b) (i) 1000 (✓)
   (ii) They would interfere with mobile phone communications (✓).

8. a) An orbit directly above the equator (✓) with an orbital time of exactly 24 hours (✓).
   b) The satellite is always in the same position over the equator (✓).

Your score: ☐ out of 49

Your improvement index: $\frac{\Box/49}{\Box/33} \times 100\% = \Box \%$

9 Test yourself (page 63)
Force and motion

1. a) 5 km/h (✓)   b) 1.4 m/s (✓)
2. a) the area under the line (✓)   b) speed (✓)
3. 0.5 m/s^2 (✓), 500 N (✓)
4. a) 9.0 m (✓)   b) −6.0 m/s^2 (✓)
   c) (i) 19 m (✓)   (ii) 28 m (✓)
5. a) (i) 4000 N (✓), 800 J (✓)   (ii) 8000 J (✓)
   b) Potential energy is converted into thermal energy (or heat) (✓) by the braking force acting on the lift cable (✓). This force is necessary to prevent the lift from falling freely (✓).
6. The force of air resistance depends on the speed and the shape of the vehicle (✓). The speed increases until the force of air resistance is equal to the engine force (✓). Changing the shape to reduce the force of air resistance enables the car to reach a higher top speed (✓).
7. The force of air resistance increases with speed (✓). As the parachutist falls, his/her speed increases until the force of air resistance is equal and opposite to the weight of the parachutist (✓). The speed therefore becomes constant as the overall force becomes zero (✓).
8. a) 80 000 N (✓), 80 000 N (✓)
   b) (i) 6000 m (✓),   (ii) 20 MJ (✓)
   c) It is carried away by the air as thermal energy (✓).

Your score: ☐ out of 27

9 Round up (page 69)
Force and motion

1. a) (i) 4320 m (✓)   (ii) 4.32 km (✓)   b) 4.3 m/s (✓)
2. a) It was steady (✓) and less than the speed of X for most of the journey (✓). Then the speed of Y was greater than that of X (✓) and Y overtook X (✓).
   b) (i) 10 m/s (✓)   (ii) 15 m/s (✓)
3. a) Speed is distance travelled per second (✓); velocity is speed in a given direction (✓).
   b) (i) 9 km north (✓) then 24 km south (✓)
   (ii) 15 km south (✓)
4. a) 1.6 m/s^2 (✓), 20 m (✓)   b) 1120 N (✓)
5. a) 2.5 s (✓)
   b) (i) 63 J (✓)   (ii) 63 J (✓)   (iii) 31 m (✓)
6. a) 9.5 m/s (✓)   b) 2.7 kJ (✓)   c) 4.5 m (✓)
   d) The pole vaulter uses his or her arm muscles to gain height (✓).
7. a) Graph to show a straight line with a negative gradient (✓) from 10 m/s to 0 in 50 s (✓).
   b) (i) 250 m (✓)   (ii) −0.2 m/s^2 (✓)
   c) −6000 N (✓)
   d) 0.02 (✓)
8. a) The car skids if the force of the brakes on the wheels exceeds the frictional force of the road on the tyres (✓).
   b) The maximum frictional force of the road on the tyres is less on a wet road (✓). This force is equal and opposite to the force of the road on the car (✓). Hence the maximum braking force for no skidding must be less on a wet road (✓), so it takes longer to stop from a given speed (✓).
   c) (i) 22.5 m (✓)   (ii) −5.0 m/s^2 (✓), 6000 N (✓)
   d) 6 s (✓), 45 m (✓)

Your score: ☐ out of 41

Your improvement index: $\frac{\Box/41}{\Box/27} \times 100\% = \Box \%$

10 Test yourself (page 71)
Forces in balance

1. your weight (✓), the support force from your chair (✓)
2. a) neutral (✓)   b) unstable (✓)   c) stable (✓)
3. a) about 1.2 m (✓)
   b) The point at which the lift force is exerted is three times further from the pivot than the centre of gravity (✓). Hence the lift force is one-third of the weight (✓).
   c) 50 kg (✓)

145

Answers

4 a) (i) The force is applied to a much smaller contact area if the knife is sharp (✓).
   (ii) Atmospheric pressure acting on the outer surface is greater than the pressure of the air trapped between the cap and the tile (✓). The pressure difference creates sufficient force to hold the cap on the wall (✓).
   b) 6 kPa (✓✓)

5 a) The original shape is regained after the removal of applied forces (✓).
   b) The original shape is not regained after the removal of applied forces (✓).

6 a) 20 cm (✓) b) 2.5 N (✓)

7 The moment of the applied force is greater with a long spanner than with a short spanner (✓). Hence less force is needed to produce the necessary moment (✓).

8 a) 0.40 N m (✓) b) 2.7 N (✓✓)

Your score: ☐ out of 23

10 Round up (page 77)
Forces in balance

1 a) The tyres are wider to create less pressure on the soft ground (✓). Also, the tractor can tilt further with big wheels before it topples over (✓).
   b) Your diagram should show a small base and a high centre of gravity (✓). The pin needs to tilt only a little before it falls over because of its high centre of gravity in relation to its small base (✓).

2 a) (i) 200 kPa (✓) (ii) 6 kPa (✓) b) 0.004 m² (✓)

3 a) The stiffness of the steel spring is constant (✓); the stiffness of the elastic band changes as it is stretched (✓).
   b) No (✓), it does not give equal changes in length for equal increases in force (✓).

4 a) (i) pure water 1.00 g/cm³ (✓); salt water 1.08 g/cm³ (✓)
       (ii) pure water 1000 kg/m³ (✓); salt water 1080 kg/m³ (✓)
   b) Salt water has a greater density than pure water (✓). This means the pressure is greater at the same depth (✓); hence the upthrust on an object is greater in salt water than in pure water (✓).

5 0.4 m (✓), 1.1 N (✓), 10 N (✓), 0.19 m (✓)

6 a) Your graph should show axes labelled correctly and units shown (✓), points plotted correctly (✓), points covering at least half of each scale (✓), a straight line drawn through the points (✓).
   b) 1.9 N (✓)

Your score: ☐ out of 27

Your improvement index: $\dfrac{\boxed{}/27}{\boxed{}/23} \times 100\% = \boxed{}\%$

11.1 Test yourself (page 78)
Dynamics equations and graphs

1 a) Constant deceleration for the first 4 seconds (✓), then a greater deceleration for the last 6 seconds (✓).
   b) (i) −2.5 m/s² (✓), 100 m (✓) (ii) −3.3 m/s² (✓), 60 m (✓)

2 a) 30 m/s (✓) b) (✓✓✓)
   c) 45 m (✓)

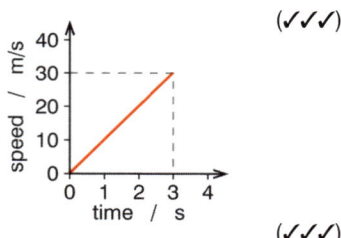

3 a) (✓✓✓)
   b) (i) −1.5 m/s² (✓) (ii) 1200 m (✓) c) 60 kN (✓) 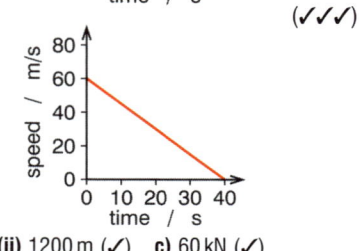

Your score: ☐ out of 17

11.1 Round up (page 79)
Dynamics equations and graphs

1 a) (i) 1.25 s (✓) (ii) 0 (✓)
   b) $a = -10$ m/s², $t = 1.25$ s, $v = 0$
      (i) Use $v = u + at$ (✓) to give $u = 12.5$ m/s (✓)
      (ii) Use $s = \tfrac{1}{2}(u + v)t$ or $s = ut + \tfrac{1}{2}at^2$ (✓)
           to give $s = 7.8$ m (✓)

2 a) Use $v^2 = u^2 + 2as$ with $a = 10$ m/s², $s = 1.5$ m, $u = 0$ (✓) to give $v = 5.5$ m/s (✓)
   b) Use $v^2 = u^2 + 2as$ with $u = 5.5$ m/s, $v = 0$, $s = 0.020$ m (✓) to give $a = -750$ m/s² (✓)

3 a) Use $v^2 = u^2 + 2as$ with $s = 65$ m, $v = 0$, $a = -7$ m/s² (✓) to give $u = 30$ m/s (✓)
   b) 30 m/s = 30 × 3600/1000 km/h = 30 × 3600/1000 × 5/8 = 68 m.p.h. (✓)

Your score: ☐ out of 13

Your improvement index: $\dfrac{\boxed{}/13}{\boxed{}/17} \times 100\% = \boxed{}\%$

Answers

11.2 Test yourself (page 80)
Force and momentum
1 480 kg m/s (✓), 1920 J (✓)

2 **a)** 12 000 kg m/s (✓)   **b)** 2400 kg m/s² (✓)   **c)** 2400 N (✓)

3 **a)** total initial momentum = 2000 × 5 (✓);
   total final momentum = (2000 + 3000)v (✓)
   5000v = 2000 × 5 (✓) so v = 2 m/s (✓)

   b) total initial KE = $\frac{1}{2}$ × 2000 × 5² = 25 000 J (✓)
   total final KE = $\frac{1}{2}$ × 5000 × 2² = 10 000 J (✓)
   loss of KE = 25 000 − 10 000 = 15 000 J (✓)

4 **a)** (i) 2000 × 1600 (✓) = 3.2 × 10⁶ kg m/s² (✓)
   (ii) 3.2 × 10⁶ N (✓)

   b) engine force − mg = ma, where m is the mass and a is the acceleration (✓). Substitute known values to give m = 1.8 × 10⁵ kg (✓)

Your score: ☐ out of 17

11.2 Round up (page 82)
Force and momentum
1 **a)** total initial momentum = 4000 × 5 + 2000 × 1
   = 22 000 kg m/s (✓)

   b) total final momentum = 2000 × 5 (✓) + 4000v (✓)
   total final momentum = total initial momentum
   giving 2000 × 5 + 4000v = 22 000 (✓)
   Solve to give v = 3 m/s (✓)

2 **a)** total initial momentum = 4000 × 5 − 2000 × 1
   = 18 000 kg m/s (✓)

   b) total final momentum = 2000 × 5 (✓) + 4000v (✓)
   total final momentum = total initial momentum
   giving 2000 × 5 + 4000v = 18 000 (✓)
   Solve to give v = 2 m/s (✓)

3 **a)** The student carries away momentum (✓), so the skateboard carries away equal and opposite momentum (✓) so that the total momentum is zero (✓).

   b) 50v = 5 × 8 (✓) gives v = 0.8 m/s (✓)

Your score: ☐ out of 15

Your improvement index: $\dfrac{\Box /15}{\Box /17} \times 100\%$ = ☐ %

11.3 Test yourself (page 83)
More about forces
1 **a)** Any two of: velocity, acceleration, force, weight, momentum (✓✓).
   b) Any two of: speed, mass, energy, power, work, time (✓✓).

2 **a)** 8000 N (✓)   **b)** 8000 N (✓)

3 1.0 N (✓) in the same direction as the 3 N force (✓)

4 5.0 N (✓) at an angle of 37° to the opposite direction of the 4 N force (✓)

5 **a)** vertically down (✓)
   b) horizontal, in the direction the satellite is moving (✓)

6 **a)** 24 hours (✓)
   b) The satellite remains directly above a point on the Earth's equator (✓).
   c) 3.1 km/s (✓)

Your score: ☐ out of 15

11.3 Round up (page 84)
More about forces
1 **a)** 17.0 N (✓)   **b)** 7.0 N (✓)   **c)** 13.0 N (✓)   **d)** 10.4 N (✓)

2 **a)** 12.8 m/s (✓)
   b) time to reach the ground = 200/8 = 25 s (✓);
   horizontal distance moved = 10 × 25 (✓) = 250 m (✓)

3 **a)** speed²/radius = 10 (✓) gives speed = 8100 m/s (✓)
   b) time for one orbit = circumference/speed (✓) = 2π × 6 600 000/8100 (✓) = 5100 s (✓)

Your score: ☐ out of 13

Your improvement index: $\dfrac{\Box /13}{\Box /15} \times 100\%$ = ☐ %

12 Test yourself (page 86)
Electric charge
1 **B** and **C** (✓✓)

2 **a)** C (✓)   **b)** B (✓)

3 **a)** A metal contains electrons which move about freely inside it (✓). These electrons carry charge and hence transfer charge through the metal when a potential difference is set up across the metal (✓).

   b) All the electrons are firmly attached to atoms (✓) and so cannot transfer charge through the material (✓).

Answers

4 If the charged rod is negative, it repels electrons from the cap onto the leaf and stem (✓) which then repel each other (✓). If the charged rod is positive, it attracts electrons onto the cap from the leaf and stem (✓). This makes the leaf and stem positive, so the leaf is repelled from the stem (✓).

5 (i) It leaks away (✓).
(ii) The plate retains its charge where it is dark. The charge attracts the particles (✓).

6 The pipe would become charged due to fluid friction, and a spark might be created (✓). This would be dangerous since it might ignite oil vapour (✓).

7 Any two from: electrostatic paint spray; ink jet printer; electrostatic precipitator (✓✓).

8 360 C (✓✓)

9 The liquid in the cell contains hydrogen ions and chloride ions (✓). Hydrogen ions are positive and are discharged at the anode (✓); chloride ions are negative and are discharged at the anode (✓).

10 Any two from: chromium electroplating; tin plating; extraction of aluminium from its ore; purification of copper (✓✓).

Your score: ☐ out of 25

12 Round up (page 92)
Electric charge

1 a) ii, iv, i then iii (✓✓✓✓) b) positive charge (✓) c) no (✓)

2 a) Electrons transfer from the electroscope to the rod (✓) so the leaf and stem both become positive (✓). Hence the leaf is repelled by the stem (✓).
b) No charge can transfer to or from the electroscope once the rod has been removed (✓).
c) Hold the rod near the electroscope (✓). Earth the electroscope cap (✓). Remove the earth connection (✓). Remove the rod (✓). (See page 88.)
d) Charge the electroscope with a known charge. Bring the unknown charge near the cap (✓). If the leaf rises, the unknown charge is the same as the charge on the electroscope (✓). If the leaf falls, it is oppositely charged (✓).

3 a) (i) The charge on the metal car body discharges to earth (✓) through a person in contact with the ground who touches the car (✓).
(ii) The car driver would be charged from the car (✓) and would discharge to earth on setting foot out of the car (✓).
b) (i) The charge on the car leaks to earth through the trailing conductor (✓).
(ii) Rainwater conducts electricity (✓) so allows the charge on the car body to transfer to earth (✓).

4 a) 180 C (✓), 1080 C (✓) b) 0.06 g (✓) c) 0.36 g (✓)
d) 0.35 A (✓)

5 a) (i) The toner cartridge is nearly empty (✓) so less and less powder reaches the plate (✓) (or the 'lighter/darker' contrast control knob is not set correctly (✓) so not enough powder is attracted on to the plate (✓)).
(ii) The powder does not dry fast enough (✓) immediately after it has been heated (✓).
b) (i) no deflection (✓)   (ii) reverse deflection (✓)

6 a) Uncharged dust particles are attracted to the live wire grid (✓) where they become charged the same as the grid (✓) and are then attracted onto the earthed tube and stay there (✓).
b) In the presence of a nearby charged object, touching a pin allows opposite charge to transfer to it from earth (✓). Removing the earth connection leaves the pin charged (✓).

Your score: ☐ out of 40

Your improvement index: $\dfrac{\Box/40}{\Box/25} \times 100\% = \Box\,\%$

13 Test yourself (page 93)
Electric circuits

1 a) (✓✓)

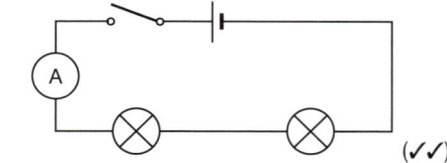

b) $0.2 \times 1.5 \times \dfrac{60}{2}$ (✓) = 9 J each (✓)

2 a) (✓✓)

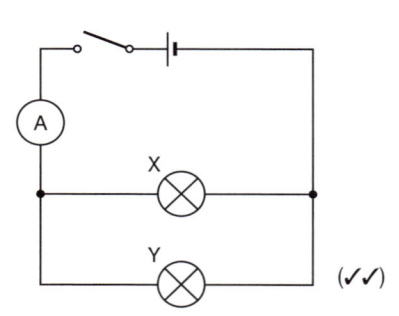

b) (i) 0.45 J (✓)   (ii) 27 J (✓)

3 a) 0.2 A (✓)   b) $\dfrac{1.0\,V}{0.2\,A}$ (✓) = 5.0 Ω (✓)

4 a) 15.0 V (✓)   b) 37.5 W (✓)

5 a)

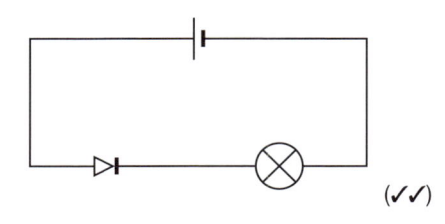

  b) The diode is now reverse biased (✓) so it will not conduct (✓).

6

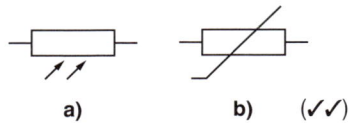

  a) An LDR's resistance depends on the incident light intensity (✓).
  b) A thermistor's resistance depends on temperature (✓).

7 a) 300 kJ (✓)   **b)** $\frac{1000\,W}{240\,V}$ (✓) = 4.2 A (✓)

8 a) A fuse is intended to protect an appliance or the connecting wires from excessive current (✓).
  b) If the current rises above a certain value, the fuse wire overheats and melts (✓) causing a gap in the circuit (✓).

9 a) $\frac{20 \times 6\,W}{240\,V}$ (✓) = 0.5 A (✓)   **b)** $\frac{240\,V}{20}$ (✓) = 12 V (✓)

10 a) 0.8 kW × 0.25 h (✓) = 0.2 kWh (✓)
  b) 1.2p (✓)

Your score: ☐ out of 34

13 Round up (page 99)
Electric circuits

1 a) 12 Ω (✓)
  b) The ammeter reading would double (✓); the voltmeter reading would be unchanged (✓).

2 a) (i) 6.3 A (✓) (ii) 3 kWh (✓)
  b) (i) It is used to earth the metal frame of an appliance connected to the ring main (✓). It therefore prevents the frame from becoming live (✓).
    (ii) 3 A (✓)
    (iii) If the fuse rating is too low, the fuse will blow when the appliance is switched on (✓). If the fuse rating is too large, the fuse will not blow if the current becomes excessive. This would create a risk of fire due to resistance heating (✓).

3 a) (i) 1.5 V (✓) (ii) 0.3 A (✓)   **b)** 0.45 W (✓)
  c) The current in P becomes less (✓); the current in Q becomes greater (✓).

4 a) 2 A (✓), 6 Ω (✓)
  b) $\frac{6\,\Omega}{5\,\Omega/m}$ (✓) = 1.2 m (✓)
  c)

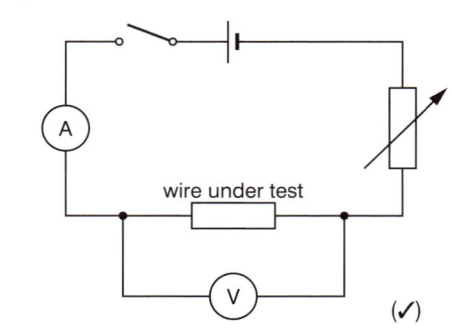

Connect an exact length of 1.0 m into the circuit (✓) and measure the current and p.d. using the ammeter and the voltmeter (✓✓). Calculate the resistance from p.d./current (✓).

5 a) (i) 1.2 kWh (✓) (ii) 10 kWh (✓) (iii) 1.0 kWh (✓)
  b) 61p (✓)
  c) 29 minutes (✓✓)

6 a) Tap water conducts electricity (✓). Water might run into the appliance and provide a conducting path to earth via the user (✓). Also, the contact resistance between the appliance and the user is reduced by water (✓).
  b) If the case became live (✓), current leakage to earth via the user might not be enough to blow the fuse (✓). An RCCB would cut the mains supply off if the leakage current exceeds 30 mA (✓).
  c) The cable would become warm due to its resistance (✓). If it overheated, the insulation might melt (✓).

Your score: ☐ out of 38

Your improvement index: $\frac{\boxed{}/38}{\boxed{}/34} \times 100\% = \boxed{}\%$

14 Test yourself (page 101)
Electromagnetism

1 a) soft iron (✓)   **b)** steel (✓)
2 a) north (✓)   **b)** north (✓)
3 a) circles centred on the wire (✓) in a horizontal plane (✓)

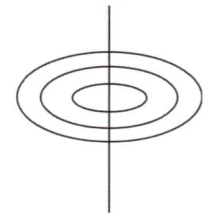

  b) field lines loop round from one end to the other (✓) and pass through the solenoid along its axis (✓)

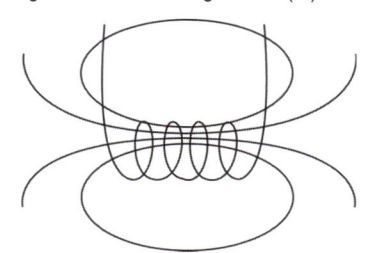

Answers

4 **a)** and **c)** permanent magnet (✓✓) **b)** electromagnet (✓)

5 **a)** the same (✓)
   b) The turning effect on the coil would reverse each time the current reversed (✓), so the coil would be unable to spin (✓).

6 **a)** The peak voltage would decrease (✓) and the time for one cycle would increase (✓).
   b) Alternating current can be stepped up to high voltage on the grid system (✓). The same power can then be delivered with smaller currents than would be necessary if the voltage was low (✓). There is less resistance heating in the grid cables and therefore less power is wasted (✓).

7 The electromagnet creates a changing magnetic field through the aluminium plate, which induces alternating current in the plate (✓). Resistance heating therefore occurs in the plate (✓).

8 **a)** 12 V (✓) **b)** 8.3 A (✓)

Your score: ☐ out of 23

14 Round up (page 107)
Electromagnetism

1 **a)** See page 102 for diagram (✓✓✓). The electromagnet attracts the iron armature when current passes through the electromagnet coil (✓). The make-or-break switch opens (✓), the current switches off and the electromagnet is no longer attracted to the armature (✓). The armature springs back and closes the switch gap (✓). Current passes again and the process is repeated (✓).
   b) (i) The iron bar is attracted into the solenoid when the switch is closed (✓).
   (ii) To ensure it is pulled into the coil when the switch is closed (✓).
   (iii) It would operate on a.c. (✓) since the bar is attracted into the coil whatever the direction of the current (✓).

2 **a)** See page 102 for diagram (✓✓✓). Current through the electromagnet coil causes magnetism in its core (✓). The armature is attracted to the core (✓). The switch is closed by the movement of the armature (✓).
   b) The alternating current in the coil of the electromagnet creates an alternating magnetic field (✓). This field induces an alternating current in any conductor it passes through (✓).

3 **a)** See page 104 for diagram (✓✓✓). The sides of the coil cut the magnetic field lines as the coil turns (✓) so a voltage is induced in the coil (✓). The voltage alternates because the angle between the direction of motion of the coil sides and field lines changes continuously (✓).
   b) (i) See page 104 (✓✓).
   (ii) any maximum or minimum (✓)
   c) The peaks are higher (✓) and nearer to each other (✓).

4 **a)** (i) A changing primary current causes a changing magnetic field in the core (✓). A changing magnetic field through the secondary coil causes an induced voltage in the secondary coil (✓).
   (ii) The secondary current is greater since the voltage is stepped down (✓).

   (iii) The plates are made of iron to make the magnetic field as strong as possible (✓). The plates are laminated to reduce induced currents in the core (✓).
   b) (i) 12 V (✓) (ii) 1.6 A (✓✓) (✓ for answer 2.0 A)

5 **a)** (i) There is less current for the same power (✓) so less heat is produced due to resistance in the cables (✓).
   (ii) UK – the higher voltage in the UK is more dangerous (✓) but smaller currents for the same power in the UK mean less risk of overheating (✓).
   b) Advantages: no underground trenches need to be dug, no waterproof insulating material needed round cable (✓). Disadvantages: liable to lightning strikes, unsightly (✓).

Your score: ☐ out of 45

Your improvement index: $\dfrac{☐/45}{☐/23} \times 100\% = ☐\%$

15.1 Test yourself (pages 109–110)
More about components and electric circuits

1 **a)** [circuit diagram: 1.5 V cell with 10 Ω and 5 Ω resistors in series] (✓)
   b) (i) 15 Ω (✓) (ii) 0.1 A (✓) (= 1.5 V/15 Ω)

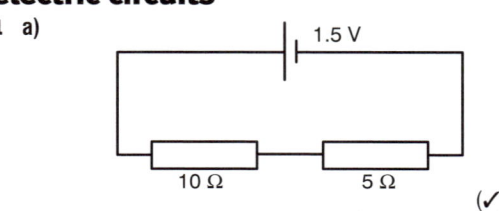

2 **a)** 3 Ω: 0.5 A (✓); 6 Ω: 0.25 A (✓); cell: 0.75 A (✓) **b)** 2 Ω (✓)

3 **a)** [circuit diagram with 1.5 V cell, mA ammeter, thermistor and resistor] (✓✓)
   b) The reading would decrease (✓) because the thermistor's resistance would increase (✓).

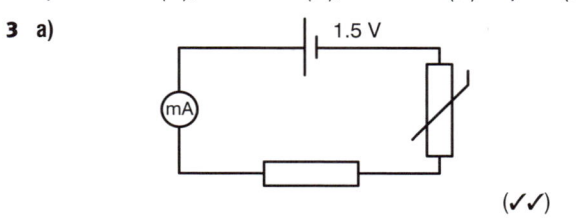

4 **a)** (i) 5.0 − 1.0 V = 4.0 V (✓) (ii) 4000 Ω (✓✓)
   b) The reading would increase (✓) because the LDR resistance would drop (✓), so the current would increase, increasing the voltage across R (✓).

5 **a)** [circuit diagram with 1.5 V cell, LED, capacitor and switch] (✓)
   b) Current passes through the LED (making it emit light) as the capacitor charges (✓), and stops when the capacitor is fully charged (✓).

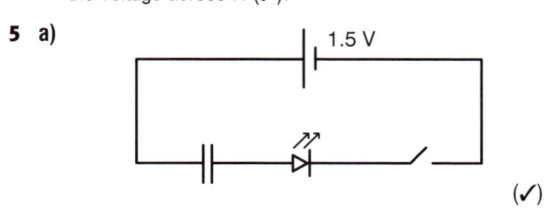

6 a) (See page 111.) (✓) **b)**

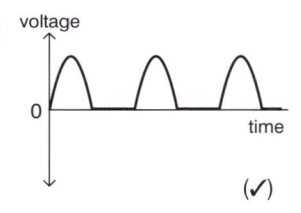

voltage vs time graph showing half-wave rectified waveform (✓)

7 The LDR's resistance falls when it is illuminated (✓), allowing current to enter the base of the transistor (✓), which causes current to enter the collector (✓), which switches on the bell (✓).

Your score: ☐ out of 26

15.1 Round up (page 113)

More about components and electric circuits

1 a) (i) in parallel (✓)   **(ii)** the same (✓)
  b) (i) 6 V (✓), 24 W/6 V = 4 A (✓)   **(ii)** 12 − 6 V = 6 V (✓), 8 A (✓)

2 a) 0.25 A (✓)
  b) total power = 20 × 12 V × 0.25 A = 60 W (✓), energy used in 1 s = 60 J (✓)

3 a) (i) It decreases (✓).   **(ii)** It decreases (✓).
     (iii) It increases (✓).
  b) $\frac{500}{1500} \times 9.0\,\text{V}$ (✓) = 3.0 V (✓)

4 a)

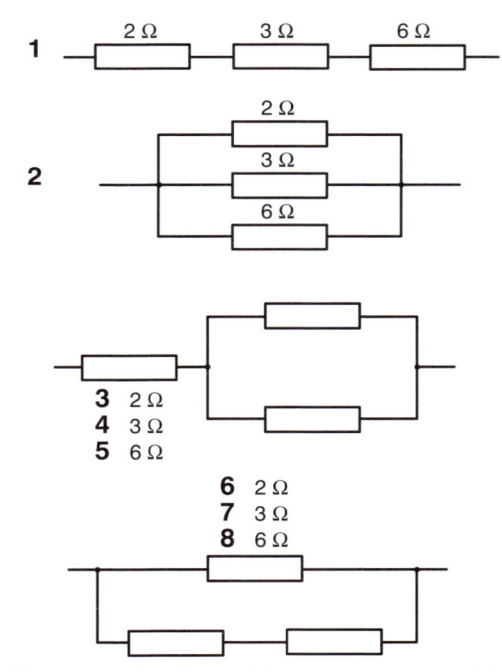

1. 2 Ω — 3 Ω — 6 Ω (series)
2. 2 Ω, 3 Ω, 6 Ω all in parallel
3,4,5. 2 Ω in series with (3 Ω ∥ 6 Ω) arrangements
6,7,8. 2 Ω ∥ (3 Ω in series with 6 Ω) arrangements

(8 arrangements: ✓ for each two correct arrangements)
  b) maximum resistance: 2, 3, 6 Ω in series = 11 Ω (✓); minimum resistance: 2, 3, 6 Ω in parallel = 1 Ω (✓)

5 a)

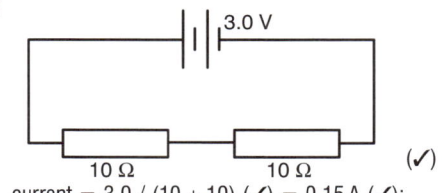

Circuit: 3.0 V cell with two 10 Ω resistors in series (✓)

current = 3.0 / (10 + 10) (✓) = 0.15 A (✓);
voltage = 1.5 V for each resistor (✓);
same for both resistors (✓)

  b)

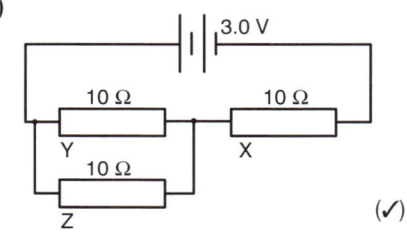

Circuit: 3.0 V cell with 10 Ω (Y) in parallel with 10 Ω (Z), in series with 10 Ω (X) (✓)

total circuit resistance = 15 Ω;
cell current = 3.0/15 = 0.2 A (✓)
current through X = 0.2 A (✓); voltage across X = 2.0 V (✓)
voltage across Y = voltage across Z = 1 V (✓);
current through Y = current through Z = 0.1 A (✓)

6 a)

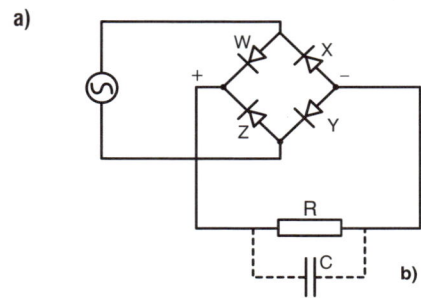

Bridge rectifier circuit with AC source, diodes W, X, Y, Z, resistor R and capacitor C

  b)

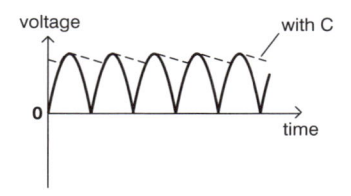

voltage vs time graph showing full-wave rectified waveform with smoothed curve "with C"

(✓✓ for circuit, ✓✓ for waveforms)
On one half-cycle, diodes W and Y conduct so current passes through R from left to right (✓). On the next half-cycle, diodes X and Z conduct, so current again passes left to right through R (✓).
  b) See diagram above ((✓) for correct connection of capacitor, (✓) for correct effect on waveform).

Answers

7 a) The resistance of the thermistor increases when it becomes colder (✓). The base current increases (✓), which allows current to flow from the collector to emitter (✓) and the relay is switched on (✓).
b) To short-circuit the back e.m.f. generated by the relay coil (✓) when it is switched off (✓).

Your score: ☐ out of 47

Your improvement index: $\dfrac{\Box/47}{\Box/26} \times 100\% = \Box\%$

15.2 Test yourself (page 114)
Electronic control

1 a) NOR (✓)
b)

input 1	input 2	output
0	0	1 (✓)
0	1	0 (✓)
1	0	0 (✓)
1	1	0 (✓)

2 a) The LED lights up when the NOT gate output is 1 (✓). This requires a 0 at the input (✓).
b) To limit the current through the LED (✓), otherwise the LED would fail due to the heating effect of the current through it (✓).

3

input 1	input 2	output
0	0	0 (✓)
0	1	1 (✓)
1	0	0 (✓)
1	1	0 (✓)

4 a) Opening the switch allows the capacitor to charge up (✓), so the capacitor voltage rises (✓). The capacitor voltage is an input to the AND gate (✓). The other input is at 1, so when the capacitor voltage reaches a certain value, the AND output switches to logic state 1 (✓) which switches the alarm on (✓).
b) Increase the resistance of the variable resistor (✓) so the current is smaller and the capacitor takes longer to reach the necessary voltage (✓).

Your score: ☐ out of 20

15.2 Round up (page 116)
Electronic control

1 a)

input A	input B	output
0	0	0 (✓)
0	1	1 (✓)
1	0	0 (✓)
1	1	1 (✓)

b)

input A	input B	output
0	0	0 (✓)
0	1	0 (✓)
1	0	1 (✓)
1	1	0 (✓)

2 a)

window sensor	key sensor	alarm
0	0	0 (✓)
0	1	1 (✓)
1	0	0 (✓)
1	1	0 (✓)

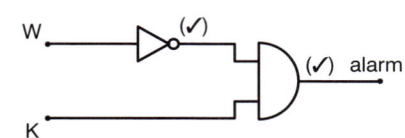

b) W → NOT gate → AND gate with K → alarm (✓)

3 a) 0 (✓)
b) The voltmeter reading stays low at first (✓). The capacitor charges up through the resistor (✓) until the capacitor voltage is high enough to switch the OR gate output to logic 1 (✓), which makes the voltmeter reading switch from low to high (✓).

4 a) The output stays at 1 even after the input condition changes (✓).
b) Y (✓)
c) Z (✓)

Your score: ☐ out of 22

Your improvement index: $\dfrac{\Box/22}{\Box/20} \times 100\% = \Box\%$

Answers

15.3 Test yourself (page 117)
Communication systems

1. a) digital (✓) b) analogue (✓) c) digital (✓) d) digital (✓)

2. a) decoder, encoder (✓), regenerator (✓)
   b) decoder, encoder (✓), regenerator (✓)

3. a) Data can be written and changed on the magnetic disc as well as read off it (✓). A CD-ROM is 'read only' and cannot be changed (✓).
   b) higher storage capacity, faster access (✓)

4. a) The dish must point directly towards the broadcasting satellite (✓).
   b) microwaves (✓)
   c) The microwave pulses are coded by the broadcasting station (✓).

5. a) less affected by noise *or* higher quality (✓)
   b) A single TV channel needs a bandwidth that would take up too much of the FM waveband (✓), leaving little space for other TV channels (✓).
   c) Each call is carried by a different frequency (✓).

Your score: ☐ out of 18

15.3 Round up (page 119)
Communication systems

1. a) reduced noise (✓) b) The signal can carry many more telephone calls in an optical fibre (✓).

2. Analogue transmission involves modulating the carrier waves with the analogue signal (✓). Digital transmission requires the carrier wave to be pulsed (✓). A code is needed to send information using pulses (✓).

3. a) 135 Gbits (✓) b) about 13 minutes (✓)

4. a) digital, copper wire for low cost (✓) b) digital, microwave for a satellite link (✓)
   c) AM radio for reception over a wide area (✓)

5. a) (i) digital (✓)
      (ii) analogue (✓)
   b) Much higher storage capacity (✓), higher quality (✓)

Your score: ☐ out of 14

Your improvement index: $\dfrac{\boxed{}/14}{\boxed{}/18} \times 100\% = \boxed{}\%$

16 Test yourself (page 121)
Radioactivity

1. a) negative (✓) b) positive (✓) c) uncharged (✓)
   d) positive (✓) e) negative (✓)

2. a) 2 p + 2 n (✓✓) b) 92 p + 143 n (✓✓)

3. positive (✓)

4. alpha, beta and gamma radiation (✓✓✓); Alpha radiation is most easily absorbed (✓).

5. Radioactivity from the surroundings or caused by cosmic radiation (✓).

6. the Geiger counter (✓)

7. Half-life – the time taken for half the atoms of a given radioactive isotope to disintegrate (✓).
   Isotope – atoms of an element with the same number of neutrons and protons (✓).

8. A nucleus of an atom splits (✓) into two approximately equal halves (✓).

9. The waste from the spent fuel rods contains radioactive isotopes with very long half-lives (✓). Radiation released by radioactive isotopes is harmful (✓).

10. See page 126 (✓✓).

Your score: ☐ out of 24

16 Round up (page 129)
Radioactivity

1. a) U-238 = 92p + 146n (✓✓); U-235 = 92p + 143n (✓✓)
   b) isotopes (✓)
   c) The time taken for half the initial number of atoms of a given isotope to decay (✓).

2. a) Smoke absorbs alpha radiation (✓) but not beta or gamma radiation (✓).
   b) If the half-life was much shorter than 5 years, the decrease in activity of the source within a year would set the alarm off (✓).

3. a) $^{220}_{82}\text{Rn} \rightarrow {}^{216}_{80}\text{Po} + {}^{4}_{2}\alpha$ (✓✓)
   b) (i) 100/s (✓) (ii) 25/s (✓)

4. a) Steel plate stops alpha and beta radiation (✓✓) but not gamma radiation (✓).
   b) (i) 200/s (✓) (ii) 160/s (✓)
      (iii) It became thicker (✓).

5. a) (i) See page 123 (✓). (ii) It produces ions (✓).
   b) X-rays, radioactive waste (✓✓)
   c) Start the Geiger counter and the stopwatch together. Stop the Geiger counter after, say, exactly 600 seconds (✓). Measure the number of counts recorded by the counter. Divide this number by 600 to give the count rate (✓).

6. Alpha and gamma radiation (✓✓), the tin foil stops alpha radiation (✓) whereas even thick lead is unable to stop the gamma radiation completely (✓).

Answers

7 a) The radiation becomes weaker with distance (✓).
b) (i) Electromagnetic radiation of very short wavelength (✓), it penetrates the body (✓).
(ii) The source is enclosed in a thick-walled lead container with a small hole to let the gamma radiation out in a thin beam (✓). The beam is directed at the tumour from different directions (✓) so as not to damage the surrounding healthy tissue (✓).

Your score: ☐ out of 35

Your improvement index: $\dfrac{\Box/35}{\Box/24} \times 100\% = \Box \%$

17.1 Test yourself (page 130)
Electrons

1 a) negative (✓)
b) (i) It is heated (✓). **(ii)** It is made positive (✓).

2 a) (✓) P → Q
b) (✓) P → Q

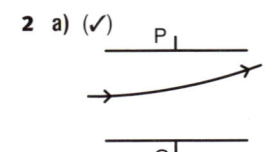

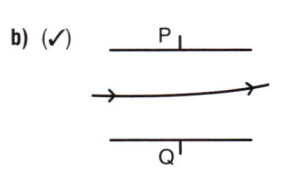

3 a) At the anode (✓) where it is struck by the electron beam (✓).
b) more intense (✓), more penetrating (✓)

4 Continuous spread (✓) of the colours of the spectrum: red, orange, yellow, green, blue, indigo, violet (✓).

Your score: ☐ out of 11

17.1 Round up (page 131)
Electrons

1 a) Electrons would collide with gas atoms if there was not a vacuum (✓), and would not be able to reach the anode (✓).
b) Most of the KE of each electron is converted to heat when the electrons collide with the anode (✓).

2 a) A spectrum consisting of narrow coloured lines (✓).
b) The pattern of lines is characteristic of the element producing the light (✓). For light from a distant galaxy, the pattern is shifted towards the red part of the spectrum because the galaxy is rapidly receding (✓).

Your score: ☐ out of 6

Your improvement index: $\dfrac{\Box/6}{\Box/11} \times 100\% = \Box \%$

17.2 Test yourself (page 132)
More about the nucleus

1 a) $A = 14$ (✓), $Z = 6$ (✓)   **b)** 88p (✓), 136n (✓)

2 a) The atoms of the foil are mostly empty space (✓).
b) The nucleus has the same type of charge as the alpha particle (✓) so it repels the alpha particle (✓).

3 a) It changes a neutron into a proton (✓) which causes a β^- particle to be emitted (✓).
b) approximately 1.5 (✓)

4 a) The nucleus splits into two approximately equal fragments (✓) and releases two or three neutrons (✓).
b) Before: the fuel is mostly U-238 which is an alpha-emitting isotope (✓). The fuel container absorbs these particles (✓). After: the fission fragments are neutron rich (✓). They therefore emit beta and gamma radiation (✓). This type of radiation penetrates the fuel container (✓).

5 a) 3 (✓)   **b)** two up quarks and one down quark (✓)

Your score: ☐ out of 19

17.2 Round up (page 135)
More about the nucleus

1 a) 8p, 6n (✓)   **b)** 8p, 8n (✓)   **c)** 8p, 11n (✓)

2 a) b (✓)
b) a is proton rich and therefore a β^+ emitter (✓). c is neutron rich and therefore a β^- emitter (✓).

3 a) two up quarks and one down quark (✓)
b) six up quarks (✓) and six down quarks (✓)

4 a) 27p (✓), 33n (✓)   **b)** 28p (✓), 32n (✓)
c) udd $\longrightarrow$ uud (✓); d $\longrightarrow$ u and emits a β^- particle (✓)

Your score: ☐ out of 15

Your improvement index: $\dfrac{\Box/15}{\Box/19} \times 100\% = \Box \%$

Equations and symbols you should know

Read, learn and inwardly digest the formulas below. To test yourself, cover each equation with a blank card after the first word and see if you can write the rest of the equation on the card.

voltage = current × resistance

electrical power = voltage × current

charge = current × time

energy transferred = potential difference × charge

energy transferred (in J) = power (in W) × time (in seconds)

energy transferred (in kWh) = power (in kW) × time (in hours)

$$\frac{\text{voltage across coil 1}}{\text{voltage across coil 2}} = \frac{\text{number of turns in coil 1}}{\text{number of turns in coil 2}}$$

$$\text{pressure} = \frac{\text{force}}{\text{area}}$$

$$\text{speed} = \frac{\text{distance}}{\text{time}}$$

$$\text{acceleration} = \frac{\text{change of velocity}}{\text{time taken}}$$

force = mass × acceleration

work done = force × distance moved in direction of force

energy transferred = work done

$$\text{efficiency} = \frac{\text{useful energy transferred by device}}{\text{total energy supplied to device}}$$

$$\text{power} = \frac{\text{work done}}{\text{time taken}}$$

weight = mass × gravitational field strength (g)

change of potential energy = weight × change in height

kinetic energy = $\frac{1}{2}$ × mass × (speed)^2

moment of a force = force × perpendicular distance to pivot

sum of clockwise moments = sum of anticlockwise moments

wave speed = frequency × wavelength

pressure × volume = constant

Electrical symbols

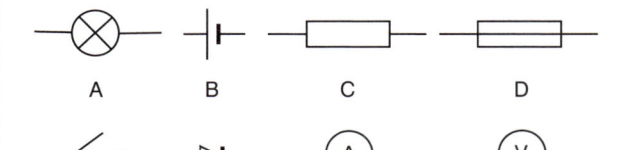

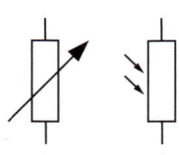

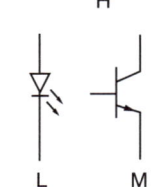

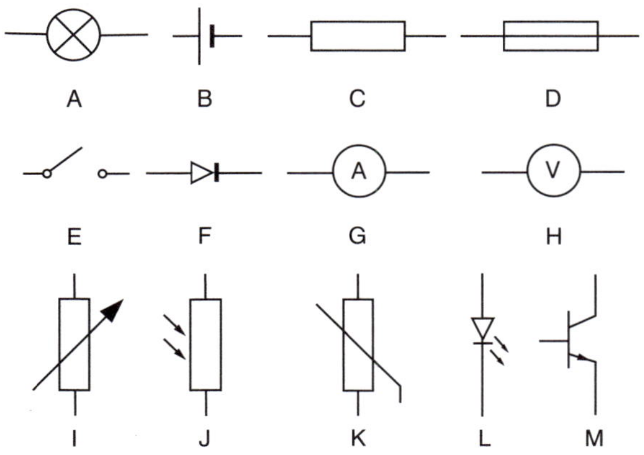

A lamp
B cell
C resistor
D fuse
E switch
F diode
G ammeter
H voltmeter
I variable resistor
J light dependent resistor
K thermistor
L light-emitting diode
M transistor

Index

absolute zero 25
a.c. generator 104–5
acceleration 65
alpha radiation 124, 128
alternating current 97, 106
ammeter 112
analogue transmission 60, 117–8
antiparticles 134
atmospheric pressure 26
atoms 87, 121

balanced forces 72
bandwidth 60
beta radiation 124, 128
Big Bang 8
Bourdon gauge 26
Boyle's law 25

cameras 55
capacitors 111
centre of gravity 72, 73
charge flow equation 90
charging by friction 87
Charles' law 25
circuit breakers 98
circular motion 84
colour 46–7
comets 5
communications 46, 60, 117–9
computer discs 119
conductors 87
conservation of energy 13
conservation of momentum 81
constellations 3
critical angle 45
critical temperature 27

density 20–1
diffraction 32, 35, 47
digital circuits 114
digital transmission 60, 118
diodes 96, 111
dispersion 51
distance–time graphs 64
drag 67
dynamo 111

Earth 3, 37
earthing 88, 98
earthquakes 37
echoes 34
efficiency of machines 14
elastic behaviour 38, 74
electric bell 108
electric circuits 94–8
electric current 90, 94, 108
electric motor 109
electrical power 14, 94
electrolysis 91

electromagnetic induction 110–11
electromagnetism 107–12
electron beams 130–1
electronic control 114–5
electrostatics 87–90
elements 121
endoscope 46
energy 12–13, 17
  internal energy of materials 23
  thermal energy 95
  transfer 12
  and work 12, 68–9
equilibrium 72–4
eyes 53–4

Faraday's law 110
fibre optics 45–6, 60
filament bulbs 96
fission 127
forces 64–8, 72–6, 80–1
frequency 31, 60, 97
fuses 98

galaxies 8
gamma radiation 59, 123, 124, 126
gas laws 25–7
Geiger counter 123
gold leaf electroscope 88
gravitational potential energy (GPE) 13, 68
gravity 5, 65

half-life 125
hearing 36
heat
  latent heat 24, 27
  specific heat capacity 23
  specific latent heat 24
  and temperature 16
  transfer 15, 16
Hooke's law 74
Hubble's law 8
hydraulics 76

information storage 119
ink jet printer 89
insulators 87
ionisation 124
infrared radiation 58
isotopes 121–3

jet engines 82

kilowatt hour (kWh) 14, 97
kinetic energy (KE) 12, 13, 68
kinetic theory 26–7

lenses 50–56

Lenz's law 110
light 44–49, 50–54
light–dependent resistor (LDR) 96
logic gates 114–5
longitudinal waves 30
loudspeakers 110

machines at work 14
magnetism 107–8
magnifying glasses 56
mains electricity 97–8
memory circuits 115
microphone 111
microscope 47
mirror images 43–4
molecules 121
moment of a force 72
momentum 80–2
motor effect 109
multimeter 112

N–Z plot 133–4
neutrons 121, 123, 134
Newton's laws of motion 67, 80
nuclear reactors 127
nucleus of atoms 121, 123, 127, 132–5

Ohm's law 95
optical instruments 55–6
optical spectra 131
oscilloscopes 34, 131

parallelogram rule 83
periodic table 121
photocopier 89
planets 4
plastic behaviour 74
polarisation 30
potential difference 94
potential divider 114
power 14, 94
pressure 26, 27, 28, 75, 76
pressure law 25
projectiles 79
protons 121, 123, 134

quarks 134–5

radioactive dating 125
radioactive waste 127
radioactivity 121–7
ray diagrams 49, 51
red shift 8
reflection 32, 43
refraction 32, 34, 44, 51
relay control 115
renewable energy resources 17
resistance 101–2, 110

resonance 38
Richter scale 37
rocket engines 82

satellites 5, 84
scalars 83
sensors 115
SETI 7
sight correction 54
slide projectors 52
solar system 4
solids 21, 80
sound 34–6
speed
  and distance 64
  of light 44
  of sound 34
  of waves 31
stability of objects 72
stars 6
stopping distances 66
strength of solids 74
Sun 2, 5
supernovae 6

tape recorder 111
temperature 15–6, 25
terminal speed 67
thermal conduction 15
thermal convection 15
thermal radiation 15
thermistor 96
time-delay circuits 115
total internal reflection 45
transformers 112
transistors 112
transverse waves 30
truth tables 114

U-tube manometer 26, 75
ultrasound 36
ultraviolet light 57
ultraviolet radiation 67
Universe 8

vectors 83
velocity 64, 67, 84
vibration 38–9, 41
visible spectrum 46
voltage 94, 114
voltmeter 94, 112
volume of solids 21

waves 29–32
  in communications 60
  electromagnetic 57–9
  light 50
  seismic 37, 41
  sound 34–6
wavelength 31
weight 13, 67
X-rays 9, 131